CONDEMN AND RESIST

Higher education is not on the sidelines – it is ground zero in the fight for democracy. At a moment of direct political assault on universities, *Condemn and Resist* powerfully exposes how attacks on knowledge, labor, and public institutions are tightly linked. A vital and compelling contribution to the growing movement of workers, students, and communities refusing the dismantling of public education and democratic life.

—*Todd Wolfson*, President of the American Association of University Professors and Vice President of American Federation of Teachers

In *Condemn and Resist*, Corey Dolgon has assembled a set of scholars deeply connected to the communities and lived experiences Donald Trump has taken aim at in his second presidential term. Each chapter provides essential historical context and analysis of the administration's current attacks and their impacts, from authors steeped in theory and the power and practice of everyday organizing. The assessments in these pages will help those trying to understand the present moment as well as those seeking inspiration for how to move forward – not back to "normal," but towards a liberatory vision of the future that we can build together.

—*Lisa Schiff*, Co-author of the *Declaration to Defend Research Against U.S. Government Censorship*

In Trump 2.0, the politics of anti-democracy have been ramped up from the first term. The result is a grave threat to the future of the republic. Corey Dolgon's edited collection captures this threat during the first year of Trump's second term, offering snapshots of a rapidly moving and well-organized reactionary movement. Chapters offer explorations of a range of topics, including public health, immigration, abortion rights, worker rights, LGBTQ, and the environment. At the same time, the book captures glimmers of hope, in part because of a resistance movement that has grown quickly and is shaping public opinion. This book is a valuable guide for assessing the destructiveness of Trump 2.0, preparing us for what comes next.

—*Peter Kivisto*, Richard A. Swanson Professor of Social Thought Emeritus, Augustana College and Author of *The Trump Phenomenon*

My friends tell me we need a revolution. I don't disagree. I'd like to know what it looks like. How do we get there? And specifically what policies work to empower and liberate others and ourselves? For all of this to happen, we need a powerful analysis. Corey Dolgon's *Condemn and Resist* gives us a blow-by-blow description of how social institutions have been attacked and dismantled over many decades – but never more rapidly and viciously than in Donald Trump's first year back in office. The autopsy is crucial – but the book's real strength is its issue-by-issue look at how political, social, economic, legal, and media activism make a difference. Particularly inspiring is each chapter's focus on what our neighbors are doing to stop ICE; to stop cuts to education, health care, and women's reproductive care; to promote labor rights; and, most of all show how grassroots efforts are building a resistance. In doing so, they also give us a glimpse of what a future society might look like. If you want to understand today better and be inspired to work for a better tomorrow, read this book!

—*Rodney Coates*, Professor of Critical Race and Ethnic Studies at Miami University

Brilliantly conceptualized and wonderfully presented, *Condemn and Resist* brings together an outstanding team of experts to analyze the breadth and depth of the Trump Administration's authoritarian assault on democracy and civil society. This book is a 'must read' for scholars, activists, and citizens who want to understand and resist the entire scope of Trump 2.0.

—*Woody Doane*, University of Hartford

With Sociology both under attack by the Trump administration and growing right-wing authoritarianism in the US and elsewhere and very well placed to analyse inequality, injustice and the operation of power (one of the reasons that it is targeted), this important collection with a range of excellent contributions is timely, necessary and welcome. Crucially, it gives us the tools to understand Trumpism and the current conjuncture, challenge its more dangerous tendencies and implications, and defend those targeted critically and collectively.

—*Aaron Winter*, Senior Lecturer in Sociology at Lancaster University and Co-author of *Reactionary Democracy: How Racism and the Populist Far Right Became Mainstream*

CONDEMN AND RESIST

SOCIOLOGISTS RESPOND TO THE FIRST YEAR OF TRUMP 2.0

EDITED BY

COREY DOLGON
Stonehill College, USA

emerald
PUBLISHING

United Kingdom – North America – Japan – India
Malaysia – China

Emerald Publishing Limited
Emerald Publishing, Floor 5, Northspring, 21-23 Wellington Street,
Leeds LS1 4DL.

First edition 2026

British Library Cataloguing in Publication Data
A catalogue record for this book is available from the British Library

ISBN: 978-1-80592-856-0 (Print)
ISBN: 978-1-80592-853-9 (Online)
ISBN: 978-1-80592-855-3 (Epub)

CONTENTS

INTRODUCTION: MAPPING, CONDEMNING, AND RESISTING TRUMP 2.0

Corey Dolgon

Stonehill College, USA

IT'S A THUG WORLD: MURDERS AND ACQUISITIONS

Early on the morning of December 31st, I finished editing the last chapter for this collection and began writing an Introduction. I hoped to complete the manuscript before my Spring semester began in late January. It seemed doable.

On Saturday night, January 2nd, Donald Trump gave orders for the US military to attack Venezuela. The next day, bombs were dropped and military special forces captured President Nicolas Maduro and his wife, Cilia Flores. By January 5th, the couple was arraigned in a New York City courtroom and placed behind bars at the Brooklyn Metropolitan Detention Center. Like several acts of the Trump 2.0 presidency, this kidnapping violated domestic and international laws, demonstrated Trump's aggressive volatility and disregard for democratic processes and human life, and allowed him to distract from his failing economy and falling poll numbers.[i] I made a note to include all of this in the introduction.

[i] Forty-seven Venezuelan soldiers killed in US attack, minister says | Reuters.

As I got back to work two days later, news broke that a young Minneapolis woman, Renee Good, was shot and killed by Immigration and Customs Enforcement (ICE) agents in an incident bound to be emblematic for what Trump's domestic militarism has become. While promising to simply deport the "worst of the worst" undocumented immigrants – "gang members, murderers, rapists and bad guys" – government enforcement agents are now terrorists in the streets of American cities. ICE and Border Control agents attack, arrest, detain, and deport documented and undocumented people alike, most of whom have no criminal records.[ii] Currently, federal officers commit daily acts of violence against workers, family members, allies, activists, neighbors, and bystanders with no end in sight.

Not only has the Trump administration blocked civil rights investigations of Good's murder and refused to allow local and State officials to examine evidence,[1] but the Department of Justice (DOJ) also immediately initiated investigations into Good *herself* and her widow, Becca Good. These efforts to disparage the victim and her wife, while ignoring persistent ICE and Department of Homeland Security (DHS) civil rights violations, inspired over a dozen DOJ resignations, including the top Minnesota State Attorney and career federal prosecutor, Joseph H. Thompson. Over 250 lawyers have resigned from the DOJ during Trump 2.0, the vast majority in protest over his weaponizing the office.[2] On January 20th, the DOJ *did* launch investigations into Minnesota Governor, Tim Walz; Minneapolis Mayor, Jacob Frey; and Minnesota Attorney General, Keith Ellison, claiming that these State officials have instigated violence and obstructed law enforcement.

Trump's strategy – defame the victim and anyone related to or defending the victim – is a predictable page from the Trump playbook: attack the accuser and then lie, lie, lie. Renee Nicole Good was a devout Christian, mother of three children, an engaged community member, volunteer, and author. But, as Baker A. Rogers (Chapter 10) explains, Trump uses the term "terrorist" to demonize

[ii] 73.6% held in ICE detention have no criminal conviction according to data current as of February 7, 2026 [TRAC (2026) *Immigration Detention Quick Facts*. https://tracreports.org/immigration/quickfacts/].

and criminalize people: “Terrorists are rhetorically subhuman, justifying exclusion and even elimination from society.” Numerous expert and forensic analyses (and multiple videos) make evident that ICE officer Jonathan Ross murdered Good by shooting into her vehicle three times – twice through the driver’s side window – as she attempted to follow ICE orders and leave the scene.[3] But Trump refuses to allow an investigation – delegitimizing any due process by demonizing Good herself. The President’s representatives (now former) DHS Kristi Noem, Vice President J. D. Vance, and Deputy Chief of Staff Stephen Miller – are on a seemingly permanent media loop characterizing Good (and all anti-ICE protestors) as extreme “domestic terrorists.”

To demonstrate the toxic vacuity of the term, “terrorist,” Vance, Noem, and Miller, like to throw a Make America Great Again (MAGA) conspiracy cocktail of modifiers into their kitchen sink of disparaging, ad hominin, character assassinations. In a series of public interviews, press briefings, and media comments following the killing of Renee Good, Vance referred to Good as a “classic terrorist,” a “deranged leftist” and part of a “lunatic fringe” that “brainwashed” her with “left-wing ideology.” Noem persistently calls Good a “domestic terrorist” and characterizes her effort to drive away as an act of weaponizing her vehicle.”[4] Appearing on Fox News in October 2025, Miller, moves quickly from referring to protestors as “extreme, leftist agitators” and “domestic insurrectionists” to assuring federal officers: “You have federal immunity in the conduct of your duties. Anybody who lays a hand on you or tries to stop you or tries to obstruct you is committing a felony.”[5] While Miller is wrong on the law and the meaning of immunity in this context, the lies make clear the administration’s purposeful strategy – reframe the ideological process that justifies murder, moving the discourse from demonizing and discrediting opposition to eliminating and exterminating them.

The persistence of Trump 2.0 lies and the dehumanization of anyone outside the MAGA mindset make it unlikely that we will see a “Have you no sense of decency, sir” moment anytime soon. This quotation comes from Senator Joe McCarthy’s 1950s anti-Communist, Red Scare campaign, where he regularly employed false claims, innuendo, threats, intimidation, and outright lies to create a national moral panic over the so-called "domestic enemies." In a "final act" moment during hearings about Communists infiltrating the US Army, McCarthy publicly accused a young Army lawyer of associating with Communists – assuming such threats would both make his case and ruin the attorney's career. In response, Lead Army counsel, Joseph Welch, famously said, "Until this moment, Senator, I think I never really gauged your cruelty or your recklessness .... Have you no sense of decency, sir, at long last?" Trump and his cohort clearly have none.

In fact, Trump has tried to co-opt the "morality narrative" itself by suggesting that the only real limitation on his use of power against sovereign nations, against US citizens, or against anyone that challenges what Onwubiko Agozino (Chapter 3) calls "executive lawlessness," is his "own morality." In an interview with the *New York Times*, reporters asked if Trump had felt any limitations on his global powers to attack other nations – Iran, Nigeria, Greenland, Canada? He replied, "Yeah, there is one thing. My own morality. My own mind. It's the only thing that can stop me .... I don't need international law."[6]

Much of this book argues that *Project 2025* – a Right-Wing Heritage Foundation playbook to radically restructure the US government and create a consolidated and all-powerful executive branch – has already succeeded, thus giving Trump an unabated autocratic abandon to use violence and intimidation at home and abroad.[7] According to Heritage's President, Kevin Roberts, *Project 2025* was an effort to "institutionalize Trumpism" and provide a "blueprint that outlines a plan to consolidate power in the executive branch, dismantle federal agencies and vet government employees to free the next Republican president from a system that Roberts views as stacked against conservative power."[8] The publication of *Project 2025* included 30 chapters on almost every major government Department, Agency, and Commission, as well as general areas such as "Trade" and the "Intelligence Communities." Despite Trump's continued claims that he knew nothing about *Project 2025*, 31 of 38 contributing authors now work for his administration.[9]

This collection responds to the ways in which *Project 2025* has acted as an ideological and strategical "blueprint" for the first year of Trump 2.0. For example, The American Civil Liberties Union

(ACLU) summarized the major issues and approaches outlined by the Conservative Playbook.[10] In early 2025, the ACLU presented (Presciently, I would say) these issues as the most volatile for the coming year. Each issue is discussed in the following chapters, as outlined below:

1. *Gutting abortion access* – Revive a 19th century law, the Comstock Act, to ban any abortion medications and materials preventing them from being sent through the US Postal Service, a reversal of the U.S. Food and Drug Administration (FDA's) approval of mifepristone (as discussed in Chapter 5 by Deborah Billings and Saphronia Carson) as well as cuts to and criminalizing a variety of women's reproductive health options (as discussed in Chapter 2 by Katrinell M. Davis).
2. *Mass deportations* – Target immigrant communities through mass deportations and raids; end birthright citizenship, continue family separation and dismantle the asylum system (as discussed in Chapter 4 by Rogelio Sáenz and Selene M. Gomez).
3. *Abusing warrantless surveillance* – Exploit the executive branch's vast and unprecedented power to spy on Americans and dismantle guardrails that prevent the president from abusing the executive branch's power (as discussed in Chapter 3 by Onwubiko Agozino).
4. *Unleashing undue force on protestors* – Violate the First Amendment to target journalists and protesters and dismantle guardrails that prevent the president from abusing executive power (as discussed in Chapter 8 by Douglas Kellner).
5. *Severely limiting voting access* – Abuse executive power to interfere in our elections by criminalizing the voting process and damaging fair representation (as discussed in Chapter 1 by Eduardo Bonilla-Silva).
6. *Censoring critical discussions in classrooms* – Censor academic discussions about race, gender, and systemic oppression and threaten educational institutions and organizations with severe funding cuts (as discussed in Chapter 6 by Corey Dolgon).

7. *Rolling back trans right* – Remove federal nondiscrimination protections; mandate discrimination against lesbian, gay, bisexual, transgender, and queer (LGBTQ) people by the federal government; exclude trans people from serving in the military; and permit faith-based, taxpayer-funded contracts to exclude trans people from disaster assistance and care for unaccompanied refugees (as discussed in Chapter 10 by Baker A. Rogers).

Along with these topics, *Project 2025* also includes critique of all public welfare programs and the use of science for health policy (also Chapter 2), coordinating tactics to disempower labor unions (Chapter 7) and delegitimizing climate science and dismantling regulatory regimes on all forms of environmental pollution (Chapter 9). This collection offers a comprehensive view of these mostly successful efforts to redesign American Democracy and public policy.

These efforts will continue unless we, the people, stand up. This book is an effort to encourage and support the work of people prepared to actively condemn *and* resist. But it's now January 20th and three more people have been shot and injured by ICE: two in Portland, Oregon and one more in Minneapolis. Yet protests have also expanded and intensified. As the body count mounts, Trump controls Venezuela, threatens military action in Iran, and has told Greenland and Denmark officials that the USA will take control of the Island "one way or another." To best challenge, this no longer *creeping* fascism[11] requires both a solid analytical autopsy of what has happened – how and why – as well as a documentation and assessment of growing resistance to Trump's brutal repression at home and violent imperialism abroad. Clearly, I need to finish this introduction.

FLOODING THE ZONE AND WRITING THIS BOOK

Scholars and critics now commonly refer to Trump's strategy of "flooding the zone" to keep critics and media off balance and ineffective.[12] Douglas Kellner (Chapter 8) suggests that the Government shutdown was an effort to distract the public from the Epstein files affair. I argue (Chapter 6) that Trump's strategy of constant threats to cancel funding from educational institutions and health and scientific research – particularly at universities – not only cast a chilling effect on academic freedom, freedom of speech, diversity programs, etc., but also forces college administrators, faculty, and affiliated professional and nonprofit organizations to play legal games of "whack-a-mole." Just as some institutions capitulated to one set of Trump 2.0 threats, another Trump agency would start a new investigation. Just as the ACLU or a State Attorneys General would file for an injunction against an Executive Order (EO), Trump would issue two new EOs that had to be addressed. Just as K–12 and higher educational institutions would change Diversity, Equity and Inclusion (DEI) policies and personnel, the Department of Education would set new rules and standards that had to be addressed or opposed in court.

On the off chance that legal opposition succeeded in temporarily halting or reversing Trump 2.0 policies, the flood would overwhelm enforcement, too, as the administration simply ignored the rulings. As Rogelio Sáenz and Selene M. Gomez (Chapter 4) explain:

> *Trump has regularly defied court orders related to deportation. Flights carrying immigrants out of the country have left without proper authorization. Many immigrants from nations that will not accept deportees have been taken to random countries in Central America and Africa where they face brutal conditions and great trauma. Some individuals have even attempted suicide.*

In the case of the Epstein files, under intense and widespread pressure, Trump signed the order forcing the DOJ to release *ALL* Epstein related materials by December 19th, 2025. Over one month later and still almost 99% of the files have NOT been turned over to Congress and, more importantly, with no repercussions.[iii] Flooding the zone is drowning democracy.

The Trump 2.0 typhoon of executive lawlessness has also made it difficult for media to maintain its focus on any issue for very long. For example, look at the plight of government workers initially caught in Elon Musk's chainsaw or simply told "Your Fired!" by Trump during the government shutdown in October 2025. Well

[iii] DOJ says millions of Epstein files have yet to be released – POLITICO.

over 300,000 government employees were fired or forced to resign or retire in 2025.[13] Tens of thousands of Department of Agriculture (USDA) workers in field offices throughout the nation no longer work for their communities. The effect? According to Zach Ducheneaux, former Farm Service Agency (FSA) administrator, losing thousands of loan analysts based in the 4,500 local USDA offices

> *make it harder for farmers to get USDA loans ... [it's] not only a waste of taxpayer investment in their training, producers will lose the opportunity to buy a farm or ranch, if not lose their existing farm or ranch .... They will not be able to get their operating money in a timely fashion. That's not hyperbole. It is actual, literal fact.*

News of Department of Government Efficiency (DOGE)'s initial cuts in February and March saturated most major, national news outlets. By April, coverage almost completely disappeared, and by the end of the year, only a handful of local media outlets and non-profit-run niche journals sustained coverage.[iv]

Similarly, labor related issues have been abandoned by traditional media outlets at the same time that public and private workers around the country have lost jobs, health protections, and had their lives and families made more precarious.[14] As Chris Rhomberg explains (Chapter 7), Trump initially claimed national security reasons for circumventing the 1978 Civil Service Reform Act and firing hundreds of thousands of federal workers without following legal procedures. He then issued an executive order revoking collective bargaining rights for more than a million federal employees at some 20 agencies. Unions charged that Trump's action not only violated federal labor law but also retaliated against them for defending the rights of their members, in what the President of the American Federation of Labor-Congress of Industrial Organizations, Liz Shuler, called "the single biggest act of union-busting

---

[iv] A year of scorched Earth at USDA with mass firings, canceled grants and reorganization; USDA lost 18% of its staff through buyouts, other attrition | Agri-Pulse Communications, Inc.; USDA begins 2026 down 20 percent in staff with plans to cut more | Agriculture | hometownsource.com.

in history." But nary a word in national and regional news media about Trump's all-out assault on labor unions.

Journalist Ashley Parker refers to the lack of critical response by public officials and traditional media as, "Trump Exhaustion Syndrome." She claims that "Americans just can't keep up."[v] Even critical sociologists have trouble. "Flooding the zone" and its attendant daily barrage of tyranny and lies are challenging this editor as I struggle to maintain the relevance of critical analyses focused on a moving target. Daily Trump policies and authorized brutality expand constitutional transgressions, violations of human rights and international law. How does one deploy scholarly tools and a critical lens to the autocratic and often "unhinged" declarations of a convicted felon and sexual abuser[15] who claims the only limitation on his use of power is his own morality? Even irony is drowning in the storm.

In this book, we respond to these conditions with the conviction that the very nature of an overwhelming maniacal tyranny requires a comprehensive, analytical *autopsy* that chronicles what has happened, how it happened, and why it happened. *Condemn and Resist* documents the specific nature and impact of Trump 2.0 actions and policies as they impact areas of health, immigration, education, labor, climate change, the criminal justice system, the safety of women and LGBTQ people, and the practice of democracy itself. While Trump's strategy is to destabilize opposition by flooding the zone, the authors here detail and analyze important executive orders, policy decisions, government actions and overreaches, autocratic fiats, and the deadly result of Trump's and his empowered acolytes' unchecked power.

Such critical portraits of Trump 2.0 inform our current historical moment with important documentation as well as crucial understandings of the political and social context surrounding these events. While autopsies are done primarily to discover the cause of death and what a deceased's body might tell us about a more general human condition, at times of dangerous epidemics, such examinations can also inform immediate strategies and vital reactions to stop the spread of plagues. Our purpose in this book is to promote as full and comprehensive a picture of what Trump

---

[v] Trump Exhaustion Syndrome – *The Atlantic*.

2.0 has done, how and why it has happened, and how this critical analysis might inform mass strategies for resistance and change. We hope the reader finds this effort useful as we prepare to put our words and our bodies on the line in the struggle for a just future.

THE BODY COUNT

At this stage in Trump 2.0, with the "flooding the zone" volume of policies, executive orders, and actions taken, it is almost impossible to keep an accurate tally of the lives impacted and ended as a direct or indirect result of the administration. No doubt much will be written on this in the years and decades to come. However, at the time of writing, in February 2026, the authors of this collection and I felt it important to outline some of the deaths recorded as a result of this administration.

January 24th 2026: Alex Pretti, a VA Nurse and much-loved son, community member, and co-worker was shot and killed by US Border Patrol agents. Once again, Kristi Noem and Stephen Miller rushed to microphones to denounce him as a "domestic terrorist" whose radical left agenda inspired him to attack ICE agents, brandishing a weapon, intending to "inflict maximum damage on officers." Miller called him an "assassin." Within 24 hours, video footage from multiple sources and angles exposed Noem and Miller as liars.[16] Eyewitness testimony continues to add to the evidence that *Pretti* was attacked by US Customs and Border Patrol (CBP) agents as he attempted to help a woman whom agents were also assaulting. As Pretti tried to assist her, a CBP officer pepper sprayed him and seven others wrestled Pretti to the pavement and assaulted him. Pretti *did* have a legal and licensed firearm holstered and agents removed the weapon without resistance. As he lay on the ground beaten and unarmed, CBP agents shot Pretti TEN times – at least once in the back of the head. Just as in the murder of Renee Good, Homeland Security refused to allow Minnesota law enforcement to investigate the killing.

On *September 12, 2025*, an ICE agent shot and killed an undocumented Mexican immigrant named Silverio Villegas González. Gonzalez was allegedly trying to flee a traffic stop and ICE officials claim he attempted to run them over. Subsequent video footage and eyewitness accounts suggest that Gonzalez *did* graze an officer as he tried to escape. After he was forcibly stopped, Gonzalez was pulled from his car and fatally shot in the back of the neck. A full investigation of the incident remains incomplete. At least five people have been shot and killed by ICE and DHS officials since the summer of 2025.[17]

Dozens of others have died in DHS custody. According to *The Guardian*, 32 people have died from

> *seizure and heart failure, stroke, respiratory failure, tuberculosis or suicide. Some died at ICE detention centers and field offices, others after they had been transferred to hospitals, but were still under ICE custody. In some cases, families and lawyers allege detainees died of neglect, after repeatedly trying and failing to get medical care.*[18]

On *January 21st 2026*, an El Paso Medical Examiner (ME) ruled the death of Geraldo Lunas Campos a homicide.[19] A Cuban immigrant, Campos was being held at Camp East Montana (Texas), when he died from "asphyxia due to neck and torso compression." While ICE officials claim they were trying to restrain Campos from hurting himself, the ME reported he became unresponsive while being "physically restrained by law enforcement." He had "scattered superficial abrasions" all over his body; a hemorrhage involving the strap muscles and connective tissues of the neck; and "petechial hemorrhages" in the eyelids and in the front and side of his neck, along with fractured ribs.

Between September and the end of December 2025, Trump's Department of Defense committed 35 lethal strikes against Venezuelan boats *allegedly* operated by "narco-terrorists." On the one hand, these strikes demonstrated Trump's willingness to use deadly force indiscriminately without offering any evidence for their claims of "narco-terrorism" or the legality of their attacks which killed 125 people in all. On the other hand, these strikes were part of the strategy to "loosen up" Venezuelan leaders in preparation for the final attack which occurred on January 3, 2026. The US military killed 80 people during their assault on the presidential compound and fighting at various Venezuelan military bases.[20]

In the wake of the Dobbs decision that overturned Roe V. Wade, states that have banned abortion outright have seen more pregnant women as well as infants die. Preliminary findings indicate an 8% increase in pregnancy-associated mortality, equivalent to 59 excess pregnancy deaths. While the relative increase was similar across all racial groups, the absolute impact was greater for Black women, who already faced higher baseline mortality rates. Infant mortality rates have increased 5.6% above expected levels in states with abortion bans, translating to 478 additional deaths. Black infants suffered disproportionately, with an 11% increase in mortality rates compared to a 5% increase for white infants.[vi] Deaths from congenital malformations and birth defects rose nearly 11%, suggesting that bans prevented termination of pregnancies with severe fetal abnormalities.

Perhaps the largest deadly impact unleashed by Trump 2.0 occurred early on as Elon Musk and DOGE bragged about feeding United States Agency for International Development (USAID) "to the woodchipper." The USAID began in 1961 as an independent agency with two main missions: "the first was to provide humanitarian assistance, and the second to assist and support the economic growth and self-resilience of developing countries, especially those deemed strategic for the US economic and geopolitical impact."[21] In the 21st century alone, estimates suggest that USAID funding programs and staff engagement saved almost 100 million lives. Primarily in areas related to health and safety, some of the organization's most successful campaigns included:

Emergency Response and Disaster Relief: Between 2017 and 2020, USAID reacted to more than 240 natural disasters and crises around the world – from famines in the Republic of South Sudan to armed conflicts in Afghanistan, Yemen, and the Lake Chad basin. From 2012 to 2017, the organization supported more than five million survivors of gender-based violence through medical care, counseling, and legal help. Following the January 2010 earthquake in Haiti, USAID helped provide housing for almost 200,000

[vi] Abortion bans linked to sharp rise in sepsis, infant death, and pregnancy-associated death, new research shows | PRB.

displaced Haitians; helped more than 10,000 farmers double the yields of staples like corn, beans, and sorghum; and provided short-term employment to over 350,000 Haitians, injecting over $19 million into the local economy. USAID provided nearly $42 million to combat cholera, helping to decrease the number of cases requiring hospitalization and reduce the fatality rate.[22]

Global Health: USAID partnered with Gavi – an international organization created to improve vaccine access to children – pledged $1.16 billion over 2020–2023 to ensure families in low- and middle-income countries have access to vaccines preventing Ebola, cholera, yellow fever, and meningitis. In 2020, USAID was mainly responsible for eradicating wild poliovirus in Africa. From 2007 to 2017, USAID saved 6 million lives through the President's Malaria Initiative and between 2017 and 2020, it gave out enough mosquito nets to protect 320 million people; distributed preventative medicine to protect 20 million pregnant women and 14 million children and sprayed homes with insecticides to protect 77 million individuals. The agency has also tackled AIDS – in 2015 alone, USAID helped 9.5 million people receive life-saving AIDS treatments in collaboration with partners through the President's Emergency Plan for AIDS Relief. According to the *Lancet*, researchers estimate that over the past two decades, USAID-funded programs have helped prevent more than 91 million deaths globally, including 30 million deaths among children.[23]

Early research demonstrates that Trump 2.0 cuts to USAID have already cost hundreds of thousands of lives. Professional medical and data analysts project that the death toll resulting from USAID could be over 14 million people by 2030, almost one-third of which will be children under 5 years old. According to Dr Brooke Nichols and her Impactcounter website (hosted by the Boston University School of Medicine), the result of cutting billions of dollars in aid to poor countries is staggering. They document illnesses and deaths on an incremental and almost immediate level derived from on-line data collecting and scientifically proven mathematical forecasting. The website demonstrates that cuts to anti-malarial programs, to childhood treatment for pneumonia and diarrhea, to immunization programs and treatment for tropical diseases, and infant and adult

HIV prevention and treatment have already resulted in almost one million deaths. *The Lancet* concludes:

> *our study demonstrates the crucial role that USAID funding has had in reducing mortality rates across LMICs [low and middle income countries] over the past two decades, and the profound effect that the recent abrupt funding cuts [83%] could have on adult and child mortality in the coming years. Beyond causing millions of avoidable deaths – particularly among the most vulnerable – these cuts risk reversing decades of progress in health and socioeconomic development in LMICs and could substantially undermine the achievement of the 2030 Sustainable Development Goals.*[vii]

Much like the impact of a mishandled and cruel set of policy decisions and public pronouncements during the Trump 1.0 response to Covid-19, preventable deaths barely surface to flood the zone as they are obscured by levels of inhumanity too perverse to measure.

WHEN WILL WE EVER LEARN: BUILDING A CULTURE OF UPRISING

It is January 28th and the face of DHS terrorism in Minnesota, Greg Bovino, has been removed from the state. Congress is debating calls to impeach DHS Secretary, Kristi Noem. The Trump administration has pledged to reduce federal forces in Minneapolis and sent border czar, Tom Homan, to try and calm things down. The people of the Twin Cities have taken to the streets every day for weeks. Americans have turned up the heat and ICE may be melting.

On a global level, nations are learning to stand up and fight as well. Recently, Trump went to Davos, Switzerland and told the World Economic Forum that Europe "wouldn't exist" without the USA; that NATO had never done anything for the USA; and

[vii] *The Lancet* (p. 292).

that he would take Greenland by appeasement or "the hard way," promising huge economic sanctions and possibly military intervention. Of course, his first two statements were false, inaccurate, and lies. But European nations refused to buckle, and Greenland and Denmark stood firm against annexation. Canadian Prime Minister, Mark Carney, issued a "wake up" call to European allies: the old order had been ruptured causing "the beginning of a harsh reality … where the large, main power, geopolitics, is submitted to no limits, no constraints." In response, however, he argued that "intermediate powers like Canada, are not powerless. They have the capacity to build a new order that encompasses our values: human rights, sustainable development, solidarity, sovereignty and territorial integrity of the various states."[viii] As an object lesson about the power of this approach – "to stop pretending, to name reality, to build our strength at home and to act together" – Europe sent Trump home empty handed and embarrassed.

As of today, February 1, 2026, we await whether Congress will be able to act to enforce the release of all the Epstein files. But like those who have taken to the streets in cities around the USA, and like smaller nations who have banded together to limit Trump's abandon, the struggle over the Epstein files paints another portrait of the power of persistent resistance. The women who refused to allow Epstein's history of sex-trafficking, extortions, and pedophilia to disappear quietly in the margins of post-scandal media detritus and to remain unexamined and uncharged, have instead continued to fight back. Daily they appear in the media and on Capitol Hill to challenge men of power and privilege to open the records and expose, condemn, and prosecute serial rapists and sex traffickers. Trump may promise to change ICE practices in Minneapolis, but even if DHS presence does decline, goons and thugs will be back on the streets of another city soon. Even if Trump signed the Epstein Files Transparency Act, his DOJ continues to stall and renege on releasing materials and explaining massive redactions. In other words, persistence and resistance have demonstrated that such tactics are the *only* actions that check Trump's claims

[viii] Davos 2026: Special address by Mark Carney, PM of Canada | World Economic Forum.

of autocracy. But we need to do even more and we can't become complacent.

This book's title emanates from the "Declaration To Defend Research Against U.S. Government Censorship" drafted soon after Donald Trump 2.0 began and his flurry of executive orders attacked academic freedom, freedom of speech, and promised to censor public resources from libraries and universities to public agencies, hospitals, and all forms of scientific and medical research. The Declaration was "a call to action for the scholarly communication community and additional stakeholders to *condemn and resist* recent acts by the U.S. government to censor scholarly research."[24] It continued:

> *Government censorship and restrictions on terminology, research topics, or methods fundamentally compromise these scholarly endeavors and their integrity. Examples of such censorship and intimidation in the U.S. include:*

- CDC's ban on including words relating to gender in research publications.[25]
- NSF's recent move to freeze funding for work touching in any way on issues of diversity, equity, or inclusion.[26]
- NSF's list of dozens of flagged words used to identify research that might violate President Donald Trump's executive orders.[27]
- Removal of publicly available research and data from governmental websites.[28]
- Targeting of particular researchers and government employees.[29]

This list of Trump 2.0 attacks is derived from just his first week of executive orders and the administration's immediate efforts to censor materials, funding, and other support from day one. These efforts to censor information, restrict research, and manufacture revisionist histories and right-wing propaganda to replace facts have only intensified over the ensuing year.

The chapters offered here, like the solid and important work of all engaged scholars, do an excellent job in providing the detailed analysis of what is happening in the USA today, how it happened, and the importance of publicly and powerfully condemning the autocratic power and violence spewing from the White House. More notable, I think, are the calls for and strategies of resistance that authors here present to the growing numbers of scholars, activists, and citizens taking action to *resist* as well as condemn. Even before Trump won the 2024 election, I wrote a piece calling for a *culture of uprising* "that links local and regional struggles to a revolutionary consciousness prepared to fight fascism and envision a more sustainable and liberatory future." I explained:

> *a culture of uprisings is nothing more than the willingness to consistently promote counterhegemonic alternatives to the negating forces of power and oppression – White supremacy, patriarchy, fascism, and so forth. This includes speaking truth to power in all its manifestations and within every nook and cranny of contemporary institutional systems of power, bureaucracy, and dehumanizing corporate practices .... Here I am suggesting that we must be prepared and organized to pressure overt and covert forms of oppression in the cause of dismantling what seems insurmountable. A culture of uprisings can expose society as never the "dead husk" of social forces that limit individual and social fulfillment. Instead, constant challenges to hegemonic power portray society as a set of constitutive processes open at any time to opposition if not full-scale change.*[30]

Unlike so much of contemporary popular culture that exists online and on screens and is consumed passively, a culture of uprising must be personal, collective, and physically engaged – not only to build the most effective resistance, but also to create and inspire solidarity and experience critical optimism.

Such was Paulo Freire's advice when arguing that hope was an "ontological need," but as an idea or concept it could never be enough.[31] For him, hope required – demanded – an anchoring in practice to acquire "historical concreteness." A critical hope steeped in political engagement could accomplish three important goals imperative to building revolutionary consciousness and organizing powerful movements:

1. First, uprisings against injustice demonstrate that historical blocs are just that, historical; they are not immutable or impenetrable. Speaking truth to power presents active lessons in struggle.
2. Second, uprisings create space for resurrecting and promoting traditional cultures and values of resistance. These tools for rebellion are often thought to be eviscerated by dominant cultures and elite knowledge production, but usually live and breathe in the hidden transcripts of past struggle.
3. Finally, mobilizing efforts create the physical and ideological practices that, in Freire's words, "unveil opportunities for hope."[32]

For the first time in a very long time here in the USA, the possibility of such a culture of uprisings seems more possible an outcome.

As suggested in Chapter 9, anti-Musk protests and direct action at Tesla plants and showrooms sent sales and stocks plummeting and eventually sent Musk packing from D.C. The campaign to stop Avelo Airlines from providing deportation flights to DHS involved a sophisticated and highly motivated multi-pronged strategy that included: (1) Boycotts; (2) Direct Action and rallies at Avelo airport terminals; (3) Political Pressure from local and state officials where Avelo had the most flights – some even forbid public funds from being used for the airline; and (4) Publicity & Legal Action where protesters used social media, online petitions, and lawsuits to highlight the, "cruelty" of the flights, all to damage the airline's reputation. Avelo terminated their DHS government contract on January 27th of 2026.[33]

While these large scale and successful campaigns demonstrated the potential of fighting back against authoritarianism, more notable has been the intensifying struggles emanating from small cities and even smaller communities around the country. A recent *Time* magazine article documents successful efforts to stop DHS from building immigrant detention centers in Salt Lake City, Oklahoma

City, and Kansas City where protesters and local officials stopped the sales or leasing facilities for ICE to use. Local backlash convinced a warehouse owner in Ashland, Virginia not to sell his property to DHS after hundreds protested and County officials refused to support the project. Growing protests also convinced Howard County Executive, Calvin Bell, in Maryland to revoke permits for a planned ICE facility. He claimed that local leaders had the responsibility to "act with clarity, restraint, and compassion ... to act before harm occurs and not after .... Together we will stand united, work collaboratively together and safeguard our community and stand up for dignity."[34]

For over a year, Journalist Rachel Maddow has chronicled the massive numbers of protests and marches and demonstrations rising up in small towns and cities all over the country, including in some of the most conservative states in the nation. On February 2nd, she reported the growing opposition to detention camps where "people are pulling out all of the stops to prevent them from being built." Maddow suggests that "If they build them, they will fill them"[35] In fact, the growing opposition to violent mass deportation, to the war on health and science, to the fear and intransigence regarding the release of the Epstein files, and increasingly to almost every aspect of *Project 2025*'s vision could intensify Trump's impetus for the camps. As government brutality increases, so will the passion and vitriol of resistance, likely causing Trump to expand the demonization of "extremists" and "dangerous insurrectionists," this legitimizing their detention or their deaths.

The stakes for struggle intensify as tyranny grows. But people in the USA now have an opportunity to condemn, resist, *and* re-envision what kind of society they want to live in. The growing size and number of protests around the country have already impacted policies and determined limits on Trump's totalitarian fever dreams. Mobilizing masses also empowers legal battles that continue to slow or even turn back lawless executive orders and undemocratic actions. But a culture of uprising also builds *new* solidarity among people across previously siloed issues and "special group" interests. The disgust and horrors of the Epstein scandals have brought together conservatives and feminists to promote empowering young women through education, culture, and justice.

And labor unions have taken up the challenge of recognizing immigration, deportation, and democracy as all workers' issues, too. According to labor activist, Emily Tulli, moments of crisis encourage acts of mutualism where "courage inspires more courage, and solidarity swells." She continues:

> *Today, that principle is being affirmed in Minnesota, where labor unions and community members are standing together in response to a tragic loss and an immigration enforcement campaign that is causing tremendous harm to workers, unions, and our communities.*[36]

Tulli believes that labor's embrace of a wider sense of solidarity across issues "builds on a longer history of unions opposing policies that seek to divide working people, and the foundational principle that an injury to one is an injury to all." Yet the crucial site of Minneapolis as a crucible for massive resistance would be impossible without the recent history of Black Lives Matter and 2020 organizing in response to George Floyd's murder. As *The Guardian* recently reported, "Much of the community response to the current ICE surge – including efforts to document actions by immigration officers, build camaraderie and communication between neighbors, and coordinate mutual aid – build on existing efforts." As one resident explained, "This is not our first rodeo."[37] From food deliveries and civil rights classes, from ICE watch to legal aid to child care expansive mutual aid efforts, dozens and dozens of neighborhood and citywide formal and informal nongovernmental organizations can trace their origins back to the 2020 Black Lives Matter protests. Truthout reporters concluded:

> *Lessons of 2020 are now being expanded upon. While building rapid response practices, community members are also attempting to train and be trained, make connections with other organizations and cities, and provide support for each other's material and emotional needs. Groups are absorbing (while trying to practice both safety and hospitality) a vast number of people – across all the city's neighborhoods – who were previously not connected to each other, and maybe not involved with organizing at all.*[38]

Condemn and Resist begins with a traditional belief that research and analysis are crucial to understand how the current political landscape came to be and why such reactionary and totalitarian policies have found support and legitimacy. Each author, however, argues that such knowledge must be forged in the fire of political engagement and social action. Thus, we offer these chapters as tools for grasping the evolution of our contemporary political context but also as weapons for assessing and assisting our potential for resistance and change. We look forward to seeing you in the streets and on the line.

POSTSCRIPT – A WORD ABOUT WORDS

Inside this book, you will read a variety of critical and scholarly approaches to analyzing the political dynamics of our current historical moment. Contributors use a variety of descriptive terms and concepts to depict political trends and governmental policies, some being perhaps more provocative or controversial. For example, *Project 2025* is very open in its focus on creating a unified and powerful executive branch with the president acquiring control over decisions and operations once held by the legislative branch, judicial branch, and state governments. Without any doubt, this approach to government embraces more authoritarianism. Does this mean that the USA has become increasingly fascist or totalitarian?

The use of such terms in reference to this administration will no doubt be analyzed by scholars for decades to come, but the events, policies, and stated intentions of the Trump administration toward immigration, educational, and environmental policies are clear in restricting constitutional protections and well-established laws regarding citizenship, academic freedom, free speech, and health and safety regulations – not to mention basic rights of due process and civil rights. The authoritarianism represented by these actions is clear. Trump may be no dictator but ignoring court judgments and trying to steal elections is ample evidence of a leader leaning toward totalitarianism. Overt and persistent violations of constitutional protections and the separation of powers suggest a president in search of absolute authority.

Umberto Eco once wrote that fascism was difficult to define in any absolute terms (something the vast majority of historians and social scientists who study fascism have agreed with).[39] Eco called fascism a "fuzzy authoritarianism" and presented 14 common features that any fascist nation might demonstrate – perhaps not all of them, but many of them in varying combinations and to different degrees. While it may be a stretch to say that Donald Trump *is* a dictator or that the USA *is* a fascist country, it seems utterly and absolutely reasonable to point out that the USA is much *more* totalitarian and becoming *more* fascistic over this past year, while our president is becoming more authoritarian and commandeering more power.

Trump's own personality and social behavior have called many highly respected psychologists and mental health professionals to diagnose him based on his public persona, pronouncements, and leadership style. These analyses include varying combinations of narcissistic and antisocial personality, malignant narcissism, bipolar disorder, paranoid personality, and paranoid psychosis, most linked to some form of cognitive impairment hinting at early dementia.[40]

Trump lies, pathologically, all the time, demands the government promote his description of reality regardless of facts that often prove otherwise. Consider the time he used a sharpie to change the National Oceanic and Atmospheric Agency's (NOA) predictions about Hurricane Dorian's path. Instead of admitting he had made a mistake in claiming Alabama would be directly impacted by the storm, Trump simply *added* Alabama by circling part of it with a marker to expand NOA's initial path predictions.[41] While citizens may be jaded to the degree that "all politicians lie," few if any have Trump's record of lying about almost anything and possibly everything. Sometimes he lies about history or policy, what he did or didn't do, what he said or didn't say, generally to skirt blame or aggrandize himself in the public eye. He lies about having ended eight wars (the few times his administration has tried to list these wars, it became clear that some were never wars, some ended before he became president, and some haven't ended). He lies about how tariffs work and who pays; he lies about consumer prices coming down and who won the 2020 Presidential election; he lies about bringing drug prices down "1000 percent" – a mathematical impossibility. But his ego does now allow him to admit being wrong. Staff must then double and triple down as they try to save the president's face, swearing to his lies or risk losing their jobs. Such volatility has left even the media at a loss on how to cover his pathological lying, but many authors in this collection call out such behavior and name the narcissism and the megalomania – the conceit and the absolute obsession with his own construction of his own truth.[42]

Eco's 14 principles of eternal or "Ur-Fascism" include the use of Orwell's "Newspeak" where power uses repetitive, "impoverished vocabulary" and "elementary syntax, in order to limit the instruments for complex and critical reasoning." It demands uncritical obedience where "disagreement is treason." Eco continues:

> *Besides, disagreement is a sign of diversity. Ur-Fascism grows up and seeks for consensus by exploiting and exacerbating the natural fear of difference. The first appeal of a fascist or prematurely fascist movement is an appeal against the intruders. Thus Ur-Fascism is by definition racist.*[ix]

Contributors throughout this book critique Trump's policies, practices, and rhetoric as racist, white supremacist, white nationalist, etc. Again, the evidence for such claims is legion – from policies that target immigrants of color (specifically those from Somalia, Haiti, and Latin America) to tweets referring to Black-led nations as "shit-hole" countries and reposting racist memes depicting the Obamas as gorillas. "Number 1 Fans"[43] like Nicki Minaj aside, tagging Trump as a racist seems hardly provocative or controversial anymore.

NOTES

1. CBS News. (2026, January 8). *Minnesota investigators say the FBI has blocked them from accessing evidence in the deadly ICE shooting*. https://www.cbsnews.com/minnesota/news/bca-withdraws-renee-good-ice-shooting-investigation/

[ix] Eco (1995, p. 8).

2. Corbett, J. (2025, July 14). *DOJ unit that defends Trump policies sees exodus of lawyers*. Common Dreams. Retrieved February 25, 2026, from https://www.commondreams.org/news/trump-doj.

3. Reuters. (2026). *New video of Renee Good's fatal encounter with ICE agent in Minneapolis*. Retrieved February 25, 2026, from https://www.reuters.com/graphics/USA-TRUMP/MINNESOTA-RECONSTRUCT/egvbbeqeevq/.

4. Stanton, A. (2026, January 8). *JD Vance calling woman shot by ICE 'deranged leftist' sparks liberal fury*. Newsweek; Levinson-Waldman, R. (2026, January 16). *Labeling Renee Good a "domestic terrorist" distorts the law*. Brennan Center for Justice; Uribe, M. R., & Sherman, A. (2026, January 10). *Experts question Noem calling Good a 'domestic terrorist.' Here's what the term means*. PBS NewsHour/PolitiFact.

5. PolitiFact. (2025, October 29). *Do ICE officers have 'federal immunity' as White House official Stephen Miller said?* https://www.politifact.com/factchecks/2025/oct/29/stephen-miller/ICE-agent-immigration-raids-legal-immunity/.

6. *The New York Times*. (2026, January 11). Transcript: President Trump speaks with reporters from *The New York Times*. https://www.nytimes.com/2026/01/11/us/politics/trump-interview-transcript.html.

7. Haberman, M., Savage, C., & Swan, J. (2023, July 17). Trump and allies forge plans to increase presidential power in 2025. *The New York Times*. Archived from the original on November 13, 2023. Retrieved November 13, 2023, from; Garcia-Navarro, L. (2024). Inside the Heritage Foundation's plans for 'institutionalizing Trumpism.' *The New York Times* (Digital Edition); Montgomery, P. (2024). *Project 2025: How Trump loyalists and right-wing leaders are paving a fast road to fascism*. Political Research Associates.

8. Garcia-Navarro, L. (2024). Inside the Heritage Foundation's plans for 'institutionalizing Trumpism.' *The New York Times* (Digital Edition), NA–NA. https://www.nytimes.com/2024/01/21/magazine/heritage-foundation-kevin-roberts.html

9. American Federation of Government Employees. (2024, November 25). New Trump administration packed with Project 2025 architects. https://www.afge.org/article/new-trump-administration-packed-with-

project-2025-architects/ For more on *Project 2025* see the following: Graham, D. A. (2025). *The project: How project 2025 is reshaping America*. Random House; Foster, J. B. (2025). The MAGA ideology and the Trump regime. *Monthly Review, 1*.

10. ACLU. (2026). *Project 2025, explained*. https://www.aclu.org/project-2025-explained.

11. Faulkner, N., Dathi, S., Hearse, P., & Syeda, S. (2019). *Creeping fascism: What it is & how to fight it*. Public Reading Rooms.

12. Abbasi, K. (2025). *How do we navigate our way to focusing on sickness, suffering, and symptoms when the zones are flooded? BMJ*, 388. Epstein, L., & Smith, R. M. (2024). Donald J. Trump, the Supreme Court, and American constitutionalism. *The Annals of the American Academy of Political and Social Science, 713*(1), 8–14; Pruszynski, K. (2025). Trump 2.0 and the new American oligarchy. *Political Insight, 16*(1), 8–11.

13. Wagner, D. (2025, December 31). More than 317,000 federal employees left US government in 2025. *USA Today*. https://www.usatoday.com/story/news/politics/2025/12/31/317000-federal-employees-left-us-government-2025/87970708007/

14. Martin, C. R. (2019). *No longer newsworthy: How the mainstream media abandoned the working class*. ILR Press.

15. Associated Press. (2023, April 26). *Trump denies E. Jean Carroll rape claim as trial begins*. AP News. https://apnews.com/article/trump-rape-carroll-trial-fc68259a4b98bb3947d42af9ec83d7db

16. Bromwich, J. E., & Hill, T. (2026, January 26). Minneapolis ICE shooting videos under scrutiny as investigators assess conflicting footage. *The New York Times*. https://www.nytimes.com/2026/01/26/insider/minneapolis-ice-shooting-videos-investigation.html

17. Associated Press. (2026, January 8). *Driver shot in Minneapolis is at least the 5th person killed in US immigration crackdown*. WTTW News. https://apnews.com/article/minnesota-immigration-enforcement-shooting-crackdown-surge-173e00fa7388054e98c3b5b9417c1e5a

18. Singh, M., Murphy Marcos, C., & Simmonds, C. (2026, January 4). 2025 was ICE's deadliest year in two decades: Here are the people who died in custody, *The Guardian*. https://www.theguardian.com/us-news/ng-interactive/2026/jan/04/ice-2025-deaths-timeline

19. Yancey-Bragg, N. (2026, January 12). Cuban immigrant confirmed dead at ICE's Camp East Montana facility in El Paso. *USA Today*. https://www.usatoday.com/story/news/nation/2026/01/22/geraldo-lunas-campos-ice-texas-autopsy-homicide/88308959007/

20. *The New York Times*. (2026, January 4). *Live: Trump says U.S. will "run" Venezuela after capturing Maduro*. https://www.nytimes.com/live/2026/01/03/world/trump-maduro-venezuela-us-strikes

21. Cavalcanti, D. M., de Oliveira Ferreira de Sales, L., da Silva, A. F., Basterra, E. L., Pena, D., Monti, C., Barreix, G., Silva, N. J., Vaz, P., Saute, F., Fanjul, G., Bassat, Q., Naniche, D., Macinko, J., & Rasella, D. (2025). Evaluating the impact of two decades of USAID interventions and projecting the effects of defunding on mortality up to 2030: A retrospective impact evaluation and forecasting analysis. *The Lancet, 406*(10500), 283–294.

22. Gostin, L. O., Friedman, E. A., & Wetter, S. (2025). Dismantling US global health aid. *Health Affairs Forefront*. https://ramaonhealthcare.com/dismantling-us-global-health-aid/ Johnston, J., & Lorentzen, A. (2022). *Capacity development for whom? An Agenda for USAID reform in Haiti*. Center for Economic and Policy Research. https://cepr. net/wp-conte nt/uploa ds/2022/01/Haiti-Aid-Reform-Final.pdf; Carpenter, C. L. (2020). USAID'S assured assistance: USAID's humanitarian aid in Latin America and the Caribbean 2001–2019. *Revista Internacional de Cooperación y Desarrollo*, 7(2), 163–176; Harold, S. W., Morris, L. J., & Ma, L. (2019). *Countering Chinas efforts to isolate Taiwan diplomatically in Latin America and the Caribbean: The role of development assistance and disaster relief* (No. RR2885). https://apps.dtic.mil/sti/html/tr/AD1096835/index.html

23. Singh, S. K., Gupta, G. K., Agrawal, D., Zaidi, S. H. N., Batra, J., Sharma, L., Juneja, S., Joshi, K. J., Sethy, G., Haile, D. A., & Syed, S. (2024). Leveraging resource centers for strengthening immunization supply chain. *Cureus*, *16*(4); Bristol, N., Simoneau, M., & Bliss, K. (2025). *Enhancing US leadership in a new era of global immunization* [Working papers]. CSIS; Cavalcanti, D. M., et al. (2025) Evaluating the impact of two decades of USAID interventions and projecting the effects of defunding on mortality up to 2030: A retrospective impact evaluation and forecasting analysis. *The Lancet, 406*(10500), 283–294.

24. Defend Research. (2026). *Defend Research: Take action to stop U.S. government censorship of academic research.* https://www.defendresearch.org/take-action

25. Faust, J. (2025, February 1). *BREAKING NEWS: CDC orders mass retraction and revision of submitted research across all science and medicine journals. Banned terms must be....* Inside Medicine (Substack). https://insidemedicine.substack.com/p/breaking-news-cdc-orders-mass-retraction

26. Garisto, D., & Kozlov, M. (2025, February 3). Exclusive: NSF starts vetting all grants to comply with Trump's orders. *Science.* https://pubmed.ncbi.nlm.nih.gov/39900798/

27. Johnson, C. Y., Dance, S., & Achenbach, J. (2025, February 4). Here are the words putting science in the crosshairs of Trump's orders. *The Washington Post.* https://www.washingtonpost.com/science/2025/02/04/national-science-foundation-trump-executive-orders-words/

28. Deming, D. (2025, February 11). DOGE is failing on its own terms. *The Atlantic*; Kauffman, K. (2025, February 4). *The fight to preserve federal government data.* MuckRock. https://www.theatlantic.com/ideas/archive/2025/02/nih-nsf-science-doge/681645/

29. Lovelace, B., Jr., & Edwards, E. (2025, February 4). *Federal health workers terrified after "DEI" website publishes list of "targets."* NBC News.

30. Dolgon, C. (2024). From social justice to revolutionary sociology: Notes toward a popular culture of uprising. In The Oxford Handbook of Sociology for Social Justice (Epilogue, pp. 601–609). Oxford University Press.

31. Freire, P. (1994). *Pedagogy of hope: Reliving pedagogy of the oppressed* (R. R. Barr, Trans.). Continuum.

32. Dolgon, C. (2024). From social justice to revolutionary sociology: Notes toward a popular culture of uprising. In C. Dolgon (Ed.), *The handbook of sociology for social justice* (pp. 605–612). Oxford University Press.

33. Aerospace Global News. (2026). *Avelo Airlines withdraws from ICE deportation flights.* https://aerospaceglobalnews.com/news/avelo-airlines-withdraws-ice-deportation-flights/

34. Greene, C. (2026, February 5). Communities fight to block new ICE detention centers. *TIME*. https://time.com/7371935/ice-immigration-trump-detention-warehouse-protests/

35. Maddow, R. (2026, February 3). *Across the country, Americans are saying no to ICE prisons in their communities.* The Rachel Maddow Show/MaddowBlog; Maddow, R. (2026, February 2). *The Rachel Maddow show*. MS NOW. https://www.ms.now/rachel-maddow-show/maddowblog/americans-protest-ice-detention-facilities-trump-mass-deportation

36. Tulli, E. (2026, February 4). *Standing together*. OnLabor. https://onlabor.org/when-workers-stand-together/

37. Oursler, A. (2026, January 20). "2020 never ended": how Black Lives Matter organizing taught Minneapolis to handle ICE surge. *The Guardian*. https://www.theguardian.com/us-news/2026/jan/20/minneapolis-organizes-trump-ice-crackdown

38. Stegall, J., & Kosseff-Jones, A. (2026, January 23). *Minneapolis's 2020 uprising laid an abolitionist groundwork for ICE resistance.* Truthout. https://truthout.org/articles/minneapoliss-2020-uprising-laid-an-abolitionist-groundwork-for-ice-resistance/

39. Eco, U. (1995). Ur-fascism. *The New York Review of Books*, 22, 12–15; Paxton, R. O. (2005). *The anatomy of fascism*. Vintage; Passmore, K. (2014). *Fascism: A very short introduction*. OUP; Stanley, J. (2020). *How fascism works: The politics of us and them*. Random House Trade Paperbacks; Payne, S. G. (1996). *A history of fascism, 1914–1945*. University of Wisconsin Press.

40. Frederickson, J. (2018). *The dangerous case of Donald Trump: 27 psychiatrists and mental health experts assess a president. Psychiatry, 81*(4), 408–414. https://doi.org/10.1080/00332747.2018.1529989; Lee, B. X. (2023). Dangerous leadership and a culture of violence: Shared psychosis in the age of Donald Trump. *cultura & psyche*, *4*(1), 109–120; Levenson, H. R. (2023). Psychological projection: Trump and Santos (Birds of a feather flock together, what every US voter should know). *Advances in Social Sciences Research Journal*, *10*(12), 357–369.

41. Freedman, A., & Samenow, J. (2020, February 1). Newly released emails show how Trump roiled NOAA during Hurricane Dorian. *The Washington Post*. https://www.washingtonpost.com/weather/2020/02/01/new-emails-show-how-president-trump-roiled-noaa-during-hurricane-dorian/ Dale, D. (2025, December 27). *Analysis: Donald Trump's top 25 lies of 2025*. CNN News; Arceneaux, K., & Truex, T. (2023). Donald Trump and the lie. *Perspectives on Politics*, *21*(3), 863–879.

42. Barkho, L. (2023). A critical inquiry into US media's fact-checking and compendiums of Donald Trump's falsehoods and "lies." In S. Tobias & A. Stein (Eds.), *The perils of populism: The end of the American century?* (pp. 259–278). Springer Nature; Dale, D. (2025, September 23). *Fact check: Trump's mathematically impossible promise to cut drug prices by '1,000%.'* CNN News. https://www.cnn.com/2025/09/23/politics/fact-check-drug-prices-trump

43. Weaver, J. (2026, January 29). *Nicki Minaj declared herself Trump's "No. 1 fan." Why is that controversial?*. CBC News.

1

CHRONICLE OF A FORETOLD MESS: THE 2024 ELECTION AND TRUMP 2.0

Eduardo Bonilla-Silva

Duke University, USA

A SORT OF INTRODUCTION

In the summer of 2024, I drafted a beautiful essay criticizing our blind support and lofty expectations for Kamala Harris – a terribly flawed presidential candidate – which I presented at the 2024 meeting of the American Sociological Association (ASA) in Montreal. The essay was sociological and historical, but it also expressed my political views. However, as people were still shocked by that November's election result, I used the opportunity given to me by the editor of *Contexts* in late 2024[i] to address Trump in the room. I titled the piece I wrote for the sociology magazine, paraphrasing the title of García Márquez's novella *Crónica de una muerte anunciada* (*Chronicle of a Foretold Death*), as Trump's victory was a chronicle of foretold mess.

[i] In late 2024, a group of sociologists was invited by the editor of *Contexts* to write short essays on the election results. See Ghaziani et al. (2025).[1]

That piece is, with some amendments, the basis for this chapter. However, before I present the analysis I produced for *Contexts*, I must restate three of the things I articulated in my ASA intervention. And I must do this because I want readers to understand that my intent in that piece was explanatory, and in no way can it be regarded as supportive of the Democratic Party as a vehicle of progressive politics. First, if "we want change we can believe in" (remember Obama's campaign slogan?), we need to stop placing *all* our political efforts in the electorally oriented Democratic Party. After all, both parties receive massive support from corporate America[ii] and, despite Democrats' liberal vanilla flavor, they ultimately agree on maintaining America's racialized capitalist order and its imperialist policies (arguably the most glaring and shameful illustration of this is the party's continued support of Israel's genocidal campaign in Gaza). On this matter, Gore Vidal's[2] oft-quoted statement still applies:

> *There is only one party in the United States, the Property Party ... and it has two right wings: Republican and Democrat. (p. 50)*

Second, progressives and radicals need to stop voting reflexively for Democrats every four years, thinking they are the "lesser of two evils." This voting pattern, which began in earnest in 1980 when we characterized Reagan as a fascist, has clouded our vision. We have demonized every Republican nominee since and said little about the always compromised Democratic Party nominees. We have done this despite having ample evidence that "liberal" Democrat Presidents have enacted very conservative policies, such as Clinton's 1996 welfare reform or his 1994 "three-strikes and you're out" Crime Bill or Obama's deporting millions of immigrants and his imperialist record abroad – drone strikes and all.[3] During Biden's administration, we witnessed how he and the party leadership remained silent while programs such as affirmative action were targeted and finally

---

[ii] Thanks to the work of Domhoff (2021),[4] we know how corporations influence both political parties directly helping maintain the class domination of the bourgeoisie. The last election cycles have shown how politically flexible corporations can be as they switched their support from Democrats in 2020 to Republicans in 2024 based on their perception of which candidate best served their class interests.[5]

eliminated. More troublesome, Democrats failed to do *anything* meaningful while conservatives attacked critical race theory, diversity, equity, and inclusion (DEI), lesbian, gay, bisexual, transgender, and queer and trans rights, and women's rights, even when they controlled the presidency and Congress between 2016 and 2018. I suspect the latter reflects the fact that far too many liberals are not unhappy to see many of these things disappear. I have dealt with this in the academy[iii] and the same is clearly happening in the corporate world. In both, DEI is being replaced with "meritocratic" approaches that ignore the effects of racism, sexism, and homophobia on groups, processes, and outcomes.[6]

Lastly, although I remain convinced of the centrality of social movements for social justice to effect change, this does not mean I advocate ignoring electoral politics altogether. Rather, we should take a more strategic, shall we say, Leninist view on the matter.[iv] Lacking large social movement organizations in place and given the strong belief of the masses in elections, we must work to influence candidate selection and policies as well as work to produce new political options (on the possibilities of democratic regimes, see Bob Jessop,[7] and on popular-democratic populism, see Stuart Hall,[8] both in Hunt).[9]

Now I can proceed with my short chronicle of the 2024 election result and its foundational purpose for understanding the Trump 2.0 mess.

THE FORETOLD MESS

Most liberal-left leaning Americans believe their MSNBC [MSNOW]-CNN God. Rather than worshipping false idols, they

[iii] When the Supreme Court ended affirmative action in college admissions, some expected pushback from Biden and Democrats in Congress. But what we heard through the grapevine was lawyers from the Administration telling Administrators that the decision would apply not just to admissions. Rather than proclaiming their willingness to fight and expressing their support for the program, they clearly signified that universities would have to fight this on their own.

[iv] See *Lenin's Left Wing Communism, an Infantile Disorder: A Popular Essay in Marxist Strategy and Tactics*,[10] particularly chapter seven, "Should We Participate in Bourgeois Parliaments?"

should have been clear that Harris' chances were slim. First, as a Black woman, she had two strikes. Men, for example, voted for Trump (55%), and Harris received significantly less support from women than Clinton or Biden.[11]

Second, they believed the polls and had no concerns with "hidden Trump" supporters or the polls' small response rate. They also disregarded that the polls had displayed a curiously 2–3 points one-sided "margin of error" *for* the Democrats. Therefore, Trump's victory by about 1.5 points was not surprising.

Lastly, the extreme focus of Harris's campaign on democracy and abortion led them to downplay the economy (whatever happened to James Carville's famous mantra, "It's the economy stupid"?). Democratic Party leaders missed badly the economic anxiety of the masses, even though all indices of consumer confidence remained *well below* their levels during Trump's first term. A good example of the working-class economic anxiety is described by Politico reporter, Jack Herrera,[12] in an article published a few days after the election.

On the ground in Starr County, and in similar places across the country, I met voters who thought of the election simply as a referendum on the economy. The schoolteachers and gardeners and ranchers didn't talk like Steve Bannon or J. D. Vance. They talked about the price of milk and gas.

Democrats' insistence that people had a "perceptual gap" was profoundly anti-sociological and politically foolish. The real gap was among party elites who assumed their base was hooked and had nowhere to go. This strategy, once known as "triangulation," had become a policy of strangulation. Democrats failed miserably to understand the political implications of their increasingly more diverse, so-called coalition.[v]

DO NOT BELIEVE THE HYPE: TRUMP'S (WHITE) VICTORY

Trump won because of Whites' support. Whites comprised 71% of the electorate, and 57% of them supported Trump (*84% of his total*

[v] I say so-called coalition as voting for a party does not make one a bona fide member or supporter.

vote came from Whites). Young White Millennials and Gen-Xers, which many sociologists (and Right-Wing pundits) have touted as *woke*, also supported Trump (54% of Whites in the 18–29 and 52% of those in the 30–44 age groups).[13]

An important clarification: Whites who voted for Harris, much like those who voted for Obama in the past, are not "beyond race." Whites in both parties share the essentials on race matters except that White Democrats express their opinions with the nicest tones of color-blind racism.[14]

The false narratives of young folks being "woke" and White Democrats being racially progressive must be reexamined. To do so, we cannot continue putting our full faith in surveys. Sociologists should rely more on mixed methods designs to study the many complex topics we need to investigate, instead of reductive data points from a small sample pool. Meanwhile, we can't solely rely on such quantitative signifiers unless we understand the qualitative human stories that inform them.

DAMNED LATINOS (OR ASIANS OR ARAB AMERICANS)! A DANGEROUS STORYLINE

For the record, except for Cubans, "Latinos" [vi] (56%) went for Harris.[15] The issue was that Latinos' level of support for the Democratic candidate was smaller in this election than in the previous two elections. My Latin Americanization argument (2004) might explain elements of their vote,[vii] but religiosity (53% of Catholic and 64% of Protestant Latinos supported Trump)[16] masculinity, anti-communism, immigration, and frankly, anti-blackness[17] were key factors, too.

[vi] There is no Latino group. There are significant communal, racial, and political differences among the people that comprise this census category.

[vii] Since the early 21st century, I argued that a reorganization of the racial hierarchy was emerging. Specifically, I claimed that segments of the Latino and Asian American communities were becoming white or "honorary white" (navigating an intermediate position and status). My argument has for the most part been corroborated and, in any case, extended to other communities. Nowadays, segments of the African American community are also working to exit "Blackness" and highlighting their bi-raciality, multiraciality, or claiming they are just American. For the original argument, see Bonilla-Silva (2004).[18]

However, blaming Latinos for Harris's defeat is wrong and risky business. Democrats' dismal work with Latinos over the years (treating them as electoral cattle) has a lot to do with how they voted. And within the designated cubicle that Democratic Party leaders assigned to people of color, Whites still regard African Americans as kings of the hill despite Latinos' population and electoral growth (Latinos comprised 12% of the electorate in the election compared to Blacks' 11% and are currently about 20% of the total US population). Not surprisingly, despite the clearly rising political significance of Latinos, they account for just 2% of elected officials nationwide, albeit their representation looks a bit better in Congress.[19] This was disastrous for the Democrats as everywhere they ran a Latino candidate, the candidate outperformed Harris.[20] Latinos must be taken seriously politically, economically, and culturally, otherwise they will continue their slow migration to the Republican Party.

Another issue seldom discussed in public is African Americans' expectation that Latinos and other groups of color will support their candidates no matter what. An illustration of this was the chaos that ensued after Chicago's mayor Harold Washington died in office in 1987. Although 75.3% of Latinos and a whopping 82.3% of Puerto Ricans had supported Washington in 1987,[21] they were not shown any love in the 1987 special election. The Black political elite ignored all possibilities and assumed Latinos were a guaranteed source of support. Not surprisingly, leaders such as Luis Gutierrez backed white Democrat Richard Daley in 1989 to advance his own community's interests (which he did). Despite imperfections, Gutierrez became arguably the most progressive, visible, and influential Latino politician during his 26-year career in Congress.

All communities of color need a less nationalistic consciousness to advance their interests and to address the racism and xenophobia in their midst. Latino leaders will have to take seriously and address the racism in their communities, illustrated by the statements leaked in 2022 by Los Angeles Council member Nury Martinez comparing the son of a Black member of Council to a monkey (the media and the public missed that she also referred to Oaxacans as "little short dark people" who were "so ugly").[22] African-American leaders will also have to tackle the growing anti-Latino and anti-immigrant sentiment in their community, a sentiment that is not new.[viii,23,24] African Americans in particular must accept that progressive Latino candidates can represent them, whether they are running for local positions on school boards or city councils or for president of the country. Love is always a two-way street for everyone!

WHAT NOW?

Democracy, updating Lenin on race, is the "best possible shell for [racial] capitalism."[ix] Therefore, voting is a tactical matter even though it is not the *best* tool for attaining social justice. If we want real change, we must return to social movement politics. We must build a multiracial, multiclass united front *against* Trump's agenda and *for* social democracy. But if we keep dancing the Democrats' electoral waltz of fear ("Us or the fascists") in upcoming elections, we will rightfully deserve Macondo's[x] fate: *100 years of solitude.*

***

This is how I ended the *Contexts* piece I referenced above. Now I end the sequel by commenting on Trump's first months in power and the always important matter of what is to be done.

[viii] For the record, the data on African-American racism against other people or color and their xenophobia are scant. This, I suspect, is the result of the long-standing tradition of analyzing racism as something affecting Blacks only. Here is a subject that, although controversial, is deserving of systematic research.

[ix] The phrase appeared in Lenin's *State and Revolution*,[25] originally published in 1918. However, this is not the place for theoretical discussions, but for the record, Lenin's claim about how capitalism is best defended through liberal democratic regimes can be expanded and improved by adding the fact that capitalism (a product of modernity), was a *racialized* system from the beginning. The fact that class formation has remained racialized in the world system is the outgrowth of how primitive accumulation was (and is) enacted. For an elaboration on this, see my 2021 "debate" with Walter Benn Michaels sponsored by the University of Pennsylvania's The Andrea Mitchell Center for the Study of Democracy.[26]

[x] This is the name of the fictitious town in García Márquez's most famous novel, *Cien Años de Soledad.*

As predicted, Trump has deepened his authoritarian tendencies and appointed a cabinet of foolish acolytes who praise him and his policies no matter what. You know Trump has overdone things when even arch-conservative commentator Ann Coulter characterizes his 90-minute, open to the press cabinet meeting as "Kim Jong Il-style."[27] We are getting what we expected and then some.

Also, as predicted, Trump has proposed a budget that will extend the tax breaks he awarded the rich in his 2017 Tax Cuts and Jobs Act and add another 3.3 trillion dollars to our national debt.[28] His "Big Beautiful Bill" will throw millions off health care and cut both Medicare and Medicaid, resulting in billions cut from social programs for poor and working class people, and make major cuts to funding for public schools and higher education. He has also gotten the US embroiled in a tariff war with all nations of the world, affecting workers via inflation[29] and market volatility that has retirees and middle-class people anxiously looking at the rapid roller coaster of their 401(k) accounts. As I finish this chapter, the consumer confidence index has spiraled downward fast and furiously, a likely indicator that a recession is looming on the horizon (and most readers probably remember how horrific things were during the 2008–2009 recession).[xi]

What most people did not expect, but I alluded to in my discussion, was the rather timid response of the Democrats to Trump's policies. On this, we need to go back to first principles – if the differences between the two corporate parties in the USA are minimal, we should not expect them to do much. Dave Zirin's piece in *The Nation*[30] is on point regarding this matter. He argues that the Democrats are not "spineless," but are interested in keeping the peace with their corporate sponsors. Besides, as he suggests, they support the substance, albeit not the style, of a lot of what Trump is doing.

The issue at hand then is not simply Trump's authoritarianism, but liberals' tacit support of many of his policies. In universities across the country, for example, the main concern of administrators

[xi] While Rugaber (AP, April 4, 2025) wrote that consumer confidence had hit a four-year low (since the onset of the COVID-19 pandemic) reports from late January show that the Conference Board's Consumer Confidence Index declined for the sixth out of seven months, "well below the threshold that usually signals a recession ahead."

seems to be overfunding. Before Harvard took a stand against Trump's interventionist agenda, other universities were accommodating to his demands (Columbia University's total capitulation is a case in point[xii]) or negotiating deals with his disciples. It remains to be seen if corporate America will follow Columbia's or Harvard's path, but as of late 2025, it seems they will likely follow Columbia's path.[31]

So "What now?" This might be the ideal opportunity to launch a frontal attack on the two-party system and try to organize a movement against the "one percent" (the 2011 Occupy Movement had the right target, albeit its tactics were diffused and, ultimately, ineffective). "We the (99 percent of the) people" need to organize, organize, and when tired, we must organize some more. We should be tactical with the Democrats, but not at the expense of ignoring that they are not too different from their Republican brethren. Hence, I reiterate my belief in the urgent need of building "a multiracial, multiclass united front against Trump's agenda and for social democracy." Nothing else will protect us against Trump's authoritarianism or the Democrats' "killing me softly" politics and, for me, the latter is truly "(the worse) of two evils."

NOTES

1. Ghaziani, A., Abrutyn, S., Laurison, D., Romero, M., Perrin, A. J., Spencer-Blume, A., Menjivar, C., & Bonilla-Silva, E. (2025) Election reflections – And what comes next. *Contexts, 24*(1), 12–21.

2. Vidal, G. (2004). *Imperial America: Reflections on the United States of amnesia*. Clairview Books.

3. Bonilla-Silva, E., Seamster, L., & Ray, V. (2015). Unpacking the imperialist knapsack: White privilege and imperialism in Obama's America. In B. Bergo & T. Nicholls (Eds.), *"I don't see color": Personal and critical perspectives on white privilege* (pp. 146–168). Penn State University Press.

[xii] In July 2025, Columbia University agreed to pay a $200m fine in order to restore its federal research funding.

4. Domhoff, W. G. (2021). *Who rules America? The corporate rich, White Nationalist Republicans, and inclusionary Democrats in the 2020s.* Routledge.

5. Savage, L. (2022, February 3). The democrats are choosing to rely on corporate donors. Jacobin. https://jacobin.com/2022/02/-gop-super-pacs-pelosi-bloomberg-warren

6. The White House. (2025, April 23). *Fact sheet: President Donald J. Trump signs landmark order to restore equality of opportunity and meritocracy.* https://www.whitehouse.gov/fact-sheets/2025/04/fact-sheet-president-donald-j-trump-signs-landmark-order-to-restore-equality-of-opportunity-and-meritocracy/

7. Jessop, B. (1980). The political indeterminacy of democracy. In A. Hunt (Ed.), *Marxism and democracy* (pp. 55–80). Lawrence and Wishart.

8. Hall, S. (1980). Popular-democratic versus authoritarian populism: Two ways of 'taking democracy seriously'. In A. Hunt (Ed.), *Marxism and democracy* (pp. 157–185). Lawrence and Wishart.

9. Hunt, A. (Ed.). (1980). *Marxism and democracy.* Lawrence & Wishart.

10. Lenin, V. I. (1988). *Left wing communism, an infantile disorder: A popular essay in Marxist strategy and tactics.* International Publishers Company, Incorporated. https://ebookcentral.proquest.com/lib/cam/detail.action?docID=6006774

11. Wolf, Z. B., Merrill, C., & Mullery, W. (2024, November 6). *Anatomy of three Trump elections: How Americans shifted in 2024 vs. 2020 and 2016: Exits polls reveal a divided country.* https://edition.cnn.com/interactive/2024/politics/2020-2016-exit-polls-2024-dg/index.html

12. Herrera, J. (2024, November 11). *Why Democrats lost Latinos.* Politico. https://www.politico.com/news/magazine/2024/11/11/why-democrats-lost-latinos-00188769

13. Center for Information and Research on Civil Learning and Engagement. (2024). *2024 election.* https://circle.tufts.edu/

14. Bonilla-Silva, E. (2019). "Racists," "class anxieties," hegemonic racism, and democracy in Trump's America. *Social Currents*, 6(1), 14–31. https://doi.org/10.1177/2329496518804558

15. Gerbaud, G., Chase, H., & Robertson, K. (2024, November 6). *How Latinos voted in the 2024 U.S. presidential election*. https://www.as-coa.org/articles/how-latinos-voted-2024-us-presidential-election

16. Foley, R. (2024, November 07). Exit polls show Latino Christians swung hard to Trump in 2024. *Christian Post*. https://www.christianpost.com/news/latino-christians-swung-hard-to-trump-in-2024-exit-polls-show.html

17. Hernández, T. K. (2022). *Racial innocence: Unmasking Latino anti-Black bias and the struggle for equality*. Beacon Press.

18. Bonilla-Silva, E. (2004). From bi-racial to tri-racial: Towards a new system of racial stratification in the USA. *Ethnic and Racial Studies*, *27*(6), 931–950.

19. Latino Policy and Politics Institute. (2024). *As more Latinos run for U.S. Congress ahead of the 2024 elections, study finds they remain significantly underrepresented in elected offices*. https://latino.ucla.edu/press/latino-representation-in-congress/

20. Piper, J., Mutnick, A., & Soni, P. (2025, March 30). *The hidden trend behind Latinos' shift toward Trump*. Politico. https://www.politico.com/news/2025/03/30/latino-voters-trump-ticket-splitting-028498

21. Sánchez, J., Jr. (2021). 'What are we?': Latino politics, identity, and memory in the 1983 Chicago mayoral election. *Modern American History*, *4*(3), 263–281. https://doi.org/10.1017/mah.2021.21

22. Uranga, R. (2022, October 17). L.A. Latinos grapple with familiar colorism against Black and Indigenous people in racist tap. *Los Angeles Times*. https://www.latimes.com/california/story/2022-10-17/l-a-latinos-grapple-with-familiar-colorism-against-blacks-and-indigenous-people-in-racist-tape

23. Buchanan, S. (2005 July 27). *Tensions mounting between Blacks and Latinos nationwide* [Report]. Southern Poverty Law Center. https://www.splcenter.org/resources/reports/tensions-mounting-between-blacks-and-latinos-nationwide/

24. Vaca, N. (2004). *The presumed alliance: The unspoken conflict between Latinos and Blacks and what it means for America*. Rayo.

25. Lenin, V. I., & Chretien, T. (2014). *State and revolution: Fully annotated edition*. Haymarket Books. https://ebookcentral.proquest.com/lib/CAM/detail.action?docID=2028937

26. RACE AND POLITICS SERIES. (The Andrea Mitchell Center for the Study of Democracy). (2021). *Checking your privilege? Perspectives on the politics of White identity* [Video]. https://www.bing.com/videos/riverview/relatedvideo?&q=benn++miachAeLs+and+bonilla-silva&&mid=64C1A83 58B457F86280164C1A8358B457F862801&&FORM=VRDGAR

27. *Times of India*. (2025, May 1). *Trump cabinet takes turns to praise him. Ann Coulter calls it 'Kim Jong Ill-style tributes*. https://timesofindia.indiatimes.com/world/us/trump-cabinet-takes-turn-to-praise-him-ann-coulter-calls-it-kim-jong-il-style-tributes/articleshow/120776498.cms

28. Luhby, T. (2025, May 19). *Here's what's in the House GOP's sweeping tax and spending cuts package*. CNN.Com. https://edition.cnn.com/2025/05/02/politics/what-is-in-trump-tax-spending-cuts-package

29. Boak, J., & Rugaber, C. (2025, February 13). *The latest inflation report shows that high prices are Trump's major economic challenge*. Associate Press. https://apnews.com/article/trump-inflation-tariffs-prices-consumer-50c473821 6756499c8cdc17ab77d6d4f

30. Zirin, D. (2025, February 2018). Why democrats won't throw a real punch. *The Nation*. https://www.thenation.com/article/politics/democratic-party-fecklessness/

31. Murray, C., & Bohannon, M. (2025, April 11). IBM reportedly walks back diversity policies, citing 'inherent tensions': Here are all the companies rolling back DEI programs. *Forbes*. https://www.forbes.com/sites/conormurray/2025/04/11/ibm-reportedly-walks-back-diversity-policies-citing-inherent-tensions-here-are-all-the-companies-rolling-back-dei-programs/

2

HOLLOWED OUT: PUBLIC HEALTH INEQUITY AND SOCIAL WELFARE RETRENCHMENT IN THE TRUMP ERA

Katrinell M. Davis

Florida State University, USA

INTRODUCTION

The social welfare state in the United States has long been shaped by policies that deepen vulnerability while deflecting institutional accountability. This pattern has persisted across party lines. Under Trump's second term, however, this process accelerated – moving from rhetorical attacks on "big government" to a sweeping dismantling of labor, education, health, and environmental protections. Branded as administrative streamlining through entities such as the Department of Government Efficiency, these efforts marked a calculated withdrawal of the state from its responsibilities to care – particularly for those most dependent on public institutions.

This chapter argues that federal policy actions – enacted and proposed – are not isolated cases of conservative governance or budget restraint. Rather, they reflect a pattern of political disinvestment that weakens public infrastructure, redistributes risk to vulnerable populations, and distances government actors from responsibility for structural harm. By examining shifts in public sector employment, disability rights enforcement, Medicaid access, environmental regulation, and early childhood development, I show how these policies function collectively to erode the social contract and expand institutional neglect.

As social protections are hollowed out, the burden of care is increasingly pushed onto individuals, families, and underfunded community organizations – deepening precarity and accelerating disparities in health, employment, and life expectancy. This moment calls for more than symbolic resistance. It demands a structural response that treats public welfare not as an entitlement to be trimmed, but as a fundamental political and social commitment to strengthen our humanity.

PUBLIC HEALTH DISPARITIES IN CONTEMPORARY SOCIETY

Public health disparities in the United States represent consequences of deliberate social policy decisions rather than mere gaps in care. Discriminatory housing policies like redlining and exclusionary zoning have systematically concentrated poverty and limited access to quality healthcare, education, and employment opportunities in communities of color. These policy-driven inequities manifest in statistics revealing elevated rates of asthma, hypertension, maternal mortality, and reduced life expectancy, particularly affecting Black, Indigenous, and low-income communities. For instance, the life expectancy gap between Black and White Americans, while narrowing over recent decades, remains substantial at 3.6 years as of 2018, down from 7 years in 1990.[1] Residential segregation – a direct result of these housing policies – significantly contributes to this disparity, with studies showing segregation increases the life expectancy gap by approximately 5 years for women and 16 years for men.[2]

In addition, Black women face a maternal mortality rate of 50.3 deaths per 100,000 live births – more than three times the rate for White women (14.5 per 100,000).[3,4] In New York State, Black women had a pregnancy-related mortality ratio five times higher than White women (54.7 vs 11.2 deaths per 100,000 live births).[5] These disparities persist across all income and education levels, demonstrating that individual factors alone cannot explain the gap.

These inequities manifest as institutional neglect disproportionately affecting marginalized groups, compounded by state retreat from public welfare responsibilities.[6,7] This systemic neglect creates patterns of wage precarity, mass incarceration, and environmental toxicity, fostering intergenerational poverty.[8] Health disparities thus function as visible symptoms of broader social welfare retrenchment affecting both support systems and healthcare access.[9,10] This retrenchment transforms public health disparities from medical problems into political crises embedded in policies governing social entitlements.[11]

Addressing these inequities requires holistic approaches that recognize health disparities cannot be resolved through medical interventions alone, but demand systemic changes to the social welfare policies that create and sustain them.[12] Despite this dynamic, House Republicans propose cutting over $600 billion from Medicaid, targeting $880 billion in reductions to federal Medicaid spending over 10 years.[13,14] The Congressional Budget Office estimates these changes could lead to 8.6 million Americans losing healthcare coverage.[15] With over 83 million people currently receiving Medicaid coverage, these cuts would affect one in five Americans.[16]

The erosion of these systems exposes vulnerable groups to intensified precarity, making survival contingent on private means rather than public support. Strong social welfare systems are not merely safety nets but essential *public* goods that extend life expectancy, improve health, and reduce intergenerational poverty when equitably administered.

BEYOND AUSTERITY: STRATEGIC RETRENCHMENT AND THE HOLLOWING OF THE SOCIAL STATE

Trump's administration has initiated a sweeping rollback of the American welfare state – dismantling labor protections, defunding programs for children and families, gutting civil rights enforcement, and accelerating environmental deregulation. From the elimination of diversity, equity, and inclusion (DEI) protections and special education oversight to Medicaid work requirements and proposed erasure of Head Start, these moves represent a deliberate weakening of state protective functions. This section outlines how these policies constitute a coordinated attack on institutional infrastructures sustaining health, equity, and public accountability.

Labor Market Policy: From Retrenchment to Abandonment

This systematic dismantling of social welfare extends into labor policy, where Trump's second administration has transformed retrenchment into a strategy of large-scale displacement. Within the first 100 days, Trump introduced significant labor changes, reducing wages for federal contractors, disproportionately impacting low-income workers. Trump rescinded an executive order that gave 390,000 low-wage federal contractors a living wage.[17] The move eliminated the $17.75 per hour minimum wage for federal contractors established under Biden, reverting to $13.30 per hour – a 25% pay cut.[18,19] For full-time federal contractors earning minimum wage, this represents a loss of over $9,000 per year. If the administration eliminates the higher minimum wage entirely and reverts to the federal minimum of $7.25 per hour, workers would face a nearly 60% pay cut – a loss of roughly $22,000 annually.[20]

The administration has also enacted widespread cuts to federal positions, impacting essential sectors such as education, health, and research. Approximately 107,000 federal jobs have been eliminated thus far under the Trump administration, with plans to reduce an additional 107,000 non-defense positions by fiscal year 2026.[21] Specifically, the Education Department faces the most significant reductions, as it prepares to lay off one-third of its workforce.[22] These actions are framed as necessary steps toward "streamlining" government operations; however, they have profound implications for public sector employment, which has historically provided avenues for upward mobility among Black and Brown communities.

Research illustrates that the public sector employment premium is particularly strong for Black women, who have long depended on federal job opportunities for economic security. The trend over several decades shows a significant decline; for instance, the proportion of college-educated Black women employed in the public sector fell from 80% in 1970 to 50% by 1990.[23] These job cuts not only disrupt economic stability but also exacerbate inequalities, as federal and state employment benefits are vital for all women, especially for those in marginalized demographic groups.[24] Thus, the ongoing layoffs and reductions in public sector jobs have an outsized impact on communities that have traditionally leveraged such jobs to achieve improved economic conditions. The elimination of these roles threatens to erode the economic foundations that many families depend on, amplifying existing disparities and risking long-term consequences for upward mobility in vulnerable populations.

These shifts in the public sector workforce aren't about efficiency but about erasing government employment's stabilizing role for vulnerable communities. This echoes earlier corporate restructuring when companies offloaded thousands of workers with pension buyouts, only for many to return to lower-paying, less secure jobs. The difference now is that the public sector, once the fallback, is being hollowed out simultaneously. Workers face precarity from both directions: eroding state support and collapsing job stability.

At the same time, the elimination of DEI programs and labor guardrails – under the guise of restoring "neutrality" – removes even the minimal protections for historically marginalized workers. Trump's 2025 DEI directive – outlined in a February "Dear Colleague" letter – represents a sweeping and ideologically aggressive shift in federal education oversight. It reframes DEI efforts as forms of racial discrimination, labeling them "repugnant," "toxic," and unlawful under Title VI of the Civil Rights Act. The Department of Education under Trump began asserting that both explicit race-based policies and "proxies" (such as test-optional admissions meant to broaden access) are illegal. The policy also launched an "End DEI" portal, effectively deputizing the public to report suspected DEI-related discrimination, thus weaponizing community surveillance against inclusive educational practices.[25]

This approach is both punitive and deliberately vague. It overturns decades of federal guidance that supported DEI as a legal and necessary framework for addressing systemic inequality. Now, cultural responsiveness, social-emotional learning, and racial literacy training are cast as suspect. The chilling effect is immediate: schools must certify compliance or risk losing federal funds, and groups like the National Education Association and the Center for Black Educator Development report disruptions to educator training and legal services. Judges have since halted enforcement of the directive, citing serious due process violations: the guidance was so unclear that institutions couldn't reasonably predict what conduct was prohibited. Courts ruled it gave excessive discretion to enforcement officials and constituted a coercive final agency action. In short, what began as a regulatory pivot has become a broader cultural attack on educational equity – one that courts found both legally and constitutionally indefensible.[26]

Dismantling Protections, Deepening Inequality: The Quiet Erosion of Childhood Development and Disability Rights Provisions

Opposition to DEI programming during Trump's first 100 days also impacted how students with disabilities are protected in local areas throughout the United States. The US Department of Education,[27] under the Trump administration, has laid off nearly 1,300 employees, including at least 240 from the Office for Civil Rights (OCR),[28] and permanently closed seven of its 12 regional enforcement offices (Chicago, Philadelphia, New York City, Dallas, San Francisco, Boston, and Cleveland). These closures affect oversight of half the country's states, nearly 60,000 public schools, and over 30 million K-12 students. With more than 6,000 active civil rights investigations disrupted, former OCR staff warn that the department has severely undermined its ability to protect students' rights, leaving critical cases unresolved and threatening the future enforcement of educational equity.[29]

The closure of the OCR offices has significant implications for families navigating special education violations and healthcare access issues at the local level. Historically, OCR has served as a critical federal entity when state and local systems fail to uphold the rights of children with disabilities, ensuring access to Medicaid-covered therapies, enforcing anti-discrimination protections in health services, and addressing systemic neglect in marginalized communities.[30] Without OCR oversight, families facing barriers to medically necessary services – such as speech, behavioral, and occupational therapies – are left with fewer avenues for redress, often forced into costly litigation or left unsupported by state agencies.[31]

The dismantling of this enforcement body removes one of the few institutional mechanisms capable of holding public systems accountable.[32] These actions may exacerbate structural inequities and leave countless children and adults with disabilities without the protections guaranteed under the Rehabilitation Act of 1973,[33] the Individuals with Disabilities Education Act of 1990,[34] and other critical civil rights statutes.[35] By reducing oversight, the administration is making it even harder for families caring for dependents with special needs – young and old – to challenge systemic failures, reinforcing cycles of exclusion and harm.[36]

Accordingly, the administration's early policies suggest plans to significantly disrupt programs designed to support children and families. Trump proposed defunding Head Start, an essential early childhood education initiative serving low-income families. Head Start currently serves approximately 800,000 children and pregnant women annually, and since its inception in 1965, has served nearly 40 million children).[37,38] Head Start provides educational, nutritional, and health services that help level the playing field for children in poverty, and these budget cuts risk widening existing achievement gaps, reducing school readiness, and negatively affecting long-term academic and economic outcomes.[39]

Erasing the Safety Net: Public Health and Environmental Deregulation

Additionally, substantial budget cuts were proposed for public health initiatives critical to child welfare, including lead poisoning prevention and pediatric mental health services. Cuts to lead poisoning programs pose serious risks, as low-income and minority children disproportionately suffer from lead exposure, causing irreversible cognitive and developmental harm, reduced academic performance, and increased likelihood of chronic health problems.[40] Likewise, reducing pediatric mental health funding threatens early interventions critical for managing emotional and behavioral challenges, potentially leading to long-term negative outcomes such as poor school performance and diminished social and economic prospects.[41]

During Trump's first year, healthcare policy shifts also included substantial reductions in Medicaid funding, aggressive introduction of work requirements, and elimination of critical health programs. The administration pushed significant budget cuts to Medicaid, paired with stringent eligibility policies requiring beneficiaries to demonstrate employment or face coverage loss. Additionally, key health-related programs like the Health Resources and Services Administration and the Administration for Community Living were targeted for severe budget reductions or complete elimination, undermining public health and healthcare infrastructure.[42]

Medicaid's direct role in mitigating social determinants of health is also being dismantled. In March 2025, Centers for Medicare & Medicaid Services rescinded guidance that allowed states to use 1,115 waivers to cover housing, nutrition, and transportation. States with current waivers may continue them temporarily, but future proposals are effectively frozen. This move abandons a broader vision of health care and returns Medicaid to narrow clinical services and fiscal restraint.[43]

Furthermore, Trump's environmental policies in his initial 100 days have heavily favored deregulation. The Environmental Protection Agency (EPA) has undergone a noteworthy transformation due in part to Trump's executive order requiring two regulations to be repealed for every new one immediately constrained environmental protection. A proposed 31% budget cut ($2.6 billion) and hiring freeze gutted operational capacity. Scientific advisory committees were dismantled, and mid-level scientists were pushed into early retirement. Nearly $100 million in EPA grants were frozen. The agency restricted scientific communication and slashed research funding – undermining not just regulatory infrastructure but environmental science itself.[44]

This wave of deregulation is not an isolated case but reflects a broader, systematic unraveling of public governance – signaling a comprehensive reevaluation of the federal government's role in addressing societal needs and supporting vulnerable populations.[45]

The attack on the EPA mirrors the administration's ongoing efforts to dismantle core components of the US social welfare system. House Concurrent Resolution 14 outlines a substantial fiscal restructuring plan that would fundamentally alter federal spending priorities over the coming decade. The resolution proposes approximately $3.661 trillion in reductions to new budget authority alongside $4.787 trillion in outlay cuts spanning fiscal years 2024–2033. These reductions strategically target numerous budget functions, creating significant decreases across diverse sectors, including national defense, international affairs, scientific research, energy initiatives, agricultural programs, commercial development, healthcare systems, educational funding, veterans' benefits, and transportation infrastructure.

The policy shifts enacted and proposed under Trump's administration signal a calculated dismantling of core pillars of the American social contract. These are not isolated budgetary adjustments but coordinated efforts to roll back the state's role in ensuring collective welfare and equity. Labor market retrenchment, environmental deregulation, Medicaid cuts, and reduced childcare and disability protections constitute deliberate withdrawals of governmental responsibility and protection from marginalized communities. These actions increase precarity, deepen inequalities, and undermine social, economic, and health equity. This dismantling threatens to normalize neglect and shift responsibility from institutions to individuals, disproportionately burdening those least able to absorb harm.

STRATEGIES FOR CONFRONTING RETRENCHMENT: BEYOND SYMBOLIC RESISTANCE

The political project of social welfare retrenchment will not be undone through rhetorical opposition alone. Trump's second term has clarified that symbolic outrage offers little insulation for communities most vulnerable to institutional neglect. As the federal government accelerates its withdrawal from public responsibility, the burden of resistance shifts to state and local actors.

Civic participation remains essential, yet voting is not a catch-all solution – particularly when elected officials in ostensibly progressive regions implement federal directives with minimal resistance. Unlike the aggressive defiance launched by conservative governors against the Affordable Care Act, many Democratic-led states have defaulted to administrative compliance with Trump-era policies, even when they contradict their stated values. This silent compliance is not a procedural necessity – it is a political choice.

Legal strategies play a role in challenging the administration's punitive agenda. Civil rights groups, labor advocates, and environmental coalitions have initiated suits targeting unlawful waivers, discriminatory enforcement, and regulatory rollbacks. But litigation is slow and reactive. Without parallel pressure – *public campaigns, investigative journalism, and grassroots mobilization* – these efforts risk becoming symbolic gestures themselves.

We must confront the performative politics of symbolic progressivism. Take sanctuary city policies as an example. While cities like New York, Philadelphia, and Chicago framed themselves as protectors of immigrant communities during Trump's first term, many continued to share data with Immigration and Customs Enforcement (ICE), honor detainer requests, or exploit policy loopholes that facilitated enforcement. Sanctuary became branding – while deportation machinery operated uninterrupted beneath it. While mayors and governors in these cities and states (and elsewhere) finally began to stand their ground during the Summer and Fall of 2025, it was local and citizen led defiance that fueled the new found courage of these officials.

States like Florida and Texas have not merely complied with Trump's agenda – they have extended it. From replicating federal DEI bans to expanding detention partnerships and undermining labor protections, these states function as laboratories for deeper austerity. Conversely, states like California and New York offer examples of intentional resistance through environmental protection and expanded public health funding.

The takeaway is simple: neutrality does not exist. States are co-architects of the social contract. Whether through silence, acquiescence, or bold divergence, they shape what remains of public obligation. What's needed now is not symbolic dissent but coordinated disruption. We have seen the cost of hollowed-out systems: poisoned water in Flint, mass Covid deaths in underfunded hospitals, and stacked bodies in privatized detention centers. These are political outcomes of a state choosing punishment over protection. The time for observation and simple critique has passed. The charge now is to condemn, resist, legislate, and reimagine.

NOTES

1. Schwandt, H., Currie, J., Bär, M., Banks, J., Bertoli, P., Bütikofer, A., Cronin, C. J., Evans, W. N., Gupta, A., Koning, R., Leive, A., Lleras-Muney, A., Meltzer, D., Richter, K., Schmieder, J., Skans, O. N., Tominey, E., Wuppermann, A., & Venkataramani, A. S. (2021). Inequality in mortality between Black and White Americans by age, place, and cause and in comparison to Europe, 1990 to 2018. *Proceedings of the National Academy of Sciences, 118*(40), e2104684118.

2. Johnson, R. C. (2024). Where does the Black-white life expectancy gap come from? The deadly consequences of residential segregation. *Demography, 61*(3), 677–701.

3. *Pearson*, C. (2024, June 4). *US has the highest rate of maternal deaths among high-income nations.* CNN Health. https://www.cnn.com/2024/06/04/health/maternal-deaths-high-income-nations.

4. Policy Center for Maternal Mental Health. (2025, February). *Maternal mortality in the U.S. declined, though disparities in the Black population persist.* https://policycentermmh.org/maternal-mortality-in-the-u-s-a-declining-trend-with-persistent-racial-disparities-in-the-black-population/.

5. New York State Department of Health. (2024, March 14). *New York State report on pregnancy-associated deaths in 2018–2020.* https://www.health.ny.gov/press/releases/2024/2024-03-14_maternal_mortality.htm.

6. Bornstein, M. B., & Harville, E. W. (2020). Racial disparity in pregnancy risks and complications in the US: Temporal changes during 2007–2018. *Journal of Clinical Medicine*, 9(5), 1414. https://doi.org/10.3390/jcm9051414.

7. Yusuf, K. S., Szabo, K., & Lee, C. J. (2020). Expected surge in maternal mortality and severe morbidity among African-Americans in the era of COVID-19 pandemic. *International Journal of Maternal and Child Health and AIDS*, 9(2), 185–195. https://doi.org/10.21106/ijma.405.

8. MacDorman, M. F., & Declercq, E. (2020). Improving US maternal mortality reporting by analyzing literal text on death certificates, United States, 2016–2017. *PLOS ONE*, *15*(11), e0240701. https://doi.org/10.1371/journal.pone.0240701.

9. Chinn, D. (2021). Health equity among Black women in the United States. *Journal of Women's Health*, *30*(10), 1452–1456. https://doi.org/10.1089/jwh.2020.8868.

10. Thomas, S. B. (2022). Trust also means centering Black women's reproductive health narratives. *The Hastings Center Report*, *52*(4), 18–25. https://doi.org/10.1002/hast.1362.

11. Phelan, J. C., Link, B. G., & Tehranifar, P. (2010). Social conditions as fundamental causes of health inequalities: Theory, evidence, and policy implications. *Journal of Health and Social Behavior, 51*(Suppl.), S28–S40. https://doi.org/10.1177/0022146510383498.

12. Chinn, D. (2021). Health equity among Black women in the United States. *Journal of Women's Health*, *30*(10), 1452–1456. https://doi.org/10.1089/jwh.2020.8868.

13. PBS. (2025, May 28). *Exploring the potential impact of Medicaid cuts in Trump's big budget bill.* PBS NewsHour. https://www.pbs.org/newshour/show/exploring-the-potential-impact-of-medicaid-cuts-in-trumps-big-budget-bill.

14. Center on Budget and Policy Priorities. (2025, March 17). *Congressional Republicans can't cut Medicaid by hundreds of billions without hurting people*. CBPP Report. https://www.cbpp.org/research/health/congressional-republicans-cant-cut-medicaid-by-hundreds-of-billions-without-hurting.

15. Al Jazeera. (2025, May 25). Fact-checking Trump's claims about Medicaid cuts in GOP bill. *Al Jazeera Health News*. https://www.aljazeera.com/news/2025/5/25/fact-checking-trumps-claims-about-medicaid-cuts-in-gop-bill.

16. Vera Institute. (2025, March 18). *Trump's Medicaid cuts would be a disaster for crime and safety*. Vera Institute of Justice.

17. McNicholas, C., Sanders, S., Bivens, J., Poydock, M., & Costa, D. (2025, April 25). *100 ways Trump hurt workers in his first 100 days*. Economic Policy Institute. https://www.epi.org/publication/100-days-100-ways-trump-hurt-workers/.

18. Federal News Network. (2025, March 19). *White house rescinds federal contractor minimum wage*. https://federalnewsnetwork.com/federal-newscast/2025/03/white-house-rescinds-federal-contractor-minimum-wage/.

19. Reuters. (2025, March 20). *Trump nixes $17.75 minimum wage for federal contractors adopted by Biden*. https://www.reuters.com/legal/government/trump-nixes-1775-minimum-wage-federal-contractors-adopted-by-biden-2025-03-20/.

20. Economic Policy Institute. (2025, March). *The blatant Trump attack on workers you may not have heard about: Cutting the wages of hundreds of thousands of workers*. https://www.epi.org/blog/trumps-blatant-attack-on-workers-you-may-not-have-heard-about-cutting-the-wages-of-nearly-half-a-million-workers/.

21. Katz, E. (2025, June 6). *Trump is planning to slash 107,000 federal jobs next year. See where*. Government Executive. https://www.govexec.com/workforce/2025/06/trump-planning-slash-107000-federal-jobs-next-year-see-where/405758/.

22. Katz, E. (2025, June 6). *Trump is planning to slash 107,000 federal jobs next year. See where*. Government Executive. https://www.govexec.com/workforce/2025/06/trump-planning-slash-107000-federal-jobs-next-year-see-where/405758/.

23. Carrington, W. J., McCue, K., & Pierce, B. (1996). Black/white wage convergence: The role of public sector wages and employment. *Industrial and Labor Relations Review*, *49*(3), 456–471.

24. Davis, K. M., & Dickerson, N. T. (2007). Postindustrial era restructuring in the public sector: The effect on Black, Latina and White women workers 1970–2000. *Social Forces*, *86*(2), 671–698.

25. U.S. Department of Education. (2025a). *Dear colleague letter: SFFA v. Harvard (No. 109506)*. https://www.ed.gov/media/document/dear-colleague-letter-sffa-v-harvard-109506.pdf.

26. NPR. (2025, April 26). *3 judges ruled Trump overstepped with school DEI crackdowns*. https://www.npr.org/2025/04/26/nx-s1-5375904/trump-dei-schools-education-courts; *National Education Association* v. *United States Department of Education*, Civil No. 25-cv-091-LM, 2025 DNH 055 P (D.N.H. 2025).

27. U.S. Department of Education. (2025b). *Office for Civil Rights: Protecting the rights of students with disabilities*. https://www.ed.gov/ocr.

28. Office for Civil Rights. (2024). *Annual report to Congress: The Office for Civil Rights, U.S. Department of Education*. https://www.ed.gov/ocr/annual-report.

29. Higher Ed Dive. (2025, March 13). *Half of OCR eliminated after Trump Education Department layoffs*. https://www.highereddive.com/news/half-of-ocr-fired-after-trump-education-department-layoffs/742384/.

30. McLean, C., Hart, A., & Cline, J. (2020). Small advances and swift retreat: Race-conscious educational policy in the Obama and Trump administrations. *Education Policy Analysis Archives*, *31*, Article 75. https://doi.org/10.14507/epaa.31.7536.

31. Wettach, J. R., & Sanders, B. K. (2021). Insights into due process reform: A nationwide survey of special education attorneys. *Connecticut Public Interest Law Journal, 20*(2), 239–288. https://cpilj.law.uconn.edu/wp-content/uploads/sites/2515/2021/07/Wettach-Final.pdf.

32. Song, L., Choi, J., & Lee, S. (2020). The effects of Title IX enforcement on sexual assaults on college campuses. *Contemporary Economic Policy*, *42*(2), 254–269. https://doi.org/10.1111/coep.12656.

33. Rehabilitation Act of 1973, P.L. 93–112, 87 Stat. 355 (1973). https://www.congress.gov/bill/93rd-congress/house-bill/3683.

34. Individuals with Disabilities Education Act of 1990, Pub. L. No. 101–476, 104 Stat. 1103 (1990). https://www.congress.gov/bill/101st-congress/house-bill/3260.

35. Raj, C. (2021). The lost promise of disability rights. *Michigan Law Review, 119*(5), 933. https://repository.law.umich.edu/mlr/vol119/iss5/3/.

36. Maviglia, S., Soffientini, A., & Rosa, A. (2023). School resource officers and students with disabilities: *Wilson* v. *City of Southlake* (2019). *Intervention in School and Clinic, 58*(2), 112–119. https://doi.org/10.1177/10534512231156891.

37. Office of Head Start. (2025, February 27). *Head Start program facts: Fiscal year 2023*. U.S. Department of Health and Human Services.

38. National Head Start Association. (2025, January 23). *Head Start fact sheets*. NHSA Resource Center.

39. Hager, E. (2025, April 23). *How kids are harmed by Trump's budget cuts*. ProPublica. https://www.propublica.org/article/how-trump-budget-cuts-harm-kids-child-care-education-abuse.

40. Centers for Disease Control and Prevention, Lead Exposure and Prevention Advisory Committee. (2024, January 12). *LEPAC 2022 annual report to U.S. Department of Health and Human Services*. https://stacks.cdc.gov/view/cdc/148232.

41. United States Senate, Office of Senator Tim Kaine. (n.d.). *Report on Trump's first 100 days harming seniors and people with disabilities*. https://www.kaine.senate.gov/imo/media/doc/report_on_trumps_first_100_days_harming_seniors_and_people_with_disabilities.pdf.

42. Fierce Healthcare Staff, Muoio, D., Tong, N., Beavins, E., & Gliadkovskaya, A. (2025, April 30). *Donald Trump's first 100 days: A pulse check on healthcare*. Fierce Healthcare. https://www.fiercehealthcare.com/providers/donald-trump-first-100-days-healthcare-presidency-doge-rfk-jr-robert-kennedy-hhs-firings; Atlanta Journal-Constitution. (2025). *President Trump spent his first 100 days mirroring Project 2025. What happens next?* https://www.ajc.com/news/president-trump-spent-his-first-100-days-mirroring-project-2025-what-happens-next/41dfb313-00e6-413c-ada4-aef5536cc8e5; National Health Law Program. (2025, January). *President Trump's day one actions threaten Medicaid and the ACA*. https://healthlaw.org/president-trumps-day-one-actions-threaten-medicaid-and-the-aca/.

43. Fierce Healthcare. (2025, March 5). *CMS rescinds Medicaid's health-related social needs guidance*. https://www.fiercehealthcare.com/payers/cms-rescinds-medicaid-health-related-social-needs-guidance.

44. Environmental Protection Agency. (2025, March 14). *EPA launches biggest deregulatory action in U.S. history*. https://www.epa.gov/newsreleases/epa-launches-biggest-deregulatory-action-us-history; National Public Radio. (2025, May 2). *The Trump administration says it will cut EPA staffing to Reagan-era levels*. https://www.npr.org/2025/05/02/nx-s1-5385272/epa-environmental-protection-agency-cuts-trump-zeldin.

45. U.S. Congress. (2025). *H. Con. Res. 14, 119th Congress*. https://www.congress.gov/119/bills/hconres14/BILLS-119hconres14enr.pdf.

3

EXECUTIVE LAWLESSNESS AND UNPOPULAR AUTHORITARIAN POPULISM

Onwubiko Agozino

Virginia Tech, USA

INTRODUCTION

Reflections beyond the beginning of Donald Trump's second term showed supporters and opponents alike that he is not a democrat. He warned us he would be a dictator on day one, but his increasing authoritarianism suggests he continued the role on day two and beyond. On a personal note, I have a view of such activity unique from most criminologists. I grew up under a series of military dictatorships in Nigeria. As a child, I survived a genocide that killed 3.1 million people in Biafra. There, the dictatorship used starvation as a "legitimate weapon" of war. This experience makes me sensitive to the emergence of dictatorial rule anywhere in the world, and especially here in the United States – a country that has historically claimed to be an exceptional bastion of democracy.

Gani Fawehinmi, a Nigerian human rights lawyer, courageously and persistently challenged Nigeria's military dictators. These acts resulted in his repeated detention without trial or due process. Fawehinmi developed a theory to explain corrupt dictators' contempt toward courts and legal systems in general. He termed this style of rule "executive lawlessness." Elsewhere, I combined Fawehinmi's observations with Stuart Hall's theory of authoritarian populism to help explain South Africa's relatively *peaceful* transition to democracy – a transformation absent punitive turns in criminology.[1] Under the leadership of Nelson Mandela and the African National Congress – in partnership with the Communist Party of South Africa – the people embraced their traditional philosophy of *Ubuntu* to achieve what Derrida called the forgiveness of the unforgivable (although Tutu & Tutu[2] retorted that there is no such thing as the unforgivable under Ubuntu). After one year of Trump 2.0, we must wonder if such a new democratic turn is possible.

As this chapter will explore, Trump 2.0 has shown contempt for the democratic tenets of US justice system, and in many actions and executive orders (EOs) sought to bypass or even undermine existing laws and processes. In this way, Trump 2.0 exhibits executive lawlessness. Trump's anti-democratic, lawless EOs eroded what has been a generally presumed and constitutionally protected lynchpin of US legal system – *due process*. Yet, his authoritarian efforts to dismantle due process could not succeed without the support of other government officials and judicial sycophants. Cabinet sycophants like Secretary for Homeland Security, Kristi Noem, claim that the President has the *right* to remove *anyone* he wants from the country.[3] The Supreme Court's conservative majority similarly sanctions his dictatorial power grabs by lifting temporary injunctions issued by lower courts whose judges tried to thwart the administration's lawlessness.[4] White House Press Secretary, Karoline Leavitt, even asserted that "America cannot function if President Trump, or any other president for that matter, has their sensitive diplomatic or trade negotiations railroaded by activist judges."[i]

The world seems baffled watching Trump test the limits of a desired imperial presidency. As other authors in this collection discuss, he violates constitutional provisions protecting birthright citizenship and equal rights; he attacks diversity, equity, and inclusion

[i] https://thehill.com/homenews/administration/5324277-white-house-court-tariff-rulings/.

(DEI) policies and other legal and ethical conventions with systemic impunity; he has violated Congressional authority at will and now investigates the possibility of ripping away citizenship based on race and ethnicity. Lawless EOs and Trump's contempt for courts and Congress wreck the principles of democratic institutions. Meanwhile, he threatens law firms, media companies, and universities, chilling free speech and academic freedom. He has even gone so far as to empower neo-fascist white South African oligarchs by granting them permanent entry into the United States, claiming they are "refugees" fleeing "white genocide."[5] Juxtapose this absurd fantasy with the real experiences of US citizens, lawful residents, and those legally seeking refugee status who have been detained in alligator concentration camps and got deported to foreign countries without due process – as explored in other chapters in this collection. Absent traditional, systemic stop gaps, only an organized and mobilized mass of people can contest executive lawlessness. Aside from direct action, the only way to neutralize Trump's hold is by winning at the ballot box in 2026. Such a victory can only occur if US electorate is educated, organized, registered to vote, and goes out to the polls.

THE FIRST 100 DAYS OF LAWLESSNESS

One of the first EOs signed by President Joe Biden was number 14006, ordering the Department of Justice (DOJ) to stop renewing contracts with private prison operators. Biden argued that for-profit detention centers persistently lack adequate safety standards and underperform public "facilities with respect to correctional services, programs, and resources." Prison abolitionists welcomed the EO, hoping it might inspire increasingly progressive policies toward making the prison industrial complex obsolete.[6] Indigenous Peoples ran orderly societies for thousands of years without building a single prison; it was European conquistadores who imposed their carceral fetish on the "new World." Activist scholars such as Angela Davis[7] and Ruth Gilmore[8] have led the call for prison abolition, but Donald Trump reversed Biden's EO and reauthorized the Justice Department to renew contracts with private detention centers.[9] Trump's recessive EO on day one indicated that he was singularly focused on pursuing corporate-backed repression with executive power.

EO lawlessness continued as the DOJ terminated consent decrees with numerous police departments around the country.[ii] Consent decrees are used as tools by the federal government to reform rogue police departments charged with corruption, discrimination, and routine brutality. Trump ended these restrictions, hoping to "unleash law enforcement" on US streets to "aggressively" enforce the law against criminals in order to keep "innocent civilians' safe."[10] This EO promised to deploy "excess" national security assets from the Department of Defense (DoD) and Department of Homeland Security (DHS) to assist local police in law enforcement on US streets. Severe and brutal DHS and Immigrations and Customs Enforcement (ICE) extra-legal activities have occurred in cities across the country: Los Angeles to New York; Washington, D.C. to Portland, Oregon; Chicago, Memphis, Charlotte, Seattle, Minneapolis, and the list grows weekly. Deploying federal troops (or state national guards with or without explicit invitation from governors) violates basic military rules – particularly the Posse Comitatus Act – which severely limits the use of federal military to police domestic areas. This overreach occurs at a time when violent crime rates have dropped to levels not seen in 30 years. But these efforts fit neatly into Trump's fascist playbook as he tries to control mostly democratic-run urban areas featuring large numbers of people of color, undocumented immigrants, and people and politicians who oppose his administration. While his authoritarian approach to law enforcement may appeal to poor, white, and often rural voters, it damages the notion that the rule of law protects all people in the United States, including non-citizens. Meanwhile, history and evidence show that fascist-style law enforcement does not improve public safety, as over 90% of crime prevention and detection is handled by communities rather than by the police or military.[11]

In the first few months of Trump 2.0, individuals and organizations filed over 220 lawsuits (over 500 by the end of 2025[iii]) against

---

[ii] Trump Moved to Dismiss Police Consent Decrees—How Can Judges Respond? | Lawfare.

[iii] https://thefulcrum.us/rule-of-law/supreme-court-rulings-2025

the administration's efforts to dismantle government agencies and traditional funding mechanisms for education, health, humanitarian aid, and dozens of other programs that support public welfare at home and abroad. In 90 such cases, the courts temporarily blocked Trump's executive lawlessness and supported established democratic and judicial due process.[12] The Supreme Court's conservative majority, however, repeatedly lifted these injunctions in what Justice Sotomayor denounced as "willful blindness" to Trump's executive lawlessness.[13] She believed the Court hid behind excuses and should let cases "play out in the lower courts" before intervening.[iv]

I argue that Trump 2.0 has been a period of executive lawlessness and *unpopular* authoritarianism. Millions of Make America Great Again (MAGA) supporters vociferously endorsed Trump's promise of dictatorship on day one because they falsely believed his policies would not affect them personally. Instead, they believed that this "Day One dictator" would be a form of retribution against liberals, immigrants, people of color, and anyone who fell into the now demonized, ideologically bloated category of "woke." However, according to an African saying, when the rain falls, it will not fall on just one man's rooftop. Similarly, Martin Luther King Jr[14] wrote, "injustice anywhere is a threat to justice everywhere." When tens of thousands of federal workers are fired without cause and when DEI initiatives are subsequently terminated by corporations, public institutions, and government agencies, and when Medicare funding is slashed by almost a trillion dollars, a majority of those affected will be poor, white workers – Trump's base.

As a result, millions of people who opposed Trump – as well as many who had supported him but now find themselves "woke" – are coming out into the streets to protest executive lawlessness. These demonstrators shout, "No Kings" in our country, a popular saying among the radically democratic and republican culture of the Igbo, where I was raised. Walter Rodney once called on historians to study such indigenous models of democracy in Africa.[15] Adiele Afrigbo

[iv] Just before this article went to press, the Supreme Court handed Trump a rare and stunning defeat, prohibiting his administration from federalizing state national guardsmen and deploying them to Chicago against the will of Illinois' Governor and the city's mayor.

agreed that nationalist historiography too often privileged "kings and kingdoms" as a vain, colonial attempt to prove that Africans were *civilized* because they had monarchs.[16] Armed with a radically democratic legacy, however, the enslaved Igbo never made good slaves. Some even argue their values may have contributed to the development of democratic ideas among the founding fathers, who themselves came from monarchical cultures.[17] Similar anti-authoritarian resistance must inform the next stage of US history if we are to avoid totalitarianism.

LAWLESS EOs AND THE COMMON GOOD

From day one, the American Civil Liberties Union (ACLU), National Association for the Advancement of Colored People (NAACP), and other organizations have tracked Trump's EOs and anti-democratic policies, often challenging his actions in court daily. The following chronicle of executive lawlessness and unpopular authoritarianism is heavily influenced by the work of the ACLU (2025a).

Day One: EOs

Trump signed about 40 EOs on day one, ranging from eliminating birthright citizenship (despite Fourteenth Amendment guarantees); opposing democratic principles of DEI (protected by existing laws); against lesbian, gay, bisexual, transgender, and queer (LGBTQ) identities; and against immigrants in a country that prides itself as a nation of them. We are reminded that EOs are not the law of the land – a President can issue such orders only to direct agencies on implementing existing statutes. But no EO can replace existing laws or constitutional provisions, nor interfere with Congressional powers to make new laws. EOs cannot prevent the courts from holding the executive branch accountable, nor prevent voters from holding referenda on errant politicians open to recall, or being voted out through the democratic process.

National and state ACLU chapters have challenged many of these EOs, as have groups such as the Asian Law Caucus, State Democracy Defenders Fund, and NAACP on behalf of New Hampshire Indonesian Community Support, League of United Latin American

Citizens, and Make the Road New York. These organizations offer hope that democracy will survive in the United States, especially with the support of Courts who have temporarily blocked dozens of EOs. For instance, the EO to end birthright citizenship (14160) and the one to end gender-affirming care for 19-year-olds (14187) were blocked by courts because they violated constitutional provisions. But the Supreme Court's conservative majority lifted those injunctions, allowing cases to play out in the lower courts with the EOs intact. The order to deny transgender citizens the right to identify their correct gender identity on US passports was also partially blocked. Other lawsuits challenged the EO that fast-tracked the deportation of immigrants and their infant US citizens without due process, as well as the order to end protection for asylum seekers at the border.

January 27th: Funding Freeze

Courts have also been persuaded by non-profits, universities, and public health officials to block Trump from freezing trillions of dollars in federal grants *already* appropriated by Congress. The Constitution and the Impoundment Control Act give Congress the power of the purse, meaning that no president has the authority to withhold funds already approved by Congress. Trump violated the constitution by threatening to block funding for states or localities that provided sanctuary for immigrants who themselves were unlawfully threatened by federal officials. Dozens of sanctuary cities have sued Trump over these funding threats. Meanwhile, a US District Court in Northern Illinois dismissed Trump's lawsuit against the city of Chicago's sanctuary policy, stating the constitution's Tenth Amendment protects the right of states to establish such policies.

February and March 2025

The Department of Government Efficiency (DOGE), led by an unelected billionaire immigrant who spent over a hundred million dollars to elect Trump, hacked into multiple federal computer systems holding the "sensitive personal information" of millions of Americans – bank accounts, health records, and social security numbers.[18] These government-sponsored acts violated the privacy rights of millions of citizens and residents by exposing them to myriad cybersecurity risks. The ACLU and other human rights organizations submitted freedom of information requests and asked Congress to investigate Elon Musk's and DOGE's phishing expedition, but the Supreme Court's conservative majority allowed the Trump administration to proceed by overturning preliminary injunctions.

On February 4th, the DHS and ICE commenced transferring non-citizens from immigration detention facilities in the United States to Guantánamo Bay, Cuba, detaining them there without due process as required by the Fifth Amendment to the constitution. The ACLU sued to gain access to these people and sued again to block such illegal transfers.[19] The state of Florida later doubled down on the illegality by constructing an alligator-infested detention center for immigrants – at a huge cost to local taxpayers.[20] In a moment of classic inhumanity, Trump visited the facility and joked that costs would be minimized because alligator security guards don't get paid but are effective because detainees cannot outrun them.[21]

On February 14th, Trump issued another lawless EO (14151) banning funds for public education programs that promoted DEI, directly violating First Amendment rights to free speech and academic freedom. The Civil Rights Division of the Department of Education issued a "Dear Colleague" letter threatening to cut federal funding from educational institutions that implement DEI programs in admission, curriculum, or research and outreach. Preliminary injunctions by the courts blocked such orders on the ground that they represented a "blatant attack on free speech and academic freedom" as Corey Dolgon explains in greater detail elsewhere in this collection.

Similarly, Trump's unprecedented drive for authoritarianism included EOs in February and March against law firms and lawyers who had worked on federal and state investigations of Trump (Mueller probe, January 6th insurrection, New York attorneys who successfully convicted him and the Trump Organization, etc.). Trump moved to terminate federal contracts for five major law firms, going so far as barring them from federal buildings and interacting with federal employees inside. While some firms capitulated, making deals delivering Trump billions in free legal services, others went to court challenging him – and won. Similar violations of free speech occurred as Trump 2.0 officials deleted scientific research on health care from government websites used by doctors and medical researchers. Any article using terms such as LGBTQ or Transgender was removed despite their effectiveness in communicating vital information to doctors and caregivers. The ACLU joined a lawsuit by Harvard University doctors pleading that such actions violated free speech.[22]

On March 8th, ICE unlawfully arrested and detained Columbia University student, Mahmoud Khalil, for his advocacy of Palestinian rights. He was a lawful resident with a Green Card, married to a US citizen, and the father of an infant US citizen. Still, he was arrested and shipped to a detention center in Louisiana without due process. Khalil eventually won release on bail, but the administration vowed to re-arrest and deport him. One week later, ICE arrested Georgetown professor Dr Badar Khan Suri, apparently "in retaliation for his speech in support of Palestinian rights and his family's ties to Gaza."[23] He was detained and said "they made a subhuman out of me."[24] Similarly, on March 25th, ICE detained Ph.D. student and Fulbright scholar Rümeysa Öztürk for being the co-author of an op-ed in her campus newspaper. She was kidnapped while on her way to have dinner with friends. She was thrown into an unmarked car and also sent to a detention center in Louisiana. Moreover, on April 14th, "ICE detained Columbia University student Mohsen Mahdawi outside of his naturalization interview in retaliation for supporting Palestinian rights." He has lived in the United States legally for over 10 years. ICE planned to fly him to Louisiana for deportation, but a temporary restraining order stopped them. The ACLU was part of the team defending these unlawfully detained scholars and their freedom to express dissent.[v]

Furthermore, on March 14th, President Trump unlawfully invoked the Alien Enemies Act, authorizing the secret deportation of hundreds of immigrants, despite lacking proof that any of them were enemies of the United States.[25] Without due process,

[v] For details of all the cases referenced in this paragraph, see ACLU (2025d,[26] 2025e,[27] 2025f,[28] 2025g[29]).

the United States deported one immigrant because he had tattoos saying "mom" and "dad" – which officials falsely alleged were gang tattoos for Tren de Aragua, an El Salvadoran gang.[30] A federal judge ordered the government to return this deportee and grant his day in court. Judges also prohibited future deportation flights without legal authorization. The Trump administration simply ignored the court order. The Supreme Court agreed that due process rights require those facing deportation to be given opportunities to challenge government allegations, but they lifted the temporary restraining order anyway. Essentially, this decision forced advocates to bring new, *individual* lawsuits in each jurisdiction where deportees were held. Despite this overt effort to stymie deportees' defense by increasing exponentially the workload of representing them, the ACLU refiled lawsuits and successfully won new temporary restraining orders. Judges eventually stopped deportations under the Alien Enemies Act.

On March 25th, Trump issued another EO (14248) giving himself the power to change election rules that potentially disenfranchised millions of qualified voters, especially those "of color, women voters, naturalized citizens, voters with disabilities, voters with low incomes, and first-time voters." The ACLU challenged this power-grab in court, arguing that the constitution specifically gave Congress and the states the power to regulate election, not the president. On April 24th, a federal judge agreed and put a partial ban on the unlawful EO, ruling that Trump has no such powers.

April 2025

On April 1st, the Trump administration withheld grants of $65.8 million for Title X federal family planning "to reproductive health care organizations that provide access to birth control, cancer screenings, testing and treatment for STIs, and other preventive health care." They alleged that funds were withheld because organizations made public statements in support of DEI and against racism. This executive lawlessness puts "hundreds of thousands of patients at risk of losing access to critical health care." The ACLU sued to force the administration to release the critical funding for public health.[31]

Also in April, the DoD began banning books and changing curricula at military academies, claiming such books and programs promoted "woke" gender and racial ideologies. Similarly, Trump accused cultural programs like Black History Month, Pride Month, Women's History Month, and National Hispanic Heritage Month for promoting "divisive equity ideology."[32] On April 15th, the ACLU sued the government in defense of academic freedom and free speech of students and professors.

On April 25th, the Federal Bureau of Investigation (FBI) arrested Milwaukee Judge, Hannah Dugan for allegedly telling an immigrant in her courtroom to walk into a public area when ICE agents came to arrest him.[33] No law requires judges to assist immigration officials to arrest anyone in their courtroom. The ACLU challenged Dugan's unprecedented arrest, explaining that the ICE action was intended to intimidate all judges into capitulating to Trump's whims and caprices. On April 28th, President Trump continued such threats by issuing an EO to prosecute state or local officials in sanctuary cities who don't cooperate with mass deportations.

On the 100th day of Trump's presidency, a federal judge ordered the government to release ACLU client, Mohsen Mahdawi, on bail and grant him due process. Beyond the first 100 days, Trump ordered national guard troops to remove unhoused people from the streets of Washington DC, subverting the power of local police. The administration backed down, however, when DC Mayor Muriel Bowers threatened to sue. Such an overreach was tested in Los Angeles *despite* the California Governor's lawsuit. Trump claims national guard and military deployments are necessary to address skyrocketing crime and chaos in each city he targets. Yet, in every case, such claims prove inaccurate, and research demonstrates local crime on the decline.

While Trump poses as the "law-and-order president," he remains a convicted criminal and sexual abuser. For months, he refused to release FBI files concerning convicted pedophile, Jeffrey Epstein (some of them again, as we go to press, Congress has forced the DOJ to release them). And Trump consistently issues EOs and policies that violate the laws and traditions of US democracy. While courts continue to claim Trump is *not* above the law, issuing injunction upon injunction against him, a conservative Supreme Court keeps suggesting otherwise. During the longest government shutdown in US history, the Trump administration refused to negotiate an extension to Affordable Care Act subsidies, without which millions of Americans will find health insurance unaffordable and will lose coverage. The administration also threatened to lay off furloughed workers (especially those affiliated with the Democratic Party) and close what Trump called "Democrat programs," such as the Supplementary Nutritional Assistance Program, Medicaid, and Medicare. During the shutdown, Trump fired almost all the workers responsible for special education programs. Meanwhile, Trump's anti-Democratic Party propaganda machine violated the Hatch Act forbidding federal employees from using government offices for partisan political purposes. Politico reported that while DOE employees were furloughed, administrators impersonated them by inserting "partisan" automatic email responses blaming Democrats for the shutdown. The American Association of Government Employees sued the DOE for Hatch Act violations, and US District Court Judge, Christopher Cooper, agreed, forcing the removal of such "partisan language."[34]

THEORETICAL DISCUSSION

Sociologist Wolfgang Streeck analyzed the first Trump administration by comparing it to Bonapartism – an authoritarian form of imperialism. Streeck then used Weberian Status Group pluralism (a theory arguing social stratification can develop from multiple categories of power – not just economic, but social, cultural, etc.) as an explanation for the emergence of politicians that he called "Trumpists."[35] However, his critical essay lacked thorough conceptual clarifications to address theoretical inadequacies and empirical errors that threatened the validity of his analysis and the policy efficacy of its implications. On Bonapartism, Streeck invoked Marx's[36] *The Eighteenth Brumaire of Louis Bonaparte* to remind us that Trump is not the *first* figure to come to power and seek absolute rule to the disadvantage of the same masses of peasants who supported them to begin with. Streeck, however, neglected to inform readers that Marx never intended this concrete historical example to be *overgeneralized,* for he counted the instances of Bonapartism on two fingers of one hand.[37] Marx used this concrete example to show that *sometimes*, the infrastructural mode of production is less a determinant of historic outcomes than the superstructural ideology of his much-abused "base-superstructure" model. Neither Bonaparte nor Trump should be understood as isolated individuals because they are actually *class representatives* – regardless of personal pathologies.

Of course, Trump is no emperor and even if he wanted to rule the United States the way that Bonaparte ruled France, Trump has to get past a Congress with anxious eyes on the mid-term elections; past the courts that block his chief executive officer style decision-making; past a still critical press revealing scoops that force government reaction and even retrenchment; and past the energized electorate ready to call his bluff from one ill-advised EO to another. Streeck understood that Trump "won" the election but ignored that he lost the popular vote by nearly three million in 2016 and over seven million in 2020.

A more suitable theoretical framework for such an inquiry would be Stuart Hall's[38] writings on *Thatcherism and Authoritarian Populism* or even Kimberly Crenshaw's[39] *Intersectionality*. Their work provides a much stronger paradigm for analyzing the race–class–gender politics of articulation, disarticulation, and rearticulation in societies structured by dominance. Streeck erred by concluding that group interests were limited to their identity interests – that is, only transgender people care about reactionary bathroom birther laws. On the contrary, many Americans oppose prejudiced laws that pick on other groups. History teaches that authoritarianism eventually escalates violence in society to the detriment of all.

In reflecting on Trump's first victory, I wrote about the evolution of political party identities in the United States.[40] For decades, US opinion polls indicated that the electorate self-identifies as 43% democrats, 43% republicans, and 14% independents, varying in some states like Virginia, where parties are 28% each and independents form the majority.[41] Parties must swing independent voters to win elections, but if they fail to turn out their base, they may still lose. US electoral maps have looked mostly red for decades, with blue regions clinging to the coastal margins and urban centers. This reality means that Trump's victory should not have been surprising. However, the almost even split in 2024 between Trump and Harris (74-71 million votes respectively) indicates his authoritarianism may not be as populist as presumed. Here is where Hall's Authoritarian Populist theory helps us understand both Trump administrations and the very *unpopular* nature of his populism.

Hall coined authoritarian populism to help explain "Thatcherism" in the United Kingdom and, by extension, "Reaganism" (and now "Trumpism") in the United States. He wrote that Thatcher and Reagan mobilized popular votes among the British and US working classes primarily because Liberals (Labour and Democratic Parties) offered no convincing alternatives to neo-liberal capitalism and its attendant policies promoted by Tories and republicans. Working class voters (primarily white) bought into anti-corporatist state rhetoric in favor of lower taxes and smaller government, despite anti-organized labor, pro zero-tolerance policing, tighter immigration control, and restrictive social welfare programs not in their class interests.

Attempts to explain conservatives' and republicans' repeated victories at the polls by *only* referencing working-class racism, xenophobia, and homophobia fail to account for the popularity of *authoritarianism* among the general electorate. According to Hall, Gramsci's concept of hegemony more adequately accounts for why the passions of working-class voters tend toward radical right-wing politicians who, unlike most left-wing parties, offer them *stronger* and more certain intellectual and moral leadership. The Right constructs a hegemony that promises to dominate or liquidate antagonistic interest groups, addressing a hegemonic crisis where ruling elites must dominate by brute force instead of moral and intellectual persuasion. They call out troops and militarize police to put down peaceful popular protests – as Thatcher did and Trump does. Even Hall, however, may have overestimated the "populism" of authoritarianism.

Such theoretical constructs often overlook the power of resistance – particularly at the most authoritarian moments. Stephen Pfohl[42] criticized C. Wright Mills' implication that America's power structure came about *without* "ideological struggles to control the masses." Pfohl noted Mills never accounted for the agency of organized masses to change the course of US history despite capitalism remaining intact. Althusser's[43] notion of "Ideological State Apparatuses" suggests that even families, educational institutions, places of employment, the media, religion, etc., all function as domains where struggles over hegemony persist. These struggles explain why elections tend to divide families, congregations, colleges, and communities. If every qualified voter voted, neo-fascist populism would be shown for the sham it is, as the vast majority would flip them the birdie. Populism is not always the absolute majority tendency in a polity, but rather the tendency capable of mobilizing enough support to prevail over even more popular opponents.

Trump 1.0 may have attracted many poor voters by depicting their plight as "living in hell," thus demonizing the opposition while anointing his campaign with an Old Testament style crusade. Struggling working-class people had nothing to lose by voting for a non-establishment candidate who recognized economic distress, unlike Clinton, who could not appeal to their visceral frustration over the impact of neo-liberal austerity. In 2024, Harris similarly could not counter the allegation that, as Vice President, she failed to fix "porous" borders. Nor could she address the general feeling of Biden's weakness – both physically and politically. Even with a democratic majority, Biden and Harris's *own* party blocked their economic and social policies. Trump's road to victory proceeded with primarily empty promises and pledges to reduce costs, reduce crime, deport "illegals," and portray strength and power at home and abroad.

Yet, his 2024 victory was narrow – one of the narrowest in history. And, as demonstrated above, Trump has faced opposition and resistance at almost every turn. It is easy to overestimate the power of reactionary populism because its arrogance and puffery are part of the program. But the level of opposition in the courts, on the streets, and even in popularity polls (under 40% as we go to press[44]) suggests not a popular authoritarianism but an unpopular one.

CONCLUSION

The Trump administration should be pressured by the electorate to seriously address the "hell" he claimed Americans experienced. US citizens should demand that Trump provide better funding for education and workforce development and universal healthcare. They should pressure Trump to move toward fair, redistributive economic policies, toward reparations for slavery and genocide, and toward ending the prison industrial complex and militarized policing. But if Trump is ideologically determined to govern only for the benefit of the 1%, he should expect opposition from even those who displayed yard signs declaring to be "Deplorable and Proud of It"[45] or "I Voted for the Felon" (a pro-Trump political slogan used by supporters after his felony conviction). If republicans prefer to wage a class war against the poor, a racist war against minorities, and a gender war against women and LGBTQ people, they should expect voters to punish them in the 2026 mid-term election and beyond.

Meanwhile, the hegemonic struggles will continue to be waged on the streets, in places of worship, within families, by unions, and through the courts. And this dynamic is my final point. Trump's unpopular authoritarianism is becoming more so by the day. To defeat his executive lawlessness requires continued pressure from groups and individuals in all institutional venues at persistent and increasing levels. But one of the most opportune strategic moments for this opposition will be the upcoming mid-term elections. As Bonilla-Silva[46] suggested here and elsewhere, electoral politics are not a solution to oppression but must remain one tool among many. Revolutionaries from Rosa Luxemburg to Malcolm X have acknowledged that voting can be a crucial part of any radical movement – particularly in democracies where elections can be powerful moments for mobilizing masses, not to reaffirm bourgeois, so-called democratic institutions, but to redesign and recast democracy itself. Let 2026 be a first step in this revolutionary process of replacing an unpopular authoritarian with a new, vibrant democracy featuring new visions and new practices of justice.

NOTES

1. Agozino, B. (2003). *Counter-colonial criminology: A critique of imperialist reason*. Pluto Press.

2. Tutu, D., & Tutu, M. (2014). The book of forgiving. HarperCollins.

3. Neuman, S. (2025, May 20). *DHS secretary misstates meaning of habeas corpus under Senate scrutiny*. NPR. https://www.npr.org/2025/05/20/nx-s1-5405144/habeas-corpus-noem-dhs-senate.

4. Kunzleman, M., & Thanawala, S. (2025, June 27). *High court ruling on injunctions could imperil many court orders blocking the Trump administration*. AP News. https://www.mypanhandle.com/news/politics/ap-high-court-ruling-on-injunctions-could-imperil-many-court-orders-blocking-the-trump-administration/.

5. Hinton, A. L. (2021). *It can happen here*. New York University Press.

6. Eisen, L.-B. (2025, January 20). *Trump reverses Biden order that eliminated DOJ contracts with private prisons*. Brennan Center for Justice. https://www.brennancenter.org/our-work/analysis-opinion/trump-reverses-biden-order-eliminated-doj-contracts-private-prisons.

7. Davis, A. (2009). *Abolition democracy*. Seven Stories Press.

8. Gilmore, R. (2022). *Abolition geography: Essays towards liberation*. Verso.

9. Eisen, L.-B. (2025, January 20). *Trump reverses Biden order that eliminated DOJ contracts with private prisons*. https://www.brennancenter.org/our-work/analysis-opinion/trump-reverses-biden-order-eliminated-doj-contracts-private-prisons.

10. Trump, D. (2025, April 28). *Strengthening and unleashing America's law enforcement to pursue criminals and protect innocent citizens*. https://www.whitehouse.gov/presidential-actions/2025/04/strengthening-and-unleashing-americas-law-enforcement-to-pursue-criminals-and-protect-innocent-citizens/.

11. Onyeozili, E. C., Agozino, B., Agu, A., & Ibe, P. (2021). *Community policing in Nigeria*. Virginia Tech Publishing.

12. ACLU. (2025a). *The first 100 days*. https://www.aclu.org/the-first-100-days.

13. McCoy, A. (2007). *A question of torture: CIA interrogation, from the Cold War to the War on Terror*. Metropolitan Books.

14. King, M. L., Jr. (1963). *Letter from Birmingham Jail*. African Studies Center, University of Pennsylvania.

15. Rodney, W. (2019). *Groundings with my brothers*. Verso.

16. Afigbo, A. (1972). *The warrant chiefs: Indirect rule in Southeastern Nigeria, 1891–1929*. Longman Group.

17. Equiano, O. (1792). *The life of Olaudah Equiano, or, Gustavus Vassa, the African*. Author.

18. Fowler, S., Joffe-Block, J., & Bond, S. (2026, March 11). *The government is investigating new claims that DOGE misused Social Security data*. NPR.

19. ACLU. (2025b). *Groups Sue Trump administration for access to immigrants sent from U.S. to Guantánamo Bay*. https://www.aclu.org/press-releases/groups-sue-trump-administration-to-halt-transfer-of-immigrants-from-u-s-to-guantanamo-bay.

20. Amnesty International. (2025). *USA: New findings reveal human rights violations at Florida's "Alligator Alcatraz" and Krome detention centers*. https://www.amnesty.org/en/latest/news/2025/12/estados-unidos-nuevas-investigaciones-revelan-violaciones-de-derechos-humanos-en-los-centros-de-detencion-de-alligator-alcatraz-y-krome-en-florida/.

21. Oh, I. (2025, July). The cartoonish cruelty of Trump's "Alligator Alcatraz". Mother Jones. https://www.motherjones.com/politics/2025/07/alligator-alcatraz-trump/.

22. ACLU. (2025c). *Doctors challenge removal of their patient safety research from federal website*. https://www.aclu.org/press-releases/doctors-challenge-psnet-removal-trump-assault-science.

23. Center for Constitutional Rights. (2025, May 5) *Federal judge rules against Trump administration, keeps Dr. Khan Suri's case in Virginia*. https://ccrjustice.org/home/press-center/press-releases/federal-judge-rules-against-trump-administration-keeps-dr-khan-suri.

24. Diaz, J., & Martínez-Beltrán, S. (2025, May 14). *Georgetown researcher released from immigration detention on federal judge's order*. NPR News (STLPR). https://www.stlpr.org/npr/2025-05-14/georgetown-researcher-released-from-immigration-detention-on-federal-judges-order.

25. ACLU. (2024). *Anti-immigrant extremists want to use this 226-year-old law to implement a mass deportation program*. https://www.aclu.org/news/immigrants-rights/anti-immigrant-extremists-want-to-use-this-226-year-old-law-to-implement-a-mass-deportation-program.

26. ACLU. (2025d). *A letter from Palestinian activist Mahmoud Khalil.* https://www.aclu.org/news/free-speech/a-letter-from-palestinian-activist-mahmoud-khalil.

27. ACLU. (2025e). *Khan Suri* v. *Trump et al.* https://www.acluva.org/cases/khan-suri-v-trump-et-al/.

28. ACLU. (2025f). *Öztürk* v. *Trump*. https://www.aclu.org/cases/ozturk-v-trump.

29. ACLU. (2025g). *Mohsen Mahdawi challenges his unlawful detention by ICE.* https://www.aclu.org/press-releases/attorneys-for-mohsen-mahdawi-challenge-his-unlawful-detention-by-ice.

30. Reichlin-Melnick, A. (2025). *United States frees Venezuelans held in El Salvador following prisoner swap*. American Immigration Council. https://www.americanimmigrationcouncil.org/blog/united-states-frees-venezuelans-el-salvador-prisoner-swap/.

31. ACLU. (2025h). *NFPRHA and ACLU challenge Trump administration over unlawful withholding of title X family planning program grants.* https://www.aclu.org/press-releases/nfprha-and-aclu-challenge-trump-administration-over-unlawful-withholding-of-title-x-family-planning-program-grants.

32. Giroux, H. (2026, April 26). *War on DEI's aim: Normalizing white nationalism.* FlaglerLive. https://flaglerlive.com/dei-war/.

33. Lybrand, H., & Boyette, C. (2025, December 2). *ICE to launch operation targeting Somali immigrants in Twin Cities, federal official says, as Trump calls community "garbage"*. CNN. https://www.cnn.com/2025/12/02/us/ice-operation-somali-migrants-minneapolis.

34. Perez, J., Jr. (2025, November 7). Judge orders Education Department to halt 'partisan' employee email messages. *Politico*. https://www.politico.com/news/2025/11/07/judge-orders-education-department-to-halt-partisan-employee-email-messages-00643270.

35. Streeck, W. (2017). Trump and Trumpists. *Inferences, 3*(1). https://inference-review.com/article/trump-and-the-trumpists.

36. Marx, K. (1852). *The Eighteenth Brumaire of Louis Bonaparte.* Joseph Wedemeter.

37. Marx, K. (1852). *The Eighteenth Brumaire of Louis Bonaparte.* Joseph Wedemeter.

38. Hall, S. (1985). Authoritarian populism: A reply. *New Left Review*, *1*, 151.

39. Crenshaw, K. (1991, July). Mapping the margins: Intersectionality, identity politics, and violence against Women of Color. *Stanford Law Review*, *43*(6), 1241–1299.

40. Agozino, B. (2016). Trumpism and authoritarian populism. In *CTheory: Theorizing 21c: 21C035,/*. http://ctheory.net/ctheory_wp/trumpism-and-authoritarian-populism.

41. Pew Research Center. (2015, April 7). *A deep dive into party affiliation*. https://www.pewresearch.org/politics/2015/04/07/a-deep-dive-into-party-affiliation/.

42. Pfohl, S. (2015). The criminological imagination in an age of global cybernetic power. In J. Frauley (Ed.), *C. Wright Mills and the criminological imagination prospects for creative inquiry* (pp. 99–133). Routledge.

43. Althusser, L. (1971). Ideology and ideological state apparatuses (Notes towards an investigation). In *Lenin and philosophy and other essays*. Monthly Review Press.

44. The Economist. (2026). *Donald Trump's approval rating*. https://www.economist.com/interactive/trump-approval-tracker.

45. Bonilla-Silva, E. (2019). Toward a new political praxis for Trumpamerica: New directions in critical race theory. *American Behavioral Scientist, 63*(13), 1776–1788.

46. Root, W. A. (2016, September 13). Deplorable and proud of it. *Las Vegas Review-Journal*. https://www.reviewjournal.com/opinion/opinion-columns/wayne-allyn-root/deplorable-and-proud-of-it/.

4

FEAR AND XENOPHOBIA: TRUMP'S FIRST 100 DAYS AND THE POLITICIZATION OF IMMIGRATION

Rogelio Sáenz and Selene M. Gomez

University of Texas at San Antonio, USA

Imagine you have been living in fear over the last several months, not sure whether Immigration and Customs Enforcement (ICE) or other masked "officers" might drive up in unmarked vehicles, bearing no credentials, and knock your door down to take you and your family away.[1] You have been working steadily for as long as you can remember, but are afraid to go to work because ICE raided your workplace.[2] Your family is hungry and needs food, but you fear going to the grocery store or local food bank because you may be apprehended.[3] Your spouse has run out of medication and needs medical care, but you are afraid to go out for fear of being apprehended.[4] You are so proud of your daughter, who excels in school, but you cannot take her there for fear of being apprehended.[5] You think of the last 30 years you've lived in this country, toiling away without complaint and expressing gratitude about being able to establish a home and future for your family. Now, you feel like a fugitive. You do not know what the future brings. If you are apprehended, where will you be sent? With much consternation, you hear about people being deported to dangerous foreign lands. You fear the worst: that your family will be separated.

This is the reality that countless unauthorized immigrants have experienced since Donald Trump began his second term. In his first presidential term, Trump deported countless numbers of undocumented immigrants, stopped unauthorized immigrants and those seeking refugee status from entering the country, and separated children from their parents at the border.[6] In his second term, Trump vowed to use immense shock-and-awe tactics to conduct the mass deportation of "millions and millions" of undocumented immigrants.[7] Over his first 100 days, he viciously targeted immigrants for mass arrest and deportation using an expanded playbook that included giving ICE access to schools, churches, hospitals, and other public and civic areas traditionally safe from ICE raids. The administration's cruelty toward immigrant populations includes mass deportation and imprisonment without due process or regard for democracy, the rule of law, and human rights. The aim is plain and simple: the exclusion and erasure of people of color portrayed as invaders who "do not belong" in the USA. Such policies are particularly attractive to white nationalists convinced "their" country has been "stolen" by "foreigners and minorities" who are not "real Americans."[8]

Despite the long history of the exclusion and minimization of immigrants and people of color in this country, one thing is clear since Trump took office in 2025: we are now living in an increasingly autocratic and fascist country whose leader is terrorizing the nation and its people with no accountability. While Trump's autocracy is widespread across the nation's institutions, it is especially apparent in his treatment of immigrants of color and his intent to remove millions of unauthorized (and even authorized) immigrants. Furthermore, he has used his favorite weapons – deceit, lies, and hyperbole – to racialize and criminalize immigrants.[9]

Ironically, Trump is conducting mass deportation at a time when the USA *needs* immigrants more than ever. The nation is an increasingly aging country with its white population already experiencing population loss for nearly a decade. Quite simply, the US economy cannot thrive without an unauthorized workforce that has been the engine of the nation's prosperity. Trump's lies about unauthorized immigrants being the bane of working-class people – especially whites – characterize foreign workers as "invaders" who have taken away white peoples' jobs and resources (unproven and untrue). Meanwhile, Trump, himself, will take billions from poor, working, and middle-class people and redistribute to the rich.[10]

In this chapter, we provide an overview of mass deportation and associated policies during the first year of Trump 2.0. We begin with a discussion of the historical context involving the exclusion of immigrants and people of color. We then provide an overview of the current context, featuring the erosion of democracy, increased violence against immigrant workers, and the general rise of fascism. We also look at various strategies for challenging these policies and the general trend toward racist authoritarianism.

THE HISTORICAL CONTEXT FOR THE EXCLUSION OF IMMIGRANTS AND PEOPLE OF COLOR

To best understand contemporary immigration policies and practices, we must recognize the nation's historical exploitation and periodic exclusion of immigrants and people of color. From the country's founding until the 1950s, only white immigrants were eligible for US citizenship[11] with people of color deemed "perpetual foreigners."[12,13] Upon their arrival in what *became* the USA, white immigrants subjugated and killed Indigenous Peoples and stole their land, placing them in reservations where they remained marginalized from the US mainstream. Ironically, even Indigenous Peoples would have to wait until 1924 to receive US citizenship. In addition, the Chinese Exclusion Acts of 1882 and 1892 barred Chinese from coming to the USA and subsequently extended the ban to all Asians. Moreover, the Immigration Acts of 1921 and 1924 established a quota system favoring Northern and Western Europeans in opposition to Southern and Eastern Europeans who were seen as "swarthy" people, inferior to "true Americans."

During the Great Depression, the USA established the Repatriation Program in the 1930s to return Mexicans to Mexico, deporting approximately one-third of the Mexican origin population in the country, including many US citizens.[14,15] Furthermore, during World War II, President Franklin Delano Roosevelt established Executive Order 9066 on February 19, 1942, which resulted in the internment of approximately 112,000 persons of Japanese origin. Moreover, the USA established "Operation Wetback" in 1954 to deport Mexican immigrants, with a peak of approximately 1.1 million deported in 1954.[16,17] More recently, the Immigration and Naturalization Service and later the Department of Homeland Security have established a series of operations to deport undocumented immigrants, particularly Mexicans and Central Americans.[18]

Trump's current mass deportation is only the latest effort to remove people from this country. Make no mistake, though; he is purposely targeting people of color to exclude them from the nation.[19]

THE CURRENT CONTEXT: THE EROSION OF DEMOCRACY AND RISING FASCISM

Throughout its history, the USA has touted itself as the greatest democracy and the envy of the world for its democratic principles. While Trump's election in 2016 threatened this national image, American democracy is now shattered. From day one, Trump 2.0 bragged about being an autocrat and actively degrading democracy.[20] As made clear in other chapters in this collection, Trump regularly makes unilateral decisions without regard to the Constitution, the practice or spirit of established law, or habeas corpus. He aggressively disregards court orders and court decisions. Trump tried to operate this way during his first term, but fortunately, some guardrails remained in place – including members of his administration who pushed back against his illegal actions. In the current administration, loyalty and obedience to Trump are the only requirements for filling top cabinet and administrative positions. Trump also dominates Republicans in Congress and his appointees to the Supreme Court. The guardrails are gone.

Accordingly, ICE has become a rogue institution. Agents commonly wear masks to cover their faces, do not show proper identification to confirm their credentials, and they storm into sites without proper protocol.[21] ICE has also used deceit to lure undocumented immigrants under the pretense that they need to show up in person to update documents or court-issued tracking devices, only to be apprehended for deportation. These and other practices have intensified fear among undocumented immigrants and their families.

Trump has regularly defied court orders related to deportation. Flights carrying immigrants out of the country have left without proper authorization. Immigrants from countries that do not agree to take back deportees are taken to random countries in Central America and Africa, where they face brutal conditions and great trauma. Some individuals have even attempted suicide.[22,23] Meanwhile, Trump specifically targets and demonizes immigrants of color. For example, he charges – without evidence – that most Venezuelan immigrants belong to the violent international organization *Tren de Aragua*. Without due process and drawing on an antiquated 1798 Alien Enemies Act, Trump deported upwards of 200 Venezuelans, accusing them of being gang members without credible evidence. They were sent early in his administration to El Salvador's infamous Terrorism Confinement Center, a large prison complex condemned for human rights violations.[24] Trump made a secret deal with El Salvador President Nayib Bukele, to hold and torture deported US immigrants in return for compensation still unreported.[25]

Furthermore, Trump has even deported US citizens. The *Washington Post* estimates that dozens of US citizens have been either detained or deported.[26,27,28,29] Several such documented cases included children with serious medical needs and adults arrested or detained by ICE.[30] Not surprisingly, all of these US citizens snared by ICE or Border Patrol have been Latino.

In fact, Trump publicly contemplated deporting US citizens convicted of violent crimes (he calls them "homegrown criminals") to El Salvador prisons.[31] *TIME* journalist Popli[32] notes that:

> *Deporting U.S. citizens would mark a dramatic escalation of the Trump Administration's already aggressive approach to immigration and criminal justice and has raised immediate legal and ethical questions from constitutional experts, who tell TIME that even suggesting the removal of U.S. citizens crosses a line long considered inviolable.*

Shortly after taking office, Trump signed an executive order to open the infamous Guantanamo Bay facility as a detention center for "the worst criminal illegal aliens threatening the American people."[33] In early February, Trump sent approximately 200 Venezuelans to Guantanamo Bay, many without criminal records. According to a lawsuit led by the American Civil Liberties Union (ACLU), those held "effectively disappeared into a black box and cannot contact or communicate with their family or attorneys."[34] Trump officials responded, claiming that they were not "detainees" because of their criminal records and, therefore, had no statutory rights to legal representation.[35] A judge hearing the case in late February removed these Venezuelan detainees from Guantanamo Bay, but they were subsequently sent to Venezuela.

Furthermore, Trump wants myriad detention centers built around the country. In early May, he ordered Alcatraz prison – closed since 1963 – reopened to hold primarily detained immigrants. Florida opened an Alcatraz-like facility, "Alligator Alcatraz," in early July. This facility occupies "an isolated Everglades airfield surrounded by mosquito-, python-, and alligator-filled swamplands."[36] Florida Attorney General, James Uthmeier, described the *ideal* location of the detention center, noting that "There's really nowhere to go. If you're housed there, if you're detained there, there's no way in, no way out."[37] Despite being in operation only a short time, guards at Alligator Alcatraz have already been accused of cruelty and violating inmates' basic human rights.[38] Many of those inmates have no criminal record.[39]

In addition, Trump issued a day-one executive order to end birthright citizenship. In late June, the Supreme Court, in a 6-to-3 vote, provided support for Trump's executive order, but did not rule on the constitutionality of the executive order. Ironically, recent population projections indicate that ending birthright citizenship would double the nation's unauthorized population from 2.7 million in 2025 to 5.4 million in 2075.[40]

Finally, the Trump administration has worked hard to quash dissent. After widespread ICE raids and arrests of immigrants in Los Angeles, local residents pushed back. In response to dissent, Trump sent hundreds of National Guard troops to Los Angeles, thus militarizing the city and bypassing California Governor Gavin

Newsom. In addition, Democrat lawmakers who opposed Trump, such as California Senator Alex Padilla and New York City Comptroller Brad Lander, have been violently arrested.[41] Resistance continues, but so have the number of brutal arrests and deportations.

The data show that from January 20 to June 30, 2025, the number of immigrants arrested grew significantly, about 25% to over 100,000.[42,43] Trump's border czar, Tom Homan, called for doubling available detention center beds from 50,000 to 100,000. Deportations during this period have also risen dramatically to somewhere between 150,000 and 240,000.[44,45] This number is expected to rise and break Obama's record of 316,000 immigrants deported in 2014. However, these numbers do not include people who have self-deported. While it is difficult to count the actual number of people who have left voluntarily, some estimates suggest that they surpass those deported by ICE. For example, a recent report from the Center for Immigration Studies,[46] an organization opposing immigration, estimates that there was a decline of nearly 1 million foreign-born persons and approximately 600,000 foreign-born persons in the workforce between January and May 2025, suggesting that many of these include people who have self-deported.

MASS DEPORTATION IMPACT ON THE US WORKFORCE

The business community, especially those in agriculture and construction, has been very concerned about Trump's mass deportation of a sizable portion of its workforce. Using data from the January and June 2024 and 2025 Current Population Survey (CPS), we observe that between January and June 2025, the US workforce grew by 0.89%, half the growth rate during the January to June 2024 period (1.72%). Moreover, the impact of Trump's mass deportation campaign can be seen by examining employment trends of non-citizen Latinos, a group that accounts for 56% of all Latino workers in the construction industry. Our analysis based on CPS data shows that the number of non-citizen Latinos in construction fell from nearly 2.4 million in January 2025 to 2.1 million in June 2025, a drop of 290,000 workers, or a decline of 12%. A total of 16 industries with approximately 40,000 workers (the average number of non-citizen Latino workers across the 235 industries in which they are employed) experienced similar declines. These included taxi and limousine services (ratio of 0.468 between the number of workers in June 2025 relative to the number of workers in January 2025), supermarkets and grocers (0.796), motor vehicles and motor vehicle equipment manufacturing (0.740), food services and drinking places, except alcoholic beverages (0.798), animal slaughtering and processing (0.885), home health care services (0.928), truck transportation (0.948), and travel accommodation (0.957).

In short, these data clearly show the major impact that Trump's mass deportation has had on the US workforce, especially in the case of non-citizen Latinos. As mass deportation increases in the coming months and years, the impact will be multiplicative. Challenges to mass deportation and immigrant detention policies have grown to protest and resist Trump 2.0's anti-immigrant ideology and tactics.

RISING SOLIDARITY AND RESISTANCE TO TRUMP'S MASS DEPORTATION

For many immigrants and policy critics, the Trump administration's mass deportation apparatus is like a declaration of war on people of color, most prominently Latinos. Many whites view Latinos and other people of color as a threat to white supremacy and their political power. Mass deportation along with militarization, racism, xenophobia, and dehumanization of the Black, Indigenous, and People of Color (BIPOC) community have the intention of putting people of color in "their place," reducing their numbers and political power. While the cruelty and inhumane treatment of undocumented immigrants "is the point" of policies in Make America Great Again (MAGA) America,[47] they have sparked an awakening in the Latino community and among their allies in many states, particularly in California. It has been heartening to see people in communities where undocumented people live standing up to the Trump administration and ICE's mass deportation efforts. Solidarity is rising through mutual aid, community-based surveillance of ICE, and protests large and small against ICE actions. But resistance has been met with ever more punitive punishment, coercion, military and local police enforcement, and a barrage of conservative media and Trump administration propaganda that criminalizes individuals who oppose Trump.

Since the protests started in Los Angeles on June 6th, 2025,[48] over 500 people have been arrested and charged with violating police orders to disperse, curfew violations, resisting, obstructing, or delaying a police officer and resisting arrest.[49] But these protests have set in motion other protests nationwide. Indeed, within the first week after the rebellion in LA, protests against ICE raids occurred in over 30 cities.[50] These spaces have not only become sites to challenge the Trump administration, but also spaces for the Latino community to plant their flag – refusing to be erased and proclaiming that they DO belong in this country. The message is that being "American" doesn't require one to forego their country of origin and ethnicity.[51]

Subsequently, on June 14th, cities and towns across the country held almost 2,000 "No King" rallies with over 5 million participants – one of the largest days of protest in US history.[52] People are also coming together and organizing to protect their local communities. For instance, the LA Taco newsroom shifted its coverage of gastronomy and culture to covering ICE raids. They now provide locals with real-time updates and on-the-ground news that has now gained the trust of LA residents.[53] The number of immigration activist organizations continues to grow as they try to halt mass deportation actions and policies.[54]

Similarly, more groups have committed to actively monitoring ICE actions, especially officials' treatment of people during ICE raids. Take, for example, the collaborative platform of "People over Papers," developed by a daughter of Mexican immigrants. This platform allows people to report ICE agents' presence in real time and shows the reports on a map. As of mid-July, the platform has over 12 million users and over 300,000 visits daily.[55] These actions illustrate a massive self-activity movement and offer a ray of hope against the anti-immigrant authoritarianism of Trump's first months in office. Given the mounting challenges, such efforts will need to expand and intensify to achieve success.

WHAT IS AHEAD?

To date, there is no sign that the Trump administration will ease up in its brutal and inhumane treatment of immigrants. Conditions are likely to get worse and unauthorized immigrants and their families will continue to bear the brunt of mass deportation, but wider segments of the nation will undoubtedly be impacted as well.

As we illustrated above, we are already seeing the impact ICE raids have had on labor in different industries, most prominently in construction. The economic consequences of labor shortages have impacted all of us with the rising cost of living and cost of basic items, like food. These and other economic hardships will only increase in intensity during the second year of Trump 2.0. To make matters worse, the labor shortages associated with mass deportation will intersect with the economic woes from Trump's draconian tariff policies to put many people in worse economic conditions.

In addition, the USA will feel the major economic pinch in supporting an increasingly aging population and in maintaining Social Security payments for a growing number of beneficiaries. According to Davis et al.,[56] undocumented workers paid an estimated $25.7 billion in Social Security in 2022. Since undocumented workers cannot collect retirement and other Social Security benefits without a change to their immigration status, US citizens and beneficiaries are essentially receiving a subsidy of billions of dollars from undocumented labor – these subsidies will decline dramatically if current policy continues.[57]

Fortunately, given Trump's unrelenting authoritarian actions, we are likely to see a greater segment of the population pull off their blinders and realize that there is a true erosion of democracy and rising fascism in this country. The challenging times will provide opportunities for the organization of people to challenge the Trump administration and attempt to restore the political structure that existed before Trump took office. The upcoming 2026 elections will be extremely important. But perhaps the mass mobilization of people will create a vision of democracy that is even more substantive and inclusive than before. Can people in the USA rise up to build such a movement?

CONCLUSIONS

The first 100 days of the Trump administration dismantled much of the last few decades' progress that improved the conditions for people of color and other marginalized groups. For example, diversity, equity, and inclusion (DEI) programs and policies to even the playing field and provide supportive environments in white and heteronormative institutions are now gone. In addition, Trump's executive orders and other new federal policies have ignited a domino effect in anti-immigrant rhetoric at the state, county, and municipal levels.

While these actions further antagonize the BIPOC immigrant community, they also set a worrisome precedent. Local governments tend to be the next line of defense against federal anti-immigrant policies. Some municipalities *have* stood up to Trump, but others are doubling down on MAGA violence and racism. For instance, in the Texas 2025 state legislative session, Senate Bill (SB) 8, mandates that local law enforcement offices collaborate with ICE, and Senate Bill 36, creates a "homeland security division" within the Department of Public Safety, and Texas terminated its law, which granted in-state tuition to undocumented students, which was first enacted in 2001. Texas has even mimicked Trump's use of the National Guard, as Governor Abbott sent the Texas National Guard to San Antonio to put down demonstrations there.

On a federal level, we also see bills like the Laken Riley Act that manipulate a tragic murder to massively expand immigration detention, further criminalize immigrants, and it encourages anti-immigrant states to sue the federal government for immigration decisions.[58] Another bill that seeks to further disfranchise BIPOC, especially Latinos, is the SAVE Act (HR 22). It increases restrictions on voting rights by requiring documentary proof of citizenship at the federal level. Like other policies to diminish political representation, it generates confusion among and intensifies the intimidation of the BIPOC population, which could lead to people not showing up to the polls where they might be harassed or even arrested. Less political power for BIPOC makes it easier to pass outrageous and increasingly racist legislation.

In the midst of this chaotic and unprecedented year of authoritarianism, we must highlight grass-roots actions and mass mobilizations that provide us with a glimmer of hope, pushing the pendulum back toward justice. Even though it has not passed yet, the John Lewis bill could work to restore voting rights. It sparked a national day of action – "Good Trouble Lives On" – mobilizing individuals across the country to make "good trouble" through peaceful marches and protests commemorating the 5th anniversary of John Lewis' death. The continuous outcries of people standing up to the Trump administration provide hope that people will wake up and use their power to push back.

We have major challenges ahead with the remainder of Trump 2.0 and the continued criminalization and dehumanization of people of color – using immigrants as scapegoats for everything wrong in this country. The reality is that our challenges remain rooted in racism, fear, and xenophobia. Even more worrisome is that such conditions will come back to affect this country in many ways and have negative consequences that will take years, perhaps decades, to overcome. Still, we must remember we can fight back! We can win and perhaps create an even *more* equitable and just country. But it is important for individuals to make plans for whatever may take place that will affect them and their families. We must take care of ourselves and our community, positioning ourselves to challenge the rest of Trump 2.0.

NOTES

1. Rampell, C. (2025, June 11). The secret police descending on Small Town, America. *The Washington Post*. https://www.washingtonpost.com/opinions/2025/06/11/immigration-arrests-ice-raid-masks/.

2. Sandoval, E. (2025, June 27). On a quiet southern border, empty farms and frightened workers. *New York Times*. https://www.nytimes.com/2025/06/27/us/politics/border-immigration-farms.html?smid=url-share.

3. Seitz, A., & Martin, J. (2025, July 27). In fear of ICE raids, some forego care. *San Antonio Express-News*. https://www.pressreader.com/usa/san-antonio-express-news-sunday/20250727/281831469783006.

4. Seitz, A., & Martin, J. (2025, July 27). In fear of ICE raids, some forego care. *San Antonio Express-News*. https://www.pressreader.com/usa/san-antonio-express-news-sunday/20250727/281831469783006.

5. Goldstein, D., & Sanchez, I. C. (2025, June 16). Immigration raids add to absence crisis for schools. *New York Times*. https://www.nytimes.com/2025/06/16/us/immigration-raids-school-absences-deportation-fears.html?smid=url-share.

6. Soberoff, J. (2020). *Separated: Inside an American tragedy*. Mariner Books.

7. Morgan, L., & Groves, S. (2025, January 23). Trump move to deport 'millions and millions' of immigrants could quickly max out ICE's detention center beds. *Fortune*. https://fortune.com/2025/01/23/trump-deport-millions-immigrants-max-out-ice-detention-center-beds/.

8. Srikantiah, J., & Sinnar, S. (2018). White nationalism as immigration policy. *Stanford Law Review Online*, *71*, 197.

9. Flagg, A. (2024, November 11). *How we reported on rhetoric about immigrants in the 2024 election*. The Marshall Project. https://www.themarshallproject.org/2024/11/20/how-we-reported-on-rhetoric-about-immigrants-in-the-2024-election.

10. Rattner, S. (2025, July 3). How bad is this bill? The answer in 10 charts. *New York Times*. https://www.nytimes.com/interactive/2025/07/03/opinion/domestic-policy-bill-in-charts.html?smid=url-share.

11. López, I. H. (2006). *White by law: The legal construction of race*. New York University Press.

12. Huynh, Q.-L., Devos, T., & Smalarz, L. (2011). Perpetual foreigner in one's own land: Potential implications for identity and psychological adjustment. *Journal of Social and Clinical Psychology*, *30*(2), 133–162.

13. Parker, K. (2015). *Making foreigners: Immigration and citizenship law in America, 1600–2000*. Cambridge University Press.

14. Balderamma, F. E., & Rodríguez, R. (2006). *Decade of betrayal: Mexican Repatriation in the 1930s*. University of New Mexico Press.

15. Sáenz, R., Morales, M. C., & Rayo-Garza, C. (2025). *Latina/os in the United States: Diversity and change*. (2nd ed.). Polity Press.

16. Hernández, K. L. (2006). The crimes and consequences of illegal immigration: A cross-border examination of Operation Wetback, 1943 to 1954. *Western Historical Quarterly*, *37*, 421–444.

17. Sáenz, R., Morales, M. C., & Rayo-Garza, C. (2025). *Latina/os in the United States: Diversity and change*. (2nd ed.). Polity Press.

18. Dunn, T. J. (2009). *Blockading the border and human rights: The El Paso operation that remade immigration enforcement*. University of Texas Press.

19. Johnson, K. R. (2023). The KKK, immigration law and policy, and Donald Trump. *UC Law Journal*, *75*, 1645.

20. Elliott, P. (2024, January 1). Polling suggests Trump's quest for revenge appeals to voters. *TIME*. https://time.com/6550686/trump-autocracy-dictator-polling/.

21. Center for American Progress. (2025). *Masked and unidentifiable: The risks of federal law enforcement operating without identification*. https://www.americanprogress.org/article/masked-and-unidentifiable-the-risks-of-federal-law-enforcement-operating-without-identification/.

22. Correal, A. (2025, May 1). Lost in the 'death realm' of El Salvador's prisons. *New York Times*. https://www.nytimes.com/2025/05/01/world/americas/el-salvador-prisons-disappearances.html?smid=url-share.

23. Foster-Frau, S., & Herrero, A. V. (2025, February 25). Invasive frisks, suicide attempts: Three migrants describe Guantánamo detention. *Washington Post*. https://www.washingtonpost.com/immigration/2025/02/25/guantanamo-trump-migrants-deportations-venezuela/.

24. Popli, N. (2025, April 15). Can a U.S. citizen be deported? Trump's comments raise legal alarms. *TIME*. https://time.com/7277884/can-a-u-s-citizen-be-deported-trumps-comments-spark-legal-debate/.

25. Montgomery, M. (2025, April 14). The real reason El Salvador's President Nayib Bukele cozied up to Trump. *Mother Jones*. https://www.motherjones.com/politics/2025/04/el-salvador-nayib-bukele-trump-deportation/

26. Barrón-López, L., Couzens, I., & Popat, S. (2025, April 28). *Children who are U.S. citizens deported along with foreign-born mothers, attorneys say*. PBS. https://www.pbs.org/newshour/show/children-who-are-u-s-citizens-deported-along-with-foreign-born-mothers-attorneys-say.

27. Halpert, M. (2025, April 28). *Three U.S. citizen children, one with cancer, deported to Honduras, lawyers say*. BBC. https://www.bbc.com/news/articles/c4g8yj2n33yo.

28. Paúl, M. L. (2025, April 5). As Trump cracks down on immigration, U.S. citizens are among those snared. *Washington Post*. https://www.washingtonpost.com/immigration/2025/04/05/us-citizens-deported-immigration/.

29. Villarroel, M. (2025, May 6). *A look at U.S. citizens who have been deported by the Trump administration so far*. Latin Times. https://www.msn.com/en-us/news/us/a-look-at-the-u-s-citizens-who-have-been-deported-by-the-trump-administration-so-far/ar-AA1EfDov.

30. Villarroel, M. (2025, May 6). *A look at U.S. citizens who have been deported by the Trump administration so far*. Latin Times. https://www.msn.com/en-us/news/us/a-look-at-the-u-s-citizens-who-have-been-deported-by-the-trump-administration-so-far/ar-AA1EfDov.

31. Popli, N. (2025, April 15). Can a U.S. citizen be deported? Trump's comments raise legal alarms. *TIME*. https://time.com/7277884/can-a-u-s-citizen-be-deported-trumps-comments-spark-legal-debate/.

32. Popli, N. (2025, April 15). Can a U.S. citizen be deported? Trump's comments raise legal alarms. *TIME*. https://time.com/7277884/can-a-u-s-citizen-be-deported-trumps-comments-spark-legal-debate/.

33. Watson, K., Montoya-Galvez, C., & Watson, E. (2025, January 29). *Trump says U.S. will send 'worst criminal illegal aliens' to Guantanamo Bay*. CBS News. https://incubator7-dev-fly.cbsnews.com/news/trump-executive-order-guantanamo-bay-for-criminal-migrants/.

34. Woodward, A. (2025, February 21). Trump administration abruptly empties out Guantanamo prison for all immigrant detainees. *Independent*. https://www.independent.co.uk/news/world/americas/us-politics/trump-guantanamo-bay-prison-immigrants-b2702448.html.

35. Woodward, A. (2025, February 21). Trump administration abruptly empties out Guantanamo prison for all immigrant detainees. *Independent.* https://www.independent.co.uk/news/world/americas/us-politics/trump-guantanamo-bay-prison-immigrants-b2702448.html.

36. Payne, K. (2025, June 25). *'Alligator Alcatraz,' immigration detention site in the Everglades, What to know.* NBC 6 South Florida. https://www.nbcmiami.com/news/local/alligator-alcatraz-immigration-detention-site-in-the-everglades-what-to-know/3645008/.

37. Payne, K. (2025, June 25). *'Alligator Alcatraz,' immigration detention site in the Everglades, What to know.* NBC 6 South Florida. https://www.nbcmiami.com/news/local/alligator-alcatraz-immigration-detention-site-in-the-everglades-what-to-know/3645008/.

38. Amnesty International UK. (n.d.). *USA: New findings reveal human rights violations at Florida's 'Alligator Alcatraz' and Krome detention centers.* https://www.amnesty.org.uk/latest/usa-new-findings-reveal-human-rights-violations-floridas-alligator-alcatraz-and/.

39. PolitiFact. (2025, July 17). *Who ended up at Alligator Alcatraz? It's not just 'worst of the worst' criminals, as officials said.* https://www.politifact.com/article/2025/jul/17/alligator-alcatraz-detain-immigration-Florida/.

40. Van Hook, J., Fix, M., & Gelatt, J. (2025, May). *Repealing birthright citizenship would significantly increase the size of the U.S. unauthorized population.* Migration Policy Institute Short Reads. https://www.migrationpolicy.org/news/birthright-citizenship-repeal-projections.

41. Tsui, K. (2025, June 18). *At least 5 elected officials have been arrested or confronted by policy while protesting Trump's immigration policies.* CNN. https://www.cnn.com/2025/06/18/us/elected-officials-confronted-immigration-enforcement-hnk.

42. Ventura, J. (2025, June 10). *Migrants choosing to self-deport from US in growing numbers.* NewNation. https://www.newsnationnow.com/us-news/immigration/migrants-self-deport-us-growing/.

43. Bennett, B. (2025, June 11). What the data reveals about Trump's push to arrest and deport more migrants. *TIME.* https://time.com/7292939/trump-deportations-ice-arrests/.

44. Montoya-Galvez, C. (2025, July 23). *ICE on track for more detentions since Obama years, but still far short of 1 million target*. CBS News. https://www.cbsnews.com/news/ice-deportations-trump-six-months/.

45. Adams, V. (2025, July 14). *Trump administration sets deportation record*. The Daily Signal. https://www.dailysignal.com/2025/07/14/obama-vs-trump-who-deported-more-illegal-aliens/.

46. Camarota. S. A., & Zeigler, K. (2025, June 19). *Illegal population down since January: Government data suggest that the number of illegal immigrants may have fallen by 1 million*. Center for Immigration Studies. https://cis.org/Report/Illegal-Population-Down-January.

47. Serwer, A. (2021). *The cruelty is the point: Why Trump's America endures*. One World.

48. Jordan, M., Karlamangla, S., Hubler, S., Nunn, E. B., Mayorquin, O., & Stevens, M. (2025, June 14). How L.A. raids ignited a new fight over immigration. *New York Times*. https://www.nytimes.com/2025/06/14/us/los-angeles-protests-buildup.html.

49. Conybeare, W. (2025, June 15). *More than 500 arrests made over 8 days of protests in Los Angeles: LAPD*. KTLA. https://ktla.com/news/local-news/more-than-500-arrests-made-over-8-days-of-protests-in-los-angeles/.

50. Dominguez, L. (2025, June 12). Where people are protesting against immigration raids. *New York Times*. https://www.nytimes.com/2025/06/11/us/us-protest-tracker-trump-ice.html.

51. Acevedo, E. (2025, June 14). Why we fly the Mexican flag at the L.A. protests. *Washington Post*. https://www.washingtonpost.com/opinions/2025/06/14/mexican-flag-california-protest/.

52. Doyle, K. (2025, June 17). *Mapping the "No Kings" demonstrations in the United States*. ACLED. https://acleddata.com/2025/06/17/mapping-the-no-kings-demonstrations-in-the-united-states/.

53. Condes, Y. (2025, July 4). *Once it was mostly a taco website. Now it's covering L.A. ICE raids. Washington Post*. https://www.washingtonpost.com/business/2025/07/04/la-taco-los-angeles-ice-protests/.

54. Ulloa, J., & Jordan, M. (2025, July 5). Under Trump's crackdown, a new crop of immigrant rights groups rises. *New York Times*. https://www.nytimes.com/2025/07/05/us/trump-immigration-rights-ice.html.

55. Guzmán, V. (2025, July 15). *Un mapa contra el miedo: Latinas crean plataforma para rastrear la presencia de ICE*. Univision. https://www.univision.com/local/chicago-wgbo/mapa-rastrea-en-tiempo-real-la-presencia-de-ice-en-estados-unidos.

56. Davis, C., Guzman, M., & Sifre, E. (2024). *Tax payments by undocumented immigrants*. Institute on Taxation and Economic Policy. https://sfo2.digitaloceanspaces.com/itep/ITEP-Tax-Payments-by-Undocumented-Immigrants-2024.pdf.

57. Bernard, T. S. (2025, January 13). How unauthorized immigrants help finance Social Security benefits. *New York Times*. https://www.nytimes.com/2025/01/13/business/social-security-undocumented-immigrants.html.

58. National Immigration Project. (2025, January 27). *Community explainer: Laken Riley Act*. National Immigration Project. https://nipnlg.org/work/resources/community-explainer-laken-riley-act.

5

ABORTION CRIMINALIZATION UNDER TRUMP 2.0 AND LESSONS FOR RESISTANCE

Deborah Billings[a] and Saphronia Carson[b]

[a]*University of South Carolina, USA*
[b]*Emory University, USA*

The first year of the Trump administration could best be characterized as a full-frontal onslaught on reproductive health, reproductive rights, and reproductive justice (RJ). But the reactionary deluge was built upon a foundation of decades of state level abortion restrictions and a burgeoning ultra-conservative, fundamentalist movement focused on the complete criminalization of abortion. While candidate Trump continually denied any familiarity with Project 2025 during the campaign, the Heritage Foundation's "Mandate for Leadership" (also known as the "Presidential Transition Project") has been the clear guide for each step of this administration in all areas of government.[1] Project 2025 begins by stating, "History teaches that a President's power to implement an agenda is at its apex during the administration's opening days."[i]

[i] (xiii) PROJECT 2025.

Thus, examining Trump 2.0's actions in relation to abortion during the initial months of his presidency is significant.

Project 2025 outlines the goals and strategies for a multi-pronged and comprehensive dismantling of abortion access. It also includes steps to treat "gender" as a biological determination, challenge the rights of lesbian, gay, bisexual, transgender, queer+ (LGBTQ+; especially Transgender) people, and terminate diversity-equity-inclusion (DEI) policies and practices. This chapter documents the trajectory toward that multi-pronged assault during Trump's first months in office in 2025. While recognizing the intersection of the administration's efforts to undermine a full range of sexual and reproductive rights, in this chapter, we focus specifically, although not exclusively, on the issue of abortion, which serves as a lens for understanding the attempted shutdown of basic human rights.

In the face of state surveillance and efforts to criminalize abortion providers, seekers, and accompaniers, we also offer examples of strategies that are working to challenge intersecting oppressions and create new possibilities for people throughout the world. This is a critical time for reproductive rights and RJ-grounded activists in the United States to learn from global activists, especially those in the Global South, where movements have focused not only on abortion-related legal reform but also, just as importantly, on abortion access and destigmatization.

THE PRESENT FEELS LIKE THE PAST

While Trump 2.0 may feel new, an examination of the past century shows that similar repressive actions were attempted. These were always confronted with multi-sector strategizing and resistance critical to radically disrupting structures that are at the foundation of reproductive and sexual oppression.

Criminalizing Abortion

In the United States, scholars refer to the period from 1821 to 1958 as the era of abortion's "criminalization,"[2] led by movements built on racist and patriarchal ideologies. The American Medical

Association (AMA) – founded in 1847 by exclusively white male medical practitioners – made outlawing abortion a major priority. The AMA claimed abortion was "immoral and violated medical ethics ... [and an] unwarrantable destruction of human life."[3] Their movement to criminalize abortion rose within the context of shrinking family size among married white, affluent women alongside the arrival of millions of immigrants to the United States. Immigrants often had larger families, which fomented panic over "immigrant fecundity," leading to the conclusion that among "American" [read white] women, abortion "strikes a blow at the very foundation of society itself."[4]

Dynak and colleagues highlight that "The need for social and ideological control over reproduction was used to justify a medical crusade against abortion."[5] The AMA formally adopted the idea that life begins at "conception" and took its restrictive ideas to legislatures throughout the country.[6] Between 1860 and 1880, states and territories passed over 40 laws prohibiting abortion; by 1900, abortion was criminalized everywhere in the nation. What followed was entirely predictable: thousands of women died from unsafe, illegal abortions, and many more were subjected to social stigma, fear of legal retribution, and negative health consequences. As Michele Goodwin states in her essay, *The Racist History of Abortion and Midwifery Bans*,[7] "Then, just as now, anti-abortion efforts have nothing to do with saving women's lives or protecting the interests of children."[ii]

Fetal Personhood and the 14th Amendment Versus Feminist and Physician Activists

By the 1960s, anti-abortion activists launched fetal "personhood" as an argument and used the 14th Amendment to ground their position that the "unborn" had rights as individuals and as a legal class.[iii] At the same time, feminist movements promoted abortion

[ii] The Racist History of Abortion and Midwifery Bans | American Civil Liberties Union. Accessed 29 September 2025.

[iii] The Racist History of Abortion and Midwifery Bans | American Civil Liberties Union. Accessed 29 September 2025, Preface.

access and reproductive services as primary pillars to their activism. The Janes, a Chicago-based movement, was among the most renowned of these groups, arguing that fighting for abortion rights and against gender discrimination were part of a civil rights agenda that included challenging racial, economic, and patriarchal oppression. From the late 1960s until 1973, The Janes linked activism with service, bringing women and abortion providers together. "We were ordinary women trying to save women's lives. But we were criminals; we were felons," states one Jane member.[iv]

Witnessing firsthand the horrifying impact of abortion restrictions on the lives of pregnant women – especially low-income patients and Patients of Color – doctors who offered reproductive services to those in dire situations risked losing their medical licenses. Increasing pressure to legalize abortion compelled the Centers for Disease Control and Prevention to publish its first Technical Report on abortion – *Surveillance of Abortions in Hospitals in the United States, 1970*.[8,9] Also in 1970, the AMA's House of Delegates voted 103 to 73 to allow licensed physicians to perform hospital-based abortions for a range of reasons, and clinical researchers began documenting the public health benefits of legal abortion.[10]

Backlash to Advances

Despite social movements, research, practices, and policies that supported progressive changes in the 1960s and 1970s, anti-abortion forces worked mainly at the local and state levels to undermine the constitutionally guaranteed right to an abortion under the 1973 landmark Supreme Court decision, *Roe* v. *Wade*.[v] The Hyde Amendment (1980) banned the use of federal funds to cover the cost of abortion services, thereby restricting services for low income people, especially those enrolled in Medicaid and

[iv] From The Janes, Official trailer. The Janes | Official Trailer | HBO. The Janes was officially named Abortion Counseling Service of Women's Liberation.

[v] *Jane ROE, et al., Appellants* v. *Henry WADE* | Supreme Court | US Law | LII/Legal Information Institute.

Medicare or in immigration detention facilities and prisons.[vi,vii] State requirements such as mandatory counseling and waiting periods,[viii] parental notification, and/or consent in the case of minors[ix] disproportionately and negatively affected youth, Black, Indigenous, and Latina women, as well as low-income immigrants. According to a Guttmacher Institute report, 1,338 abortion restrictions were enacted between 1973 and 2021 – 44% just in the last decade.[11] In 2021 alone, 663 provisions were introduced to restrict abortion access – 108 were enacted; while of the 218 provisions introduced that would protect or expand access to abortion care, only 10 were enacted.[12]

The Dobbs Decision

The steady and consistent anti-abortion activism reached a critical moment in 2022 when the US Supreme Court ruled to overturn both *Roe* v. *Wade* (1973) and *Planned Parenthood v. Casey* (1992) in the *Dobbs v. Jackson Women's Health Organization* case.[x] This decision devolved authority to the state level for any aspect of abortion that federal law does not preempt. Restrictive abortion laws at the state level that had never been amended during *Roe* and *Casey* (known as Trigger Laws) immediately went into effect; legislators in other states proposed and successfully passed similarly restrictive or even *more* restrictive bills. In 2024, as Trump ramped up his presidential campaign, at least 16 states had highly restrictive laws in place, with new proposals emerging on a regular basis.[xi]

[vi] From 1981 to 1993, the Hyde Amendment prohibited the use of federal funds unless "the life of the mother would be endangered if the fetus were carried to term." In 1993, President Clinton signed into law an expansion of the exception to include cases of rape and incest, where Medicaid funds could be applied to cover the cost of the abortion.

[vii] https://www.reproductiverights.org/sites/crr.civicactions.net/files/documents/Hyde_Report_FINAL_nospreads.pdf.

[viii] Counseling and Waiting Period Requirements for Abortion | Guttmacher Institute.

[ix] Minors' Access to Abortion Care | Guttmacher Institute.

[x] Docket for 19-1392; 597us1r58_gebh.pdf.

[xi] For most recent information, consult Interactive Map: US Abortion Policies and Access After Roe | Guttmacher Institute and Abortion Every Day, with Jessica Valenti Abortion, Every Day | Jessica Valenti | Substack.

TRUMP 2.0 TRENDS AND PROJECT 2025

January 2025 marked a seismic shift in defining abortion policy. Over a century of local, state, and federal restrictions on abortion and reproductive health lay the foundation for Trump 2.0's rapid assault on women's health – Project 2025 became his de facto blueprint.[xii] The term "abortion" appears 199 times in the document, demonizing the practice and aiming to completely criminalize the procedure as well as those who choose it, health care professionals who provide it, family–friend–support networks, and anyone who might provide information about it.

Trump 2.0 further restricts abortion access (domestically and internationally), potentially limits access to contraceptives, and challenges reproductive rights, all by buoying ultra-conservative/fundamentalist religious ideologies. As presented in numerous articles in the collection, the first week of Trump 2.0 enacted multiple executive orders (EOs), memoranda, and policy directives – instead of *legislative* actions – as tools for making radical and rapid change, notably EOs on gender inequality,[xiii] transgender rights,[xiv] DEI,[xv] and abortion.

Beyond the 100-day mark, Trump has continued to attack access to reproductive health, under the guise of "banning abortion." For example, in September 2025, a federal appeals court ruled that the administration could move forward to block Planned Parenthood from receiving reimbursements from Medicaid, thereby prohibiting people from using Medicaid to pay for *any service* offered at Planned Parenthood clinics, including pap smears, sexually

---

[xii] Project 2025 Tracker – Home; see Project 2025 Tracker is creating a tracker for all things Project 2025, for how it was created, with the intent of providing free and accessible information to all.

[xiii] Federal Register: : Defending Women from Gender Ideology Extremism and Restoring Biological Truth to the Federal Government (January 20, 2025).

[xiv] Federal Register: : Defending Women from Gender Ideology Extremism and Restoring Biological Truth to the Federal Government (January 20, 2025).

[xv] Federal Register: : Ending Radical and Wasteful Government DEI Programs and Preferencing (January 20, 2025).

transmitted infection screening and testing, cancer screening, and contraceptives.[xvi]

The attack on people's bodily autonomy shifted significantly after the 2022 *Dobbs* decision and went into high gear as the Trump administration took control. Restricting abortion access through legislation and budgetary actions, along with the undermining of access to gender-affirming care, are actions that have gone hand-in-hand, proposed and passed by legislators emboldened by Trump's implementation of Project 2025.

According to the Center for Reproductive Rights, as of November 2025, abortion has shifted radically in terms of legality and access as compared to the 49 years of *Roe* v. *Wade*, with only 26 states having legal protections to the right to abortion and 13 states banning abortion entirely and enforced with criminal penalties.[xvii] "Abortion care deserts," which correlate with restrictive legislation, leave populations without access, not only to abortion but also to a significant range of women's reproductive health care. The South, with the exception of Virginia, is the most restrictive region of the United States, with either hostile laws or total abortion bans. The majority of these states make performing an abortion a criminal offense with penalties ranging from one to 99 years in prison. Fear among health care providers is grounded in penalties already in place and those being proposed throughout the country.[xviii] Restrictive laws post-*Dobbs* correlate with fewer maternity care providers overall, including a decrease in residency applicants and Ob/gyns and maternal–fetal medicine specialists leaving states with abortion bans.[xix,xx,13]

[xvi] It is important to highlight that Planned Parenthood never received Medicaid payments for abortion services, given the restrictions of the Hyde Amendment.

[xvii] After Roe Fell: U.S. Abortion Laws by State – Center for Reproductive Rights.

[xviii] See, for example, South Carolina's S.474, provocatively named, The Fetal Heartbeat and Protection from Abortion Act. 2023–2024 Bill 474: Abortion – Fetal Heartbeat.

[xix] Doctors Leaving Anti Abortion States | Commonwealth Fund.

[xx] As Abortion Laws Drive Obstetricians from Red States, Maternity Care Suffers – *The New York Times*.

In this post-*Dobbs* setting, combined with a zealous movement led and supported by Make America Great Again (MAGA) advocates, pregnant people in need of abortion care experience the most harrowing consequences. These include needing to find ways to travel and access abortion care in other states, sometimes far from home, being forced to wait until a complication becomes "bad enough," as determined by hospital legal teams, to warrant intervention, and being judged, stigmatized, or even accused and convicted of a felony for interrupting the pregnancy.

Abortion funds – a form of mutual aid – have become increasingly important as pregnant people need to seek services in other locales, sometimes many states from where they live. Self-managed abortion using medications, namely mifepristone and misoprostol, ordered through online networks have taken pregnant people beyond dependence on medical institutions to rely on themselves and solidarity networks.

GLOBAL IMPACT OF TRUMP POLICIES ON ABORTION

During his first week in office, Trump acted in many notable areas, all predictable under Project 2025. We highlight three actions to provide a detailed sense of the depth and breadth of the dismantling.

First, Trump issued a presidential memorandum to reinstate The Mexico City Policy, otherwise known as the "global gag rule," a policy dating back to 1984 that effectively blocks US global health funding for non-US non-governmental organizations from providing, referring, counseling, or advocating for safe abortion, even with non-US funds.[xxi,xxii] For decades, this intimidation tactic has caused confusion and distress among organizations around the

[xxi] Memorandum for the Secretary of State, the Secretary of Defense, the Secretary of Health and Human Services, the Administrator of the United States for International Development – The White House (January 24, 2025).

[xxii] Abortion and Family Planning-related Provisions in U.S. Foreign Assistance Law and Policy | Congress.gov | Library of Congress. In 1984, President Ronald Reagan issued what has become known as the "Mexico City policy," which required foreign non-governmental organizations receiving USAID family planning assistance to certify that they would not perform or actively promote abortion as a method of family planning, even if such activities were conducted with non-US funds.

world, including those working in contexts where abortion is legal or where legal indications are enshrined in existing law, resulting in organizations either losing funding, leading to many shuttering services, or compromising the care they offer.[xxiii] Since the Reagan administration, the global gag order has been reinstated under every Republican President and paused by every Democratic President.

Second, on July 2, 2025, the United States Agency for International Development (USAID) was shut down, fulfilling one of Project 2025's major objectives. This was preceded by a suspension of all foreign aid during Trump's first week in office, as well as a prohibition on USAID from funding "sexual and reproductive health and reproductive rights" as well as "gender equality" programs, eliminating the USAID Chief Diversity Officer and eliminating funding for partners that "promote discriminatory DEI practices."[xxiv] These cuts were part of the so-called Department of Government Efficiency (DOGE) sweep, despite analyses clearly demonstrating the impact of US investment on *preventing* abortion through funding of family planning/contraceptive access initiatives.[xxv]

Third, the Trump administration renewed US support for the 2020 Geneva Consensus Declaration, never formally adopted by the United Nations (UN), which outlines anti-abortion, anti-LGBTQ positions under the guise of "promoting women's health," "protecting life," and "defending family rights."[xxvi,xxvii] The Declaration as a whole runs counter to established human rights principles and UN-based global Conventions and Agreements. Renewed

---

[xxiii] 2023: The Lingering Harm of the Global Gag Rule – The Global Gag Rule.

[xxiv] Project 2025 Tracker: Project 2025 Tracker – Home.

[xxv] A 2024 analysis by Guttmacher showed the impact of US investment in family planning on reproductive health outcomes. Congress appropriated $607.5 million for fiscal year (FY) 2024, that would have served 47.6 million women and couples, prevented 17.1 million unintended pregnancies leading into 5.2 million abortions performed under unsafe conditions and/or by untrained providers, and averted an estimated 34,000 women dying from pregnancy-related complications.

[xxvi] United States Renewed Membership in the Geneva Consensus Declaration on Promoting Women's Health and Strengthening the Family – United States Department of State.

[xxvii] Geneva-Consensus-Declaration-GCD-English-2024.pdf; The Geneva Consensus Declaration – The Institute For Women's Health.

support is consistent with the Trump administration's decision to stop participation in the UN Human Rights Council and denouncing UN agencies for promoting "gender ideology" and DEI.

RESISTANCE

As the discussion so far makes clear, Trump 2.0 has furthered the United States' ongoing project of limiting access to abortion, expanded the criminalization of healthcare provision, produced an atmosphere of fear and uncertainty surrounding abortion services, and withdrawn much US financial support for abortion healthcare outside the United States. It is important to note that this is not a break from historical patterns of reproductive oppression but is in fact an extension of ongoing efforts to control and restrict people's rights, especially those of women and gender non-conforming People of Color. Yet, where there is oppression, there is almost always resistance. Looking towards genealogies of resistance to reproductive oppression by women and gender non-conforming People of Color within and outside of the United States offers a framework for imagining and building spaces of reproductive liberation within, outside of, and beyond this conservative moment. This section examines three examples of feminist resistance to reproductive oppression and explores what practical and theoretical strategies these resistances offer to help us understand and push back against Trump 2.0.

RJ is arguably the most significant movement resisting reproductive oppression in the United States. RJ is a theory, political orientation, and social movement generated by Black women and other women and People of Color, which seeks to critique the ways in which structures of power, such as white supremacy, patriarchy, capitalism, ableism, colonialism, and heterosexism work to control people's reproductive lives and expose many people to forms of reproductive violence.[14] Originating in Black women's activism in the mid-1990s, RJ has grown into a flourishing social movement and robust body of theory highlighting that people's reproduction must be understood in the context of social structures of power that create the conditions under which people have sex, reproduce, have families, or do not do any of these things.[15] As such, it has produced a social movement which is capacious in the ways it conceptualizes reproductive oppression and liberation.

This capaciousness allows activists and advocates to tackle multiple issues impacting people's reproductive lives at once. For example, the RJ strategy has helped to keep the doors of clinics open to provide abortion healthcare in settings where they otherwise would not have been able to due to a lack of political and financial feasibility, while also expanding the reach of the clinic into communities it otherwise might not have served, such as Queer and Trans communities.[xxviii]

Theory and practice work together in the RJ movement to produce material policy changes, as well as cultural and community changes. The RJ movement emphasizes that the *how* of political process matters just as much, if not more than, the *what* of political outcomes because it can lead to social and cultural changes that can shift people's social conditions without having to resort to the state.[xxix]

Feminists in Mexico also offer pathways to thinking about reproductive liberation differently. Abortion was decriminalized in Mexico City in 2007, opening widespread access to a procedure which had prior to that point been difficult to obtain in Mexico but also spawning a backlash and intensification of abortion criminalization in other Mexican states.[16] In 2023, the Mexican Supreme Court ruled that criminalizing abortion in state level penal codes is unconstitutional, grounded in human rights to life and health, among others.[17] Nevertheless, access to services within medical/clinical systems remains a challenge. Mexican feminists have developed two interlinked strategies to address the need for access: accompaniment and self-management. Accompaniment encompasses the notion of feminists working with people seeking abortions to get them access to the procedure, including offering counseling, referrals, and physically going with people to their procedures.[18] Amy Krauss argues that this is an ephemeral kind of feminist politics, which aspires to building long-term networks but often ends up looking

[xxviii] Feminist Center for Reproductive Liberation, Atlanta, GA.

[xxix] Feminist Center for Reproductive Liberation, Atlanta, GA.

like a brief intervention in a life which the feminist accompaniers know little else about. In its ephemerality, activists participate in a practice and politics of care which temporarily allows pregnant people greater access to freedom of movement and myriad services. Krauss argues that such work represents a form of feminist liberation which is no less important for its temporariness.[19]

Self-management also seeks to support pregnant people in their quest for greater autonomy over their reproductive bodies, this time by giving them access to abortion in a way that de-medicalizes the process. Accompaniment becomes part of the process of self-management when feminists assist people seeking self-managed abortion to access the mifepristone and misoprostol, which they can then take at home.[20] *Acompañantes* must negotiate an increasingly neoliberalized and pharmeceuticalized medication abortion terrain but resist these corporate forces by providing medication and accompaniment for free and supporting pregnant people's decisions.[21] This is a values-driven process which seeks to enact feminist principles of solidarity, justice, and collective care within and beyond an abortion landscape heavily governed by state and capital.[22] These spaces of feminist collective action offer pathways towards thinking about what forms of reproductive liberation could look like, even beyond the narrow scope of abortion legalization.[23]

Finally, the work to destigmatize reproductive and sexual health more broadly has strengthened over time. Stigma surrounding sexual and reproductive health and wellness is one form of reproductive oppression that is not necessarily or exclusively reliant upon law and policy. For example, abortions can be stigmatized in contexts where they are legal or seen as relatively normal in contexts where there are policies restricting access to them.[24] Thus, destigmatization can be one way to resist reproductive oppression even in contexts where laws are restrictive and governments are authoritarian. Inroads – International Network for the Reduction of Abortion Discrimination and Stigma – for example, works in 120 countries to connect grassroots community organizers, lawyers, researchers, healthcare providers, and funding organizations to foster transnational collaboration to destigmatize abortion.[xxx]

[xxx] Inroads Illustrated Report 2024.

Their strategies include community resourcing, solidarity and power building, amplifying voices of "the abortion stigma busting community," and shifting power and narratives.[xxxi] The organization is supported through collaborative efforts and an array of resources – including donors, internships, and in-kind work – making it possible to have a global reach with very limited funding.

These three examples demonstrate the ways in which resistance to reproductive oppression has been consistent across time and space. Reproductive oppression is a core element of forms of power such as white supremacy, patriarchy, heterosexism, classism, ableism, and colonialism, and as such becomes intensified in the context of authoritarian governments as a core strategy to consolidate power. Resisting reproductive oppression is one fundamental way in which we can resist oppressive power structures that are intensified under authoritarianism, including Trump 2.0.

NOTES

1. Dans, P., & Groves, S. (2023). *Mandate for leadership. The conservative promise*. Project 2025: Presidential Transition Project. The Heritage Foundation. 2025_MandateForLeadership_FULL.pdf.

2. Dynak, H., Weitz, T. A., Joffe, C. E., Stewart, F. H., & Arons, A. (2003). *Celebrating San Francisco's abortion pioneers*. UCSF Center for Reproductive Health Research & Policy.

3. Minor, S., Tapia, A., & Stumbar, S. E. (2025). Abortion in the nineteenth century through the lens of Ann Lohman. *AMA Journal of Ethics*, 27(2), E149–E158. https://doi.org/10.1001/amajethics.2025.149 (p. 153).

4. Storer, H. R. (1868). *Why not? A book for every woman*. Lee and Shepard; In *Women & The American Story*. Abortion Debate – Women & the American Story. Accessed 29 September 2025; Harris, R., & Lewis, R. (2001). The geography of North American cities and suburbs, 1900–1950: A new synthesis. *Journal of Urban History*, 27(3), 262–292.

[xxxi] Inroads.

5. Dynak, H., Weitz, T. A., Joffe, C. E., Stewart, F. H., & Arons, A. (2003). *Celebrating San Francisco's abortion pioneers* (p. 7). UCSF Center for Reproductive Health Research & Policy.

6. Ziegler, M. (2025). *Personhood: The new civil war over reproduction.* Yale University Press.

7. Goodwin, M. (2020). *The racist history of abortion and midwifery bans.* ACLU. https://www.aclu.org/news/racial-justice/the-racist-history-of-abortion-and-midwifery-bans.

8. Kahn, J. B., Bourne, J. P., Asher, J. D., & Tyler, C. W. (1970). Surveillance of abortions in hospitals in the U.S. *HSMHA Health Reports, 86*(5), 423–430. https://stacks.cdc.gov/view/cdc/62826.

9. Kahn, J. B., Bourne, J. P., Asher, J. D., & Tyler, C. W. (1970). Surveillance of abortions in hospitals in the U.S. *HSMHA Health Reports, 86*(5), 423.

10. Stewart, G. K., & Goldstein, P. J. (1971). Therapeutic abortion in California. Effects of septic abortion and maternal mortality. *Obstetrics and Gynecology, 37*(4), 510–514.

11. Nash, E. (2021). *State policy trends 2021: The worst year for abortion rights in almost half a century.* Guttmacher Institute.

12. Nash, E. (2021). *State policy trends 2021: The worst year for abortion rights in almost half a century.* Guttmacher Institute.

13. Howard, D, Bornstein, M., Wascher, J., Norris, A. H., & Rivlin, K. (2025). Relocation post-Dobbs among clinicians providing abortions. *JAMA Network Open, 8*(6), e2514884. https://doi.org/10.1001/jamanetworkopen.2025.14884.

14. Ross, L., & Solinger, R. (2017). *Reproductive justice: An introduction.* University of California Press.

15. Ross, L., & Solinger, R. (2017). *Reproductive justice: An introduction.* University of California Press.

16. Krauss, A. (2019). The ephemeral politics of feminist accompaniment networks in Mexico city. *Feminist Theory, 21*(1), 37–54. https://doi.org/10.1177/1464700118755660.

17. Human Rights Watch. (n.d.). *Mexico's Supreme Court orders federal decriminalization of abortion*. Retrieved February 20, 2024, from https://www.hrw.org/news/2023/09/08/mexicos-supreme-court-orders-federal-decriminalization-abortion.

18. Krauss, A. (2019). The ephemeral politics of feminist accompaniment networks in Mexico city. *Feminist Theory*, *21*(1), 42.

19. Krauss, A. (2019). The ephemeral politics of feminist accompaniment networks in Mexico city. *Feminist Theory*, *21*(1), 50.

20. Belfrage, M. (2023). Revolutionary pills? Feminist abortion, pharmaceuticalization, and reproductive governance. *International Feminist Journal of Politics*, *25*(1), 6–25. https://doi.org/10.1080/14616742.2022.2154688.

21. Belfrage, M. (2023). Revolutionary pills? Feminist abortion, pharmaceuticalization, and reproductive governance. *International Feminist Journal of Politics*, *25*(1), 6–25. https://doi.org/10.1080/14616742.2022.2154688.

22. Belfrage, M. (2023). Revolutionary pills? Feminist abortion, pharmaceuticalization, and reproductive governance. *International Feminist Journal of Politics*, *25*(1), 6–25. https://doi.org/10.1080/14616742.2022.2154688.

23. Inicio – Acompañando abortos; Comité de Planeación. (2022). *Explorando el activismo vinculado al aborto seguro a través de las experiencias e historias de feministas que integran Redes de Acompañamiento en América Latina* (2020–2021). Primer informe de resultados – Mayo del 2022. Informe-Activismo-MAYO-2022.pdf.

24. Kumar, A., Hessini, L., & Mitchell, E. M. H. (2009). Conceptualizing abortion stigma. *Culture, Health, and Sexuality*, *11*(6), 1–15. https://doi.org/10.1080/13691050902842741.

6

DUMBING DOWN OR RISING UP: EDUCATION MUST BE ANTI-FASCIST

Corey Dolgon

Stonehill College, USA

> *The Professors are the Enemy. Write that on the blackboard 100 times and never forget it.*[1]
>
> *They Haven't Seen truth at Harvard in 100 Years.*[2]
>
> *I love the poorly educated.*[3]
>
> *I think if any of us want to do the things that we want to do for our country and for the people ... we have to honestly and aggressively attack the universities ....*[4]

On February 14, 2025, the Department of Education (DOE) issued a letter to every college, university, and K–12 public school district in the United States. The letter threatened these institutions stating that future federal funding would be jeopardized if they failed to meet the "nondiscrimination obligations" supposedly spelled out in Title VI of the 1964 Civil Rights Act, the Constitution's Equal Protection Clause, and the *2023 Supreme Court Decision in Students for Fair Admissions* v. *Harvard University* (*SFFA* v. *Harvard*). In that latter case's Majority Opinion – essentially banning any use of racial considerations in college admissions – Chief Justice John

Roberts wrote, "Eliminating racial discrimination means eliminating all of it."

SFFA v. *Harvard* was a trigger point for the conservative movement as it not only promised an end to affirmative action but also provided an ideological and political wedge to attack every progressive educational policy from the past half-century. This opportunity arose by recasting historical and structural forces such as racism and sexism as simply "individual experiences."[5] Conservatives claim that social and political acts cannot be framed by the history and culture of policies that shaped our laws, our schools, and our social practices. Instead, equality means that every individual begins with, and is entitled to, a blank slate as if past inequalities had never existed or had any impact on the present. Thus, in his concurrent opinion on *SFFA* v. *Harvard*, Justice Clarence Thomas claimed the Court's decision would bring the nation closer to the "colorblind Constitution" originally conceived of by its framers. "I hold out enduring hope," he wrote,

> *that this country will live up to its principles so clearly enunciated in the Declaration of Independence and the Constitution of the United States: that all men are created equal, are equal citizens, and must be treated equally before the law.*[6]

Despite such a belief, the Supreme Court struck down a policy intended to manifest this principle and operationalize such hope.

Of course, Thomas's proclamation was absurd – the Constitution was not colorblind nor was it intended to be. In fact, the whole notion of "colorblindness" represents little more than a contemporary form of racist discourse. Essentially, colorblind ideology allows institutions and individuals to ignore how historical elements of racism persist today, both structurally and ideologically. The guiding premise and principle of colorblindness suggests that ending slavery, Jim Crow, and the Civil Rights Movement "did the trick," thus ridding the country of racism. This belief underlies recent court decisions rolling back not only affirmative action, but also the Voting Rights Act, any remnant of civil rights legislation, and anything related to diversity, equity, and inclusion (DEI). Lingering inequalities, according to conservatives, now result from natural, cultural, or individual pathologies, not persistent structural and social forces that stigmatize and discriminate against non-whites. In fact, to even mention race is in and of itself an act of racism.[7]

Justice Thomas's claim that by banning anti-discriminatory measures, the country somehow gets *closer* to equality reeks of what Jennifer Mueller called a "willful racial ignorance." Erasing laws and policies that address historical and systemic inequalities by claiming the measures *themselves* discriminate against the very same individuals who *still* benefit from historical inequalities seems naïve and disingenuous at best. Within the context of Make America Great Again (MAGA) politics, however, the colorblind narrative must also be understood as a very *overt* and purposeful part of rebuilding white supremacy. This goal informs almost every aspect of Trump 2.0's educational policy.[8]

Still, given its references to *SFFA* v. *Harvard*, the DOE's "Dear Colleague Letter" (DCL) should not have caught anyone by surprise. *Project 2025* (P2025), arguably Trump's 2.0 playbook, included an education chapter focused on three primary objectives: (1) Cut federal funding for *any* educational initiatives supporting public and private research universities with *any* curricular or programmatic links to DEI; (2) Defund programs that strengthen K–12 public education in hopes of dismantling public schools and expanding school choice and privatization; and (3) Reverse decades of initiatives that addressed racial, gender, and other forms of historical and contemporary discrimination, especially efforts to create a more inclusive and multicultural understanding of American history and identity.

In fact, P2025 laid the groundwork for integrating all three of these goals within an overall "anti-anti-discrimination" framework, increasingly fueled by generating fear and paranoia *about* universities in general, and scholarly fields such as gender studies and critical race theory in specific. The DCL wrongly states that schools use these theories to discard "biology in favor of political indoctrination and apply critical race theory to advocate[9] for *more* [emphasis added] racial discrimination." The letter claims that such "course material attempts to indoctrinate students with radical ideas about race and the ambiguous concept of 'gender.'" While almost half a century of educational policy focused on *dismantling* the power and privilege of white, male, and heteronormative academic ideas, structures, and cultures, the federal government is now stating unequivocally that such efforts *themselves* are discriminatory against cis-white men. Thus, they cannot be tolerated, supported, or taught.

While neither economic nor ideological attacks on education lacked precedent in traditional conservative politics ("reverse discrimination" claims and anti-affirmative action proposals were prevalent even before the 1978 Bakke case), Trump 2.0 bodes far more ominous in its threats to defund schools and its willingness to not only test the limits of the law (and the imagination) but also completely obliterate any relationship between educational policy and research, facts or the truth. For example, the DCL threatens to cut funds from educational institutions supporting *any* policy, program, or event that recognizes the history of racial discrimination and the structural roots of contemporary prejudices based on race, gender, or sexual orientation. The DCL equates graduation ceremonies celebrating students of color and residence halls for lesbian, gay, bisexual, transgender, and queer+ (LGBTQ+) students with slavery and Jim Crow. The Letter explained,

> *institutions have discriminated against students on the basis of race [and] embrace pervasive and repugnant race-based preferences and other forms of racial discrimination [that] have emanated throughout every facet of academia .... In a shameful echo of a darker period in this country's history [emphasis added], many American schools and universities even encourage segregation by race at graduation ceremonies and in dormitories and other facilities.*[10]

The DCL and its threats to defund institutions inspired dozens of lawsuits, many of which have already resulted in temporary injunctions and even summary judgments against DOE efforts. Federal courts have so far prohibited the majority of these efforts and the outright ineffectiveness of the DCL policies may simply be more evidence – like so many other policy areas discussed in this book – where the very *intention* of the threats is more about *intimidation and fear* than about the executive branch's ability to violate the law, assume dictatorial powers, and tell educators what they can and cannot teach. Yet, as more colleges, universities, and K–12 school districts capitulate to DCL demands, the greater a fascist pawl spreads over the academic landscape. In the case of education, Trump 2.0 portends to dismantle public education to enhance private profit and redistribute public funds through tax breaks for the wealthy.[11] But even more notable is the authoritarian drive to change the content of educational policy and curriculum by literally rewriting and whitewashing US history. As Jason Stanley argues, authoritarian regimes must conceal history to consolidate power: erasing history "allows [them] to misrepresent it as a 'single story, a single perspective' narrated and controlled by those in charge."[12]

In this chapter, I begin with a framework that places Trump 2.0's educational policy in the historical context of corporate and conservative racial politics, neoliberal economics, and the rise of neofascism in the United States. Next, I look at the specifics of Trump's war on education as part of a fascist project to separate the production of knowledge from the basic tenets of science, research, and the pursuit of evidence and truth. Instead, Trumpism understands facts as merely what the President *wants* to be true – pro*claims* to be true – and then threatens anyone who would espouse otherwise. The ways in which we educate students and create knowledge have become not only politicized and polarized, but they are now completely at odds with even the basic tenets of research, science, and fact. In the final section, I offer strategies for resistance and examine the signs of critical hope that come not only from universities under attack, but also from the students, faculty, and communities that recognize the fight *is* against fascism.

"WHAT ABOUT THE CHILDREN?"

> *The history of American educational reformers often seems to be the history of men fighting against an uncongenial environment. The educational jeremiad is as much a feature of our literature as the jeremiad in the Puritan sermons.*[13]

Sociologists have long studied education as an institution responsible for the reproduction of a society's most pervasive values and necessary skills. Schools teach children what they need to know to operate effectively in an ever-changing economic, social, and political system, one that demands their work, participation, and general obedience. Schools socialize students into the existing dominant culture and ruling ideas. But education is also charged with providing students the critical intellectual tools to compete and innovate, create and change the society around them. Thus, schools are a "contested terrain" on which multiple opposing political and social interests collide.[14] Such contradictions could be found in the earliest efforts at mass public education in the United States.

Led by Horace Mann, states like Massachusetts sought to effectively train a new workforce by instilling in young people an *industrial morality* – the kind of discipline needed by the owners of burgeoning factory towns across New England. While mid-19th century schools focused on values such as "attention, order, neatness, politeness and punctuality," Mann suggested there was a kind of *manufactured consent* even more primary to the purpose of education. He wrote:

> *A stable body politic and a smoothly functioning factory alike required citizens and workers who had embraced and taken as their own the values and objectives of those in authority. Schools might do better than to instill obedience; they might promote self-control.*[i]

"Educated" workers not only became more effective, efficient, and obedient; but they also saw their own futures linked to the power and success of their bosses in the workplace and their municipal leaders in the community. Such were the tenets of bourgeois democracy.

These rationalized goals remained dominant throughout the history of American education. In the early 1800s, Reverend Thomas Edson designed a special clock for classroom use, which divided up the school day neatly into thirty-two ten-minute recitation periods. A century later, Sociologists Robert S. Lynd and Helen Merrell Lynd found schools in Muncie, Indiana, similarly organized:

---

[i] Quoted in Bowles and Gintis (1976),[15] Katz (2001),[16] and Rice (1912).[17]

> *The school, like the factory, is a thoroughly regimented world. Immovable seats in orderly rows fix the sphere of activity of each child .... Bells divide the day into periods [and] ... practically all movement is forbidden except the marching from one set of seats to another between periods, a brief interval of prescribed exercise daily, and periods of manual training or home economics once or twice a week.*[18]

While reform efforts to "open up" school structures and practices came and went, most public education mimicked corporate America's need for a highly stratified, rationalized, and obedient labor force.

Schools did, however, promise to solve other social problems, such as racial and ethnic tensions. In the mid-1800s, "industrial schools" for Native Americans and Mexican Americans were built to "civilize" or "assimilate" groups into the culture of American capitalism and "middle class" values. Indian Commissioner George Manypenny explained that assimilation mandated "Indians learn to say 'I' instead of 'we,' 'me' instead of 'us,' 'mine' instead of 'ours.'"[19] Similar forays into forced assimilation occurred in the southwest, as corporations and legislators built Chicana boarding schools specifically designed to house, educate, and train young Mexican women. Not only did founders hope to create a ready supply of female domestic workers, but they also pursued women as the purveyors of cultural values and social practices in their own families and communities. "Go after the women," wrote educator Alfred White, "and you may save the second generation for America."[20]

Similar 20th century goals inspired a rapid expansion of public education to address massive immigration from Eastern Europe, Asia, and Mexico. "Americanization" remained largely about Anglo conformity and subservient assimilation. Thus, educational policy deemed schools as the proper institution,

> *to break up these groups or settlements, to assimilate and amalgamate these people as a part of our American race, and to implant in their children ... the Anglo-Saxon conception of righteousness, law and order, and popular*

> *government ... to awaken in them a reverence for our democratic institutions.*[21]

According to historian Roger Daniels, the Americanization Movement "was an organized campaign to insure political loyalty and cultural conformity." Schools not only taught English and Civics, but they also promoted hygiene and fitness, "middle class values, and discipline more appropriate to the factory than the classroom."[22] Education remained an institution that linked the ideas of capitalism, free markets, and workforce development to bourgeois democratic values and patriotism.

Higher education also followed these economic and social functions as the rise of public colleges and universities inspired new sites for industrial education. Founded well before the American Revolution, elite universities like Harvard, Yale, Princeton, and Columbia produced knowledge that legitimized Jefferson's "earned aristocracy" to occupy the upper echelons of government, church, industry, and finance. But the 1862 Morrill Act establishing public land grant institutions sought to give working class, white men more advanced technical and managerial training. These graduates would drive an expanding agricultural and industrial sector and build what would become the first American middle class. While knowledge production fueled economic growth, higher education also professed democratic participation, encouraging students' commitment to patriotism and "the American Project" of unlimited global expansion – economically and politically.[23]

Significant educational reforms in the post-WWII period saw a second major expansion in higher education as the G.I. Bill flooded colleges and universities with new, still mostly white male, students. Meanwhile, the federal government and corporations saturated campuses with previously unseen levels of funding to build up weapons research and produce new consumer-oriented technology and commodities.[24] Eventually, universities became powerful engines for local and national economic growth inspiring University of California Chancellor Clark Kerr to claim that,

> *What the railroads did for the second half of the last century, and the automobile for the first half of this century, may be done for the second half of this century by the*

> *knowledge industry; and that is, to serve as the focal point for national growth.*[25]

As higher education grew larger, more complex, and more stratified, a professional middle class of highly educated, upper level managers, engineers, doctors, lawyers, and a financial elite solidified a late 20th and early 21st century class of experts that directed economic, political, and social institutions.[26]

Post-WWII universities were also changed by social movements that demanded access and opportunity for non-whites and women. Affirmative action policies initiated in the late 1960s and 1970s changed both the demographics of student bodies and the monopoly of Anglo men over curriculum and college policies. According to Anthony Platt, "activism and government intervention made quite a difference" for Black Americans and all women:

> *between 1970 and 1990, the number of African American college graduates more than doubled; between 1964 and 1994, the number of female Ph.D.'s increased more than ten-fold; and with the ensuing diversification of the faculty, the canon was opened up to new ideas and, in some disciplines at least, the university began to approximate what it is supposed to be: a market-place of ideas.*[27]

Higher education not only became more diverse, but also programs focused on African American, Ethnic and regional studies, women's, and LGBTQ studies reshaped historical and social scientific knowledge. New insights emerged exposing the layers of social and political oppression faced by women and non-white populations, and how this discrimination had stilted the accuracy and possibility of scientific inquiry itself.[28] Such investigations also explained the historical power and capacity these groups had in resisting oppression and fighting for change.

By the turn of the 21st century, however, a neoliberal sensibility about these conflicts had found a kind of stable consensus in higher education. On the one hand, corporatization and austerity recast colleges and universities as revenue producing institutions – essentially companies themselves – committed to economic efficiencies and development initiatives. Increasingly, students became consumers; faculty became content providers and platform managers. Crippling student debt further transformed graduates into deeply indebted, indentured workers, while the bureaucratization of teaching and "outcomes-based" learning meant more administrative staff to do quantitative evaluations and more precarious, part-time instructors to offer a modicum of subject matter. Knowledge production itself focused primarily on private profits, corporate ideology, and institutional marketability.[29]

On the other hand, demands for public institutions to address generations of discrimination and limited access forced schools at all levels to implement policies that would advance diversity – not only based on race and gender, but also to support people with disabilities, LGBTQ identities, veterans and other groups designated as disadvantaged. A kind of détente was reached between conservative corporate interests – education as the site for training all levels of workers and conducting private sector research for economic growth – and progressive social interests that demanded educators and innovators be increasingly open to a more pluralistic and non-discriminatory campus.[30,31,ii]

But Trump 2.0 has changed all this. The détente is over. Most colleges and universities are now under attack for preaching even the possibility of a multicultural democracy comingled with a corporate driven, capitalist economy.[32] Private sector interests, such as upper-level workforce development and research shaped by corporate funded imperatives, remain dominant. Yet, efforts to diversify the professional middle class and encourage more critical social and political perspectives on historical and structural inequalities (especially as they relate to race and gender) are now over. While some major corporations and institutions have pledged to maintain diversity goals, most have relinquished equity initiatives either quickly without hesitation ("phew, that's over"), or reluctantly in fear of governmental retribution and MAGA backlash. And schools have been at the forefront of these conflicts and institutional capitulations.

[ii] 'Illegal' DEI: See Which States Told Trump Their Schools Don't Use It.

FOR GOD, FOR COUNTRY, FOR MARKETS

> *DeSantis' law prohibits Florida teachers from ... classroom discussions about America's racial history that can cause white students to "feel discomfort, guilt, anguish or any other form of psychological distress" about their race .... [T]he Florida Board of Education adopt[ed] new teaching standards that frame slavery as an employment opportunity that gave slaves a chance to learn valuable occupations free of charge.*[33]

> *If America's public schools cease to exist tomorrow, America would be a better place.*[34]

DeSantis's 2022 Stop Woke Act [HB7] may have been a practice run for Trump 2.0, but it was an effective one. Despite numerous lawsuits that have chipped away at a complete DEI ban, most public institutions in Florida now restrict programs, policies, and curricula related to issues of race, gender, ethnicity, or encourage any criticism of past oppression linked to present inequalities or identities. But like Trump's myriad executive orders (EOs) and DCL threats, it's the vague language, organizational confusion, and manufactured fear that seem most daunting. According to Schoorman and Gatens, HB7 went "beyond book banning," curricula restrictions, and whitewashed history lessons to include K–16 institutional funding threats, job losses, and professional intimidation on all levels.[35,36,iii] In other words, the attack on the so-called "Wokeness" was in reality a wholescale effort to dismantle public education from top to bottom in hopes of establishing a privatized system committed to a *patriotic* curriculum driven by the worship of private markets all controlled by a totalitarian, white supremacist regime.

Since 2022, more than 20 states have passed (and 25 others have tried to pass) similar bans on DEI policies, critical race theory, and other educational efforts intended to address historical inequalities and discrimination against women, LGBTQ, and non-white students. For the first 100 days of Trump 2.0, school districts across the nation scurried to develop the certification protocols demanded

[iii] Anti-DEI Legislation Tracker | BestColleges.

by the DOE, all in hopes of solidifying federal funding – even funds *already* allotted but suddenly threatened or cut off. DEI offices were closed, personnel were fired, and humanities and social science curricula were hastily revamped. Superintendents have called on schools to scrub websites of anything remotely related to DEI, and teachers have radically changed reading lists and assignments. Daniel Crowley, a ninth-grade English teacher from Ann Arbor, Michigan, worried about the "chilling effect" on teachers explaining, "It's effectively saying that naming current racialized problems is itself not just racist but is illegal … and that's really scary to me as someone who teaches African American lit, specifically."[37,38,iv]

A total of 25 states *refused* to comply with DCL demands and threw their lot in with a major lawsuit initiated by the American Federation of Teachers. On August 14, 2025, Trump-appointed US District Court Judge Stephanie Gallagher *rejected* the DCL requirements to restrict classroom speech and curriculum. Gallagher noted that Title VI had "never been interpreted to preclude teaching about concepts relating to race," and that DOE's efforts to expand the definitions of "stereotyping," "stigmatizing," and "discrimination" could not be enforced. The judge also found the government in violation of academic freedom and free speech, taking issue with DCL's vagueness and its failure to *define* DEI or clearly identify what "prohibited DEI-related activity" might be. This murkiness gave DOE power to enforce the DCL arbitrarily while creating a chilling effect on free speech. Most importantly, Judge Gallagher determined that race-neutral efforts to promote diversity and increase opportunity for all students are not presumptively illegal under Title VI.[v]

Still, in district after district, schools have not only shuttered DEI offices, eradicated DEI programs, and altered DEI policies, but they now prepare to accept a new "Patriotic" curriculum based on a presentation of American history that the DOE claims is

---

[iv] Educators Speak Out on Harms of Unlawful Education Department Directive | American Civil Liberties Union; 'A step backwards': How federal threats to DEI are impacting California schools | EdSource; Michigan standing by DEI in schools despite Trump threat to pull US funding - Bridge Michigan.

[v] Federal Court Judge Vacates Department of Education's "Dear Colleague Letter" Relating to Diversity, Equity and Inclusion (DEI): Implications for Higher Education Clients | Buchanan Ingersoll & Rooney PC.

"grounded in an accurate, honest, unifying, inspiring, and ennobling characterization of the American founding." This educational package advances the "concept that commitment to America's aspirations is beneficial and justified." In response, many historians now refer to the DOE as an Orwellian "ministry of Truth."[vi] But most K–12 schools fear losing funding if they don't comply. Meanwhile, the paranoia generated by conservative think tanks and right-wing protests has left local school boards beleaguered by vitriolic, yet poorly informed parents, convinced that schools are blaming white children for slavery and plotting to turn their children gay or trans.

For example, take the case of the Williamson County school district outside of Nashville, Tennessee. Moms for Liberty (M4L), a national right-wing educational organization trained by the conservative American Legislative Exchange Council, set its sights on challenging what they deemed an "anti-white" and "pro-gay" agenda in the district's schools.[39] As Paige Williams reported for *The New Yorker*, despite the overwhelming success of the District's English and Language Arts curriculum entitled "Wit & Wisdom," M4L complained that units on seahorses threatened to "normalize that males can get pregnant" by explaining that male seahorses give birth; the Moms suspected a covert endorsement of "gender fluidity." The group also complained about civil rights assignments that exposed white students to "psychological distress" because they described angry white mobs or had "historical photographs – segregated drinking fountains, firefighters blasting Black Americans with hoses – that might make kids feel bad."[40] School Board meetings became shouting fests with some M4L parents threatening violence. Over one thousand school districts across almost every state have been targeted by right-wing calls for critical race theory and gender identity bans.

Such ideological missions by MAGA-related activists help explain the seeming conflicts between traditional conservative efforts to dismantle DOE and ideologues (particularly Christian fundamentalists) hoping to use DOE to radically transform education in the United States. During his first 100 days, Trump signed an

[vi] ED Wants Grants to Advance "Patriotic Education".

EO to disband the DOE, and Secretary Linda McMahon called its dissolution "the final mission." Still, the DOE remains very active despite significant budget cuts and mass firings. Essentially, Trump has *repurposed* the agency to meet P2025's goals – privatizing public education while expunging DEI and related policies. The growing post-WWII white Christian nationalist movement had always combined a corporate free-market primacy with a racist patriarchal hegemony and fundamentalist Christian agenda.[41]

A recent Pro Publica report makes this radical right-wing agenda frighteningly clear as the DOE punishes public schools for diversity efforts by redirecting funds toward private entities, Christian charter schools, virtual educational start-ups, and homeschooling. Reporters O'Matz and Richards explain that, in just over eight months, DOE "officials have opened a $500 million tap for charter schools ... [and] repeatedly urged states to spend federal money for poor and at-risk students at private schools and businesses" while simultaneously threatening funding cuts for "public schools that offer programs to address historic inequities for Black or Hispanic students."[42] In other words, the DOE is effectively combining school privatization initiatives with anti-DEI policies to create a corporate-led revisionist history shaped by blind patriotism, Christian fundamentalism, and a repackaged version of white supremacy. While critics of the DOE funneling public tax dollars into private industry pockets call such efforts a "great American heist," *combining* privatization with white Christian fundamentalism is now the agency's stated mission. For example, DOE has hired almost a dozen members from the America First Policy Institute (AFPI), an organization O'Matz and Richards report has "sweeping education priorities" that include "advocating for school vouchers and embedding biblical principles in schools." Such goals are clearly articulated in the AFPI policy publication, *Biblical Foundations*, a guide to end the separation of church and state and "plant Jesus in every space." The reporters continue:

> *The paper rejects the idea that society has a collective responsibility to educate all children equally and argues that "the Bible makes it clear that it is parents alone who*

shoulder the responsibility for their children." It frames public schooling as failing, with low test scores and "far-left social experiments, such as gender fluidity."[43]

Along with a conglomeration of similar right-wing conservative groups, AFPI has received substantial funding from billionaire donors such as Richard Uihlein, Charles Koch, and Leonard Leo to supplement the DOE's transformation of public dollars into for-profit Christian education.[44]

One might have hoped that higher education would have fared better in this battle, but universities' miserable failure during the McCarthy Era may end up simply being prologue for academia's wreckage in the wake of Trumpism. Initially using "antisemitism" as a Trojan Horse to attack academic freedom and free speech, Trump's threats to defund billions in federal research money (much of it already passed by Congress and slated for distribution) forced Columbia University to "crackdown" on protest and free speech as well as restrict academic freedom in regional studies departments and completely restructure programs related to Middle Eastern Studies. The school also agreed to pay $200 million in "fines" to the US government while paying another $20 million to Jewish employees and students who have "complained" of antisemitism. In addition, Columbia granted Trump-approved officials the right to review the university's admissions records to ensure that it does not engage in affirmative action.

Soon after Columbia's capitulation in late July 2025, Brown University agreed to pay $50 million to statewide workforce development programs, ban transgender athletes from women's sports, stop gender affirming care in its Medical School, and terminate all affirmative action policies in admissions and hiring. The University of Pennsylvania also agreed to prohibit trans athletes and expunge victories and records achieved by Lia Thomas, a trans woman swimmer, and adopt definitions of "male" and "female" that align with Trump's EOs. The University of Virginia signed an agreement to comply with US Department of Justice (DOJ) policy that threatens to withhold federal funds if schools engage in DEI practices deemed unlawful. The DOJ memo from July 29th not only bans the use of DEI criteria for admissions but also prohibits race-based scholarships or programs, mentorship programs, or leadership initiatives reserved for members of certain racial groups. The memo also addresses university hiring policies, cautioning schools not to ask applicants to "demonstrate 'cultural competence,' 'lived experience,' or 'cross-cultural skills' in ways that effectively evaluate candidates' racial or ethnic backgrounds rather than objective qualifications."[45]

The Chronicle of Higher Education has tracked almost 300 higher education institutions that have eradicated or significantly altered their approach to DEI policies and curricula. From the Kentucky Community and Technical College System to Muskegon Community College in Michigan, to the Air Force Academy, Emory University, Northeastern University, and the University of California system, higher education DEI offices have been closed, hiring policies altered, mission statements revised, and curricula reconstructed to meet the narrowest of proscriptions on issues related to race, ethnicity, gender, and LGBTQ. As one sociology professor at the University of Central Florida explained, most faculty are afraid to even use the word "gender" in class.

In probably the longest, most comprehensive, and most expensive "proposed" agreement, the Trump administration will require the University of California, Los Angeles (UCLA) to terminate all admissions, hiring, training, student support, and service programs and policies that relate to DEI initiatives or identity in general. The DOJ also wants UCLA to institute policies that regulate and or prohibit student demonstrations and restrict admissions to only foreign students who sign a pledge NOT to criticize US policies. Finally, Trump wants the school to pay the government $1 billion as well as establish a fund of over almost $1.75 million for those who claim they have been discriminated against based on race or gender. Despite the obvious rollback on DEI, it's impossible not to characterize so many of these threats as simply the bully wants his lunch money. However, Trump has successfully wrangled UCLA to provide almost 200 names of faculty and students (as well as a plethora of personal and professional information) to be investigated for antisemitism, charges primarily related to their participation in Pro-Palestinian and anti-genocide demonstrations on campus. According to Judith Butler, a UC Berkeley philosophy professor and Jewish critic of the Israeli government, "There is no good evidence that antisemitism is rampant on campus." To oppose genocide "is certainly not an antisemitic thing to do ... we were taught to be against genocide, and we were taught, as well, that 'never again' is a slogan that should apply to all people."

Trump 2.0's education policy has not proceeded unchecked, as I will turn to in the next section. Yet, the attack on public education as a "great equalizer" for all Americans and on universities as sites of elite knowledge production focused on scientific and humanistic innovation continues almost unabated. On October 1st, the DOE issued a new "Compact" proposal asking nine institutions to sign on to a "wide-ranging plan that would supposedly give them preferential treatment for funding if they enact a number of policy changes." But like most Trump EOs, the benefits, qualifications, and punishments for violating or even ignoring the Compact are vague, yet ominous. The document mandates universities agree to strict admissions and hiring procedures, free speech and protest guidelines; ideological and curricular restrictions, clear definitions of two genders, and delineations between "men" and "women" and tuition freezes, among other items. But the last line of the first paragraph gives the "tell": "Institutions of higher education are free to develop models and values other than those below, *if the institution elects to forego federal benefits*" [emphasis added]. The DOE gives no specific benefits for signing the Compact, only a series of vague threats for violations or avoidance. Undoubtedly, Trump will succeed in bullying more institutions to adopt his dictates, but six of the initial nine invitees have rejected the Compact, and a few others who were later asked have also done so. Could this be the beginning of a resistance?

ANTI-FASCISM: FROM THE COURTROOM TO THE CLASSROOM; FROM THE STATEHOUSE TO THE STREETS

> *In an age of growing authoritarianism, education takes on a new sense of urgency and becomes central to politics itself .... Fascist politics are emerging across the globe, disseminating toxic racist and ultra-nationalist images .... [I]t is essential to reclaim the critical pedagogy of democracy as a moral and political project. This is especially true ... when historical amnesia, censorship, the banning*

> *of books, and a full-scale assault on teacher autonomy have become primary tools of those attacking public and higher education. Critical pedagogy has become the enemy of authoritarians out to destroy the institutions that create informed and critical citizens.*[46]

The DOE was not the only Trump agency deployed to destroy academic freedom and free speech at universities. Just before the DCL's release, the Justice Department formed a *Task Force to Combat Anti-Semitism* led by Leo Terrell – an attorney best known as a loud-mouthed, right-wing Fox News talking head. Boasting that he would be Harvard's "worst nightmare," Terrell promised, "We're going to bankrupt these universities. We're going to take away every single federal dollar .... If these universities do not play ball, lawyer up, because the federal government is coming after you." The DOJ initially investigated claims that "antisemitism" was rampant on over 60 college campuses. Columbia became the first institution to receive grant cancelations of over $400 million before subsequently capitulating to administration demands in return for funds.

Although Harvard did agree to government demands to provide international student disciplinary records, staff employment files, rename DEI offices, and defund affinity-group graduation celebrations, the university was the first major institution to *reject* the DOE's and DOJ's more stringent requirements to revise curricula, restrict free speech, dismantle all diversity efforts, and allow government supervision over admissions, employment, and other administrative practices. Trump threatened to cut off over $8 billion in federal grants, but Harvard's president stood firm, rejecting demands and stating: "No government – regardless of which party is in power – should dictate what private universities can teach, whom they can admit and hire, and which areas of study and inquiry they can pursue." Eventually, Harvard sued the government to restore funding and autonomy. Judge Allison Burrough recently ruled in Harvard's favor, writing that Trump's cuts and threats,

> *violate the law and infringe on Harvard's First Amendment rights .... A review of the administrative record makes it*

> *difficult to conclude anything other than defendants used antisemitism as a smokescreen for a targeted, ideologically-motivated assault on this country's premier universities.*

Twenty-Four other institutions, including Yale, Penn, Princeton, MIT, Stanford, and Johns Hopkins all filed *amici curiae* briefs in support of Harvard's lawsuit. The number of colleges and universities rejecting the DOE's recent Compact letter and rebuffing attempts at increased curricular restrictions from right-wing ideological think tanks continues to increase. As of November, 2025, only two institutions have signed on to the Compact – The New College of Florida and Valley Forge Military College in Pennsylvania. While most institutions await the outcomes of numerous lawsuits, more and more colleges and universities are taking Trump to court over DOE and DOJ threats of lost federal funding. On November 14, 2025, a federal court in the Northern District of California issued a *preliminary injunction* against Trump's campaign to coerce the University of California into ideological conformity – a move the court recognized as a grave threat to academic freedom and free speech.

In September, the State of New York sued the DOE over cuts to their federal grants, and that suit has been remanded to the District Court. Washington State won a preliminary injunction against the Department of Health and Human Services' efforts to dismantle the Head Start Program. A coalition of over two dozen states led by California sued the DOE over the freezing of almost $7 billion in education funding for K–12 schools and adult education, and received a temporary stay against threatened cuts. And 21 states plus the District of Columbia have sued the DOE overruled changes to student loan forgiveness, which would punish those who work for organizations that support "illegal immigration, child trafficking, pervasive damage to public property and disruption of the public order."

Meanwhile, professional organizations of faculty and teachers continue to challenge Trump in the courts. American Educational Research Association, The Council for Opportunity in Education, and many other education-based groups have staved off budget cuts – at least temporarily – and argued the illegality of DOE demands around DEI, imposed gender policies, and other infringements on academic freedom and free speech. Most notably, as mentioned before, was the AAUP's successful suit against the DOE and the DCL's threatened cuts – a case that was conjoined with Harvard's suit. But the AAUP has significant legal resources and continues to file suits in conjunction with multiple professional organizations, labor unions, and university administrations. The AAUP maintains a complete list of education-related lawsuits at https://www.aaup.org/about/programs/legal-program/aaup-litigation.

All told, the courts remain a powerful place for resistance to the encroachment of US educational policy. Radical right-wing efforts to fuel the fascist attacks on public schools and higher education persist, but academics, administrators, professional and non-profit organizations, unions, and students are ramping up the fight. In March 2025, students and faculty at UC Berkeley rallied to protest Trump threats, and in April, thousands of students at dozens of campuses around the country held rallies in hopes of emboldening their administrations to reject capitulation agreements and follow Harvard's lead. Professional organizations such as the Coalition for Action in Higher Education – which includes groups such as Higher Education Labor United and the American Federation of Teachers, the American Association of University Professors, myriad teachers' unions, and graduate student unions have helped organize these demonstrations and coordinate significant activity. In Colorado, faculty have urged administrators to form a statewide Compact to defend against Trump administrative threats, and in California, UC system faculty, staff, and students have demonstrated to embolden their administrations to avoid the massive settlement agreement mentioned above.

Most of these organizations continue to participate in the organizing and coordinating of major, national efforts such as the No Kings rallies in June and October of 2025. And in the greatest effort at coalition building toward mass mobilization and resistance, many academic labor unions, student organizations, and faculty and staff professional groups have formed Students Rise Up (SRU). Member groups include the AAUP, the Campus Climate Network, College Democrats of America, Florida Youth Action Fund, Frontlines for Freedom, Higher Education Labor United, Ohio Student Association, and the Sunrise Movement. Supporters include students, faculty and community organizations including: Dissenters, Feminist Generation, Gen-Z for Change, Generation Vote (GenVote), March For Our Lives, Oil & Gas Action Network, Socialist Alternative, Jewish Voice for Peace, Together Across America, Voters of Tomorrow, Blue Future, Get Free, NOW Young Feminists, and the New Hampshire Youth Movement.

On November 7th, SRU coordinated demonstrations on over 100 campuses around the United States involving tens of thousands of students, faculty, and other supporters. SRU has articulated three major areas of concern that include: Affordability (free public universities and affordable housing at and around campuses); Security (job security for workers; safety at school no matter our gender or immigration status or skin color); and Freedom (freedom to speak out and engage in protest without surveillance and militarized police; freedom to teach truthfully; and the freedom for workers to organize and form unions). SRU is now organizing students and campuses toward a mass student strike on May 1st, 2026, to correspond with the May Day Strong coalition's efforts to mobilize a workers' general strike on that day as well. Increasing numbers of people all across the United States are hitting the streets to protest against specific policies regarding education, Immigration and Customs Enforcement (ICE) and immigration, health care, as well as just general dissent over Trump's authoritarian rule. While we may look to courts and the campuses for resistance, mobilized masses of people will not only be the best defense against fascism, but also the site where visions of real democracy and freedom will arise.

NOTES

1. Nixon, R. (1971). Tricky Dicky: Nixon recordings confirm popular view. *The Guardian*.

2. Santorum, R. (2012). *Santorum: Colleges have become "indoctrination centers"*.

3. Trump, D. (2015). *Trump overwhelmingly leads rivals in support from less educated Americans*. PBS News.

4. Vance, J. D. (2021). *Trump taps J.D. Vance, sharp critic of higher ed, for VP.*

5. Warikoo, N. (2025). The demise of affirmative action in college admissions. *Annual Review of Sociology, 51*, 463–483; Forde-Mazrui, K. (2004). Taking conservatives seriously: A moral justification for affirmative action and reparations. *California Law Review*, 92, 683.

6. Supreme Court of the United States. (2023). *Students for Fair Admissions, Inc.* v. *President and Fellows of Harvard College*, No. 20-1199, Slip Opinion. https://www.law.cornell.edu/supct/pdf/20-1199.pdf.

7. Bonilla-Silva, E. (2022). Color-blind racism in pandemic times. *Sociology of Race and Ethnicity*, *8*(3), 343–354; Ortiz, S. M. (2021). Racists without racism? From colourblind to entitlement racism online. *Ethnic and Racial Studies*, *44*(14), 2637–2657.

8. Coates, R. (2011). *Covert racism*. Brill Publishers; Mueller, J. C. (2020). Racial ideology or racial ignorance? An alternative theory of racial cognition. *Sociological Theory*, *38*(2), 142–169; Diamond, J. B. (2024). Defending the color line: White supremacy and the legacy of Brown. *Educational Researcher*, *53*(3), 135–145; Brown, M. K., Carnoy, M., Currie, E., Duster, T., Oppenheimer, D. B., Shultz, M. M., & Wellman, D. (2023). *Whitewashing race: The myth of a color-blind society*. University of California Press; Burke, M. (2018). *Colorblind racism*. John Wiley & Sons.

9. Carter, J. S., & Lippard, C. D. (2020). Affirmative action and higher education. In *The death of affirmative action?* (pp. 19–40). Bristol University Press; Rubio, P. F. (2009). *A history of affirmative action, 1619–2000*. University Press of Mississippi.

10. Garcia, C., & Duran, A. (2023, May 17). *Attacks on 'segregated' graduation ceremonies overlook the history of racism on campus.* The Conversation. Attacks on 'segregated' graduation ceremonies overlook the history of racism on campus. https://theconversation.com/attacks-on-segregated-graduation-ceremonies-overlook-the-history-of-racism-on-campus-204991. Salai, S. (2024, April 17). Colleges double down on 'segregated' graduations amid DEI backlash. *The Washington Times*. https://www.washingtontimes.com/news/2024/apr/17/colleges-double-down-on-segregated-graduations-ami/. Klawans, J. (2025, May 30). Colleges are canceling affinity graduations amid DEI attacks but

students are pressing on. *The Week*. https://theweek.com/education/colleges-canceling-affinity-graduations-dei-attacks.

11. Baltodano, M. (2023). Neoliberalism and the demise of public education: The corporatization of schools of education. In B. M. A. Jones & S. J. Ball (Eds.), *Neoliberalism and education* (pp. 78–98). Routledge; Dolgon, C. (2017). *Kill it to save it: An autopsy of capitalism's triumph over democracy*. Policy Press.

12. Stanley, J. (2024). *Erasing history: How fascists rewrite the past to control the future*. One Signal Publishers; Praeger, S. (2025, September 18). *Trump Ed Dept. partners with Right-groups to spread white-washed civics lessons in 'schools across the nation*. Common Dreams; Solomon, P., & Fritz, M. (2025, July 1). *A look at what's behind the efforts to reshape how American history is taught*. PBS News Hour. A look at what's behind the efforts to reshape how American history is taught | PBS News. https://www.pbs.org/newshour/show/a-look-at-whats-behind-the-efforts-to-reshape-how-american-history-is-taught. Palmer, K. (2025, September 19). *ED wants to grants to advance 'patriotic education.'* Inside Higher Education. https://www.insidehighered.com/news/government/politics-elections/2025/09/19/ed-wants-grants-advance-patriotic-education. Groetzinger, K., Ho, L., & Coutant, L. (2025, October 1). *Erasing history, silencing science*. National Parks Conservation Association. Erasing History, Silencing Science · National Parks Conservation Association. https://www.npca.org/articles/10871-erasing-history-silencing-science. Schiff, L. (2025). Resisting censorship and defending the integrity of federally supported information. *DttP: Documents to the People*, *53*(2), 8.

13. Hofstadter, R. (1966). *Anti-intellectualism in American life*. Vintage.

14. Durkheim, E. (1956). *Education and sociology*. Simon and Schuster; Lagemann, E. C. (1997). Contested terrain: A history of education research in the United States, 1890–1990. *Educational Researcher*, *26*(9), 5–17, Harding, S., & Kershner, S. (2022). Contested terrain. In K. J. Saltman & N. Nguyen (Eds.), *Handbook of critical approaches to politics and policy of education*. Routledge.

15. Bowles, S., & Gintis, H. (1976). *Schooling in capitalist America* (Vol. 57). Basic Books.

16. Katz, M. B. (2001). *The irony of early school reform: Educational innovation in mid-nineteenth century Massachusetts*. Teachers College Press.

17. Rice, J. M. (1912). *Scientific management in education*. Hinds, Noble and Eldredge.

18. Lynd, R. S., & Lynd, H. M. (1929). *Middletown*. Harcourt, Brace Company.

19. Adams, D. W. (1995). Education for extinction. *Lawrence: University Press of* Kansas, 23, 164.

20. Sanchez, G., & Sanchez, G. J. (1984). *"Go after the women": Americanization and the Mexican immigrant woman, 1915–1929* (No. 6). Stanford Center for Chicano Research, Stanford University.

21. Pai, Y., & Adler, S. A. (1997). *Cultural foundations of education*. Merrill.

22. Daniels, R. (2002). "Coming to America." *A history of immigration and ethnicity in American life* (2nd ed.). HarperCollins Publishers.

23. Sorber, N. M. (2018). *Land-grant colleges and popular revolt: The origins of the Morrill Act and the reform of higher education*. Cornell University Press; Merry, M. S. (2009). Patriotism, history and the legitimate aims of American education. *Educational Philosophy and Theory*, *41*(4), 378–398.

24. Stanley, M. (2003). College education and the midcentury GI Bills. *The Quarterly Journal of Economics*, *118*(2), 671–708; Dolgon, C. (1998). Rising from the ashes: the Michigan Memorial Phoenix Project and the corporatization of university-based scientific research. *Educational Studies*, *24*(1), 5–31.

25. Kerr, C. (1964). The frantic race to remain contemporary. *Daedalus*, 93(4), 1051–1070.

26. Larson, M. S. (2017). The rise of professionalism: A sociological analysis. In S. Aronowitz & M. Roberts (Eds.), *Class: The anthology* (pp. 263–286). Wiley; Hanlon, G. (1998). Professionalism as enterprise: service class politics and the redefinition of professionalism. *Sociology*, 32(1), 43–63; Saks, M. (2012). Defining a profession: The role of knowledge and expertise. *Professions and Professionalism*, 2(1), 1–10.

27. Platt, A. M. (1997). End game: The rise and fall of affirmative action in higher education. *Social Justice*, *24*(2), 103–118; Fischer, M. J., & Massey, D. S. (2007). The effects of affirmative action in higher education. *Social Science Research*, *36*(2), 531–549.

28. Sprague, J. (2016). *Feminist methodologies for critical researchers: Bridging differences*. Bloomsbury Publishing PLC; Harding, S. (2015). Objectivity for sciences from below. In F. Padovani, A. Richardson, & J. Y. Tsou (Eds.), *Objectivity in science: New perspectives from science and technology studies* (pp. 35–55). Springer International Publishing; Bernal, D. D. (2002). Critical race theory, Latino critical theory, and critical raced-gendered epistemologies: Recognizing students of color as holders and creators of knowledge. *Qualitative Inquiry*, *8*(1), 105–126.

29. Dolgon, C. (2017). *Kill it to save it: An autopsy of capitalism's triumph over democracy*. Policy Press; Giroux, H. A. (2014). Austerity and the poison of neoliberal miseducation. *Symplokē*, *22*(1–2), 9–21; Ross, A. (2013). Mortgaging the future: Student debt in the age of austerity. In *New Labor Forum*, *22*(1), 23–28.

30. Dei, G. (2016). Decolonizing the university: The challenges and possibilities of inclusive education. *Socialist Studies/Études Socialistes*, *11*(1), 23–23.

31. Sweet, S. F. (2023). Leading transformational change in diversity, equity, and inclusion in higher education. In G. Jean-Marie & H. Tran (Eds.), *Leadership in turbulent times* (pp. 13–35). Emerald Publishing Limited.

32. Goldberg, D. T. (2023). *The war on critical race theory: Or, the remaking of racism*. John Wiley & Sons; Bennett, E. (2024). Carrying the CRT legacy in perilous times: Research and practice in the social sciences under Florida's Stop WOKE Act. *Annals of Social Studies Education Research for Teachers*, *6*(1), 5–14.

33. Cerebino, F. (2023). *DeSantis filters Black history to ease White student shame in Florida*.

34. Justice, T. (2025). *Moms for Liberty's "Toxic" Tiffany Justice is out at Heritage*.

35. Schoorman, D., & Gatens, R. (2025). Understanding Florida's HB7: A policy of intimidation by confusion. *Educational Policy*, *39*(2), 464–493.

36. Russell-Brown, K. (2023). "The Stop WOKE Act": HB 7, race, and Florida's 21st century anti-literacy campaign. *NYU Review of Law & Social Change*, *47*, 338.

37. Carroll, T. (2025). "It feels like white supremacy losing control": Gleaning local perspectives on "anti-woke" legislation." *Journal of Race, Ethnicity, and Politics*, *10*(2), 603–631.

38. Harper, S. (2025). Leveraging research and demanding proof in response to legislative attacks on DEI in U.S. Higher Education. *AERA Open*, *11*. https://doi.org/10.1177/23328584251355514 (Original work published 2025).

39. Dolgon, C. (2017). *Kill it to save it: An autopsy of capitalism's triumph over democracy*. Policy Press; Nagin, E. (2022, June 29). *How the American Legislative Exchange Council turns disinformation into law*. The Equation: Union of Concerned Scientists; Youseff, O. (2023, June 7). *Moms for Liberty among conservative groups named 'extremist' by civil rights watchdog*. National Public Radio; Gay and Lesbian Alliance Against Discrimination. (2023, December 5). Moms for liberty uses false and inflammatory language to vilify LGBTQ people. GLAAD.

40. Williams, P. (2023, October 31). The Right-wing mothers fueling the school-board wars. *The New York*.

41. Gorski, P. S., & Perry, S. L. (2022). *The flag and the cross: White Christian nationalism and the threat to American democracy*. Oxford University Press; Hedges, C. (2006). *American fascists: The Christian right and the war on America*. The Free Press; Diamond, S. (1995). *Roads to Dominion: Right-wing movements and political power in the United States*. The Guilford Press.

42. O'Matz, M., & Richards, J. S. (2025, October 8). *These activists want to dismantle public schools. Now they run the Education Department*. Pro Publica.

43. O'Matz, M., & Richards, J. S. (2025, October 8). *These activists want to dismantle public schools. Now they run the Education Department*. Pro Publica; Bensinger, K. (2024, October 24). The group at the center of Trump's planning for a second term is one you haven't heard of. *New York Times*.

44. Giroux, H. A. (2022). Resisting fascism and winning the education wars: How we can meet the challenge. *A Development Education Review*, *35*, 111–126; Burke, K. J., Juzwik, M., & Prins, E. (2023). White Christian nationalism: What is it, and why does it matter for educational research? *Educational Researcher*, *52*(5), 286–295.

45. Office of the Attorney General. (2025, July 29). *Memo for all federal agencies: Guidance for recipients of federal funding regarding unlawful discrimination.*

46. Giroux, H. (2025). *Critical pedagogy in dark times.*

7

DESPOTISM UNLEASHED: THE TRUMP ADMINISTRATION'S ASSAULT ON WORKERS' RIGHTS AND WHY IT MATTERS

Chris Rhomberg

Fordham University, USA

Imagine you are a citizen of the United States and you move from one state to another. In your former home, you took for granted your democratic rights of freedom of speech and association, the right to vote in state elections, and the right to criticize the state government. In your new home, however, a single party controls all levels of state government, and you can be deported if you openly criticize those in power or associate with people who do. Elections rarely occur because the incumbent party can legally, vigorously, and often successfully prevent any vote from happening. If an election is held, the incumbents can compel you to attend meetings where they campaign forcefully for their right to retain unilateral power. No opposing parties or views are allowed, and if you refuse to attend, you can be disciplined or deported. Even under those rules, the incumbents routinely violate your rights, but the penalties are weak and often come too late to matter.

This metaphorical scenario may sound shockingly authoritarian, but it is not unlike what many Americans experience every day at work. In the contemporary United States, employers routinely exercise effectively despotic rule, with almost absolute control over the organization of the labor process and the rules governing relations on the job, even in so-called "flexible" or gig work.[1,2] This chapter begins by reviewing why the workplace and workers' rights matter for our society and democracy. I then briefly discuss trends in US labor law and policy to highlight the meaning of events in the first year of President Donald Trump's second term. The administration has dramatically escalated a longstanding assault on workers' rights and collective organization that, in many ways, has contributed to our current crisis.[3]

WHY LABOR MATTERS

Most working Americans in the private sector are employed "at-will" in non-union jobs where they experience what philosopher Elizabeth Anderson[4] (p. 55) calls "private government." As Anderson writes, workers on the job "in effect, cede *all* of their rights to their employers, except those specifically guaranteed to them by law, for the duration of the employment relationship." Employers typically wield disproportionate power in the labor market and hierarchical authority in the workplace, affecting wages, working conditions, access to health insurance and pension benefits, and freedoms of speech, association, political preference, and even personal appearance.[5] When workers try to exercise their rights to collective action, American law allows employers to use a wide range of resources to prevent them from voting for unions, including legal tactics like procedural delays and "captive-audience" meetings, and all too often, illegal "unfair labor practices" that can include simply firing union activists, the equivalent of deportation from the workplace.

The impact spreads beyond the workplace into politics and society. Around the world, the extent and forms of unionization are strongly associated with the growth and retrenchment of democracy.[6] Rising concentrations of elite wealth threaten democratic institutions, while unions reduce wage inequality and reinforce a "moral economy" of standards in the labor market.[7,8] American unions are essential for representing the interests of non-elites and fostering popular civic and political skills and participation, particularly for minority, lower income and less educated groups.[9,10] In the workplace, regular face-to-face communication and often a greater diversity of co-workers than in neighborhoods or faith communities can make unions a critical network and vehicle to promote solidarity and cooperation across groups and counter the appeals of right-wing, ethnonationalist ideologies.[11]

Under neoliberalism, unions have faced growing pressure from employers throughout the industrialized world, yet the United States stands out both for the severity of the assault and its repressive legal turn. For decades, an increasingly conservative US Supreme Court has aggressively reinterpreted the law to favor employers. The process reached a landmark in 2018 when the Court reversed more than 40 years of precedent and mandated "right-to-work" in public sector jobs nationally, allowing employees to "free ride" on collective bargaining contracts and undermining union resources.[12] At the same time, conservatives in Congress have repeatedly stymied attempts at modernizing the 1935 National Labor Relations Act (NLRA) to better protect workers.[13] Even when Democrats held Congressional majorities under Presidents Carter, Clinton, Obama, and Biden, they failed to pass even modest pro-union labor law reform.

These trends have contributed to rising inequality, stagnant wages, and precarious employment conditions, particularly for younger Americans. Recent years have seen an upsurge of labor militancy, including strikes of workers in public schools, health care, and manufacturing, as well as high-profile union organizing campaigns of workers at Starbucks and Amazon, among others. Yet workers who try to unionize continue to face steep institutional barriers and intense hostility from employers.[14] Although public opinion polls have shown some of the highest approval ratings for unions since the 1960s, the proportion of private sector workers belonging to unions ("union density") has been driven down to less than 6%, lower than before the NLRA was passed.[15,16]

THE CURRENT JUNCTURE

Without achieving more pro-union legislation in Congress, the Biden administration nonetheless took a number of actions to counter the neoliberal drift of federal labor policy. Biden's appointees to the National Labor Relations Board (NLRB), and NLRB General Counsel Jennifer Abruzzo, broadened and strengthened enforcement of protections for workers and stiffened penalties for employers' unfair labor practices. They also streamlined procedures allowing workers to choose unions, restricted captive audience meetings, and stepped up efforts to reinstate workers fired for union activity at Starbucks and elsewhere.[17] Biden issued executive orders (EOs) to protect labor rights and raise wages for employees of federal contractors, and began implementation of strategic plans to increase diversity, equity, inclusion, and accessibility (DEIA) in hiring and other practices for the federal civilian workforce.[18]

Such actions were incremental but took important steps toward reasserting the normative role of government in regulating employment, maintaining minimum standards for workers, protecting their rights on the job, and, in the words of the NLRA, affirming their "full freedom of association, self-organization, and designation of representatives of their own choosing" to negotiate "the terms and conditions of their employment or other mutual aid or protection."[19] Regardless of their implementation, those norms highlight the choices at stake in the current juncture and the possibility of alternative visions. As executive actions, however, the Biden administration's reforms remained vulnerable to reversal by a change in government. Trump's second administration has accelerated efforts to impose a sharply opposing and challenging path for labor and the nation.

MEET THE NEW BOSS: TRUMP 2.0'S FIRST HUNDRED DAYS

Upon his inauguration in January 2025, Trump immediately began rescinding Biden's EOs, eliminating wage increases along with job quality and equal opportunity standards for federal contractors and on federally funded major projects. He also terminated what he described as "all DEI, DEIA, and 'environmental justice' offices and positions" as well as all "'equity-related' grants or contracts; and all DEI or DEIA performance requirements for employees, contractors, or grantees." His appointees even reversed policy decisions at the Department of Labor and the NLRB.[20,21] Perhaps the broadest initial labor action by the second Trump administration, however, was the overwhelming push to fire government employees and reduce the federal workforce.

On his first day in office, Trump moved to strip civil service protections from an estimated 50,000 career federal workers and make them "at-will" employees easier to fire.[22] In late January, the federal Office of Personnel Management (OPM) emailed more than 2 million federal employees offering a "deferred resignation" plan with salary paid through the end of September, while reserving the option to eliminate the jobs of workers who stayed on. By the end of May, an estimated 75,000 federal employees had taken the offer.[23,24]

Trump also created an informal body called the Department of Government Efficiency (DOGE), led by billionaire government contractor and Trump campaign donor Elon Musk. Despite its name, DOGE was not an official government department (which only Congress can create), and Musk never faced Senate confirmation, yet both assumed extraordinary powers. In early February, DOGE furloughed nearly all of the 10,000 employees at the US Agency for International Development (USAID) and around 85% of the 1,700 employees of the Consumer Financial Protection Bureau – effectively shutting down both agencies. Working with OPM, DOGE also tried to indiscriminately fire nearly 25,000 recently hired or promoted "probationary" federal employees, who have fewer civil service protections, though often years of experience in their field.[25]

On February 11, Trump ordered departments across the executive branch to initiate large-scale "reductions in force" (RIF), not including public safety, immigration control, or law enforcement.[26] The Department of Veterans Affairs set an initial goal to cut more than 80,000 employees, or 15% of its workforce. The Department of Health and Human Services announced cuts of 20,000 jobs, including 3,500 employees from the Food and Drug Administration, 2,400 from the Centers for Disease Control, and 1,200 from the National Institutes of Health.[27] The Department of Education (DOE) cut nearly half of its staff, including hundreds of workers at its Civil Rights and Federal Student Aid offices.[28] By April, according to an independent professional estimate, 27 agencies had laid off or planned to lay off as many as 280,000 federal workers, not including probationary employees.[29]

This was not the traditional partisan unraveling of a Democratic predecessor's policies by an incoming Republican administration. Trump's elimination of federal workers embodied the unilateral authoritarianism of a despotic boss, deploying a fundamental power of employers over at-will employees – *you're fired*. Not unlike President Ronald Reagan's 1981 firing of striking air traffic controllers, but on a vastly larger scale, Trump's actions signaled to all employers that the government now promoted (and would support) the most aggressive attitude toward workers' rights and due process in decades. Many of the discharges openly violated the law or the Constitution or both, and were met with a flood of litigation, conflicting court rulings, and passive complicity from the Republican majority in Congress.

The job cuts also went beyond simply downsizing federal employment, and functioned to "so degrade agency capacities that they would effectively end congressionally mandated activities and violate statutory requirements" with which the administration disagreed.[30] In April, the OPM proposed new hiring rules for career positions, which would permit agencies to quickly remove such employees if they were deemed to engage in, among other things, "subversion of Presidential directives."[31] OPM guidelines issued in May called for most federal job applicants to answer essay questions on how they would help advance Trump's agenda, which of his policy priorities and orders they thought were most significant, and how they would help implement them. As critics noted, these and other actions aimed to make public servants into political vassals who owed their jobs and primary allegiance not to the Constitution or the rule of law, but to Trump.[32,33]

A MASSIVE WAVE OF FEDERAL UNION-BUSTING

The unions representing federal employees immediately rose to challenge the administration, organizing protests and filing lawsuits to block the dismantling of USAID, stop DOGE's access to sensitive data, and prevent the mass firings of probationary employees. Soon, they too found themselves under attack. On March 7, Homeland Security Department Secretary Kristi Noem announced the Transportation Security Administration would no longer honor the seven-year contract it had signed the previous May with the American Federation of Government Employees (AFGE), representing some 45,000 airport security screeners.[34]

Less than three weeks later, citing a national security exemption under the 1978 Civil Service Reform Act (CSRA), Trump issued an EO revoking collective bargaining rights for more than a million federal employees at some 20 agencies, including the departments of Agriculture, Veterans Affairs, Health and Human Services, State, Interior, Treasury, Defense, and others. For 47 years, the CSRA exemption had applied almost exclusively to intelligence agencies and select federal law enforcement; no president had ever ordered the exclusion of entire cabinet-level departments. The same day, the OPM directed agencies to disregard union contract provisions governing RIF, grievance procedures, and deduction of union dues.[35]

The unions charged that Trump's action not only violated federal labor law but also retaliated against them for defending the rights of their members, in what the President of the American Federation of Labor-Congress of Industrial Organizations (AFL-CIO),[36] Liz Shuler, called "the single biggest act of union-busting in history." The White House Fact Sheet accompanying the order specifically targeted the "hostile Federal unions" that "have declared war on President Trump's agenda," citing the (legal) filing of grievances under their contracts, and warned that President Trump "will not tolerate mass obstruction" that opposed his unilateral authority.[37] The campaign of union-busting took its toll: the AFGE, the largest federal workers' union representing a total of some 800,000 employees, announced in April that it would lay off more than half its staff nationwide, after the cutoff of dues deduction weakened the organization's finances.[38]

Alongside the attack on federal workers' unions, the administration has sought to dismantle the government's capacity to protect workers' rights. On January 27, Trump fired Biden-appointee Gwynne Wilcox from her position as a member of the NLRB. The first Black woman to serve on the Board in its 90-year history, Wilcox's term was not due to expire until 2028. Under the statute, members can be fired only "for neglect of duty or malfeasance in office" and only after notice and a hearing.[39] Wilcox received no hearing, and the emailed letter to her made no allegations of misconduct. Rather, it cited ideological differences with Trump's agenda and faulted her for "unduly disfavoring the interests of employers."[40]

Similarly, on January 29, Trump fired two members of the Equal Employment Opportunity Commission (EEOC), Charlotte Burrows and Jocelyn Samuels, years before the end of their terms. Unprecedented in the EEOC's 60-year history, the move left the agency that enforces civil rights in the workplace without a quorum and unable to vote on rulemaking or issue new policies.[41] For federal workers, the Federal Labor Relations Authority (FLRA) adjudicates disputes between the government and its employee unions, while the Merit Systems Protection Board (MSPB) provides due process if workers are wrongly fired, demoted, or disciplined. On February 10, Trump illegally fired MSPB member Cathy Harris (whose term was not set to expire until 2028), and the next day, he fired FLRA Chair Susan Tsui Grundmann (whose term extended until July 2025). The discharges left both agencies effectively paralyzed in the midst of Trump's massive purge of the federal workforce.[42]

THE LOGIC OF AUTHORITARIANISM

Many observers saw the removals as a deliberate attempt to seize power over independent federal agencies – including the NLRB, the Federal Trade Commission, and the Federal Reserve Board – by overturning *Humphrey's Executor*, the 90-year old Supreme Court precedent protecting their autonomy. Not surprisingly, judges in both District and Appellate Courts enjoined Wilcox's removal, but the administration appealed to the Supreme Court's emergency (or "shadow") docket for immediate review without full briefing or oral argument, to stay the order while the litigation continued. The Court likewise used unsigned and unexplained opinions in the shadow docket to stay lower courts from restraining the administration's mass RIFs and its efforts to dismantle the DOE.[43]

On May 22, the Court's conservative majority stayed the order to reinstate Wilcox in a short, unsigned decision with scant justification, but hinting at their willingness to uphold Trump's power under the "unitary executive" theory promoted by the Federalist Society and the Heritage Foundation's Project 2025.[44,45] The Court's actions raised deep constitutional issues affecting the separation of powers and the checks and balances between branches of government. As Justice Sonia Sotomayor wrote in her dissent (joined by Justices Ketanji Brown Jackson and Elena Kagan) in the DOE case, "When the Executive publicly announces its intent to break the law, and then executes on that promise, it is the Judiciary's duty to check that lawlessness, not expedite it."[46]

In addition to the Wilcox case, the NLRB faces other legal threats. In 2024, corporations owned by two of the richest men in the world, Elon Musk's SpaceX and Jeff Bezos' Amazon, sued the NLRB after it issued complaints that the companies had violated their employees' rights. Disregarding the facts of the complaints, SpaceX and Amazon challenged the Board's constitutionality, originally upheld by the Supreme Court in 1937, on grounds similar to the unitary executive doctrine. Federal courts across the country had refused to rule against the NLRB on those grounds, but SpaceX and Amazon maneuvered the case into the more conservative Fifth Circuit covering Louisiana, Mississippi, and Texas. In August 2025, citing the Supreme Court's emergency stay in the Wilcox case, the Fifth Circuit Court of Appeals became the first federal appeals court to rule the NLRA unconstitutional.[47,48]

CONCLUSION: WHICH WAY OUT?

The Trump administration's attacks on workers and labor rights are inseparable from its broad right-wing offensive against civil rights and immigrants and other vulnerable groups. The movement of resistance likewise crosses over with the struggles described in the other chapters of this book. In June 2025, the Service Employees International Union (SEIU) California President David Huerta was arrested by federal agents at a protest against Immigration and Customs Enforcement (ICE) raids in Los Angeles and held for three days, prompting demonstrations for his release led by SEIU in cities nationwide.[49] The SEIU later conducted a cross-country "Justice Journeys" bus tour to educate members on the anti-immigrant raids and civil rights movement history that ended with a protest at a detention center in Louisiana.[50] As the ICE raids escalated and Trump ordered military troops into cities like Washington, D.C., Los Angeles, and Chicago, local teachers' unions led "know your rights" trainings and distributed leaflets to students. In New York City, several of the largest unions and civic organizations formed a "Hands Off NYC" coalition to defend against an anticipated federal intervention.[51,52]

For the federal workers, their unions' tenacious litigation has mainly succeeded in the lower courts but faces seemingly inevitable reversal by the conservative majority on the Supreme Court. After nine months, though, federal workers themselves may be increasingly willing to speak out. Jenna Norton was furloughed from her job as a program director at the National Institutes of Health, yet she joined a press conference outside the US Capitol before the government shutdown that began on October 1. "As a federal worker," she said, "I am here to tell you that every awful thing that would happen in a shutdown – shuttering programs that Americans rely on, damaging our economy, firing federal workers – all of this is already happening."[53] Monica Gorman, a data scientist at National Aeronautics and Space Administration and a member of the International Federation of Professional and Technical Engineers, said, "I'm done being afraid of [the Trump administration.]" Gorman and other federal workers expressed a readiness to mobilize and bring public attention to the loss of institutional knowledge, funding for vital services and research, and means for holding power holders accountable. "They say the best organizer is a bad boss," she said, "and we all have the same bad boss."[54]

Trump's agenda at the start of his second term has been to bring the authoritarianism of the non-union workplace into the world of politics and government. Whether or not the Supreme Court overturns the constitutionality of the NLRB or affirms Trump's decimation of federal workers' rights, it is likely their decisions will dramatically alter how the federal government regulates labor relations in both the private and public sectors.[55] The institutions of law and the state do not create labor solidarity or militancy, but they can impose greater or lesser levels of repression, or allow private employers the unrestrained power to do so. The next few years may witness levels of such repression we have not seen in nearly a century, making it harder for workers to form unions and exercise their rights to act collectively.

A broad, united, and active coalition will be needed to turn back the depth and scale of this authoritarian challenge. Overcoming the threat calls for *not* a retreat from the federal government but a renewed vision of national labor institutions for the 21st century. The great reforms of the New Deal drew from Progressive Era innovations in government and the established and emergent forms of union organization and industrial regulation in the labor movement. We are far from a resolution of the current juncture, and, in many ways, the struggle for a new labor order is a struggle for American democracy.

NOTES

1. Burawoy, M. (1983). Between the labor process and the state: The changing face of factory regimes under advanced capitalism. *American Sociological Review*, *48*(5), 587–605.

2. Wood, A. J. (2020). *Despotism on demand: How power operates in the flexible workplace*. Cornell University Press.

3. Rhomberg, C. (2023). Authoritarian innovation in the United States: The role of dual subnational systems of labour governance. *Journal of Industrial Relations*, 66(4), 519–537. https://doi.org/10.1177/00221856241260770.

4. Anderson, E. (2017). *Private government: How employers rule our lives (and why we don't talk about it)*. Princeton University Press.

5. Cornell, A. (2022). Labor's obstacles and democracy's demise. In A. Cornell & M. Barenberg (Eds.), *The Cambridge handbook of labor and democracy* (pp. 46–65). Cambridge University Press.

6. Rueschemeyer, D., Stephens, E. H., & Stephens, J. (1992). *Capitalist development and democracy*. University of Chicago Press.

7. Page, B., & Gilens, M. (2017). *Democracy in America? What has gone wrong and what we can do about it*. University of Chicago Press.

8. Western, B., & Rosenfeld, J. (2011). Unions, norms, and the rise of U.S. wage inequality. *American Sociological Review*, *76*(4), 513–537.

9. Kerrissey, J., & Schofer, E. (2013). Union membership and political participation in the United States. *Social Forces*, *91*(3), 895–928.

10. Wilkerson, T. (2022). 'A question of freedom': Black workers, union membership, and political participation. *Labor Studies Journal*, *47*(4), 408–432.

11. Newman, L., & Skocpol, T. (2023). *Rust belt union blues: Why working-class voters are turning away from the Democratic Party*. Columbia University Press.

12. Cornell, A. (2022). Labor's obstacles and democracy's demise. In A. Cornell & M. Barenberg (Eds.), *The Cambridge handbook of labor and democracy* (pp. 46–65). Cambridge University Press.

13. Roof, T. (2011). *American Labor, Congress, and the welfare state, 1935–2010*. The Johns Hopkins University Press.

14. Logan, J. (2023, January 28). *Corporate union busting in plain sight: How Amazon, Starbucks, and Trader Joe's crushed dynamic grassroots worker organizing campaigns*. Economic Policy Institute. https://www.epi.org/publication/corporate-union-busting/.

15. Saad, L. (2023, August 30). *More in U.S. see unions strengthening and want it that way*. Gallup. https://news.gallup.com/poll/510281/unions-strengthening.aspx.

16. Romero, P., & Whittaker, J. (2023, June 16). *A brief examination of union membership data*. Congressional Research Service. file:///C:/Users/cdrho/Downloads/R47596.4.pdf.

17. Rhinehart, L., McNicholas, C., & Poydock, M. (2024, May 1). *The Biden Board: How President Biden's NLRB appointees are restoring and supporting workers' rights*. Economic Policy Institute. https://www.epi.org/publication/bidens-nlrb-restoring-rights/.

18. McNicholas, C., Sanders, S., Bivens, J., Poydock, M., & Costa, D. (2025, April 25). *100 ways Trump has hurt workers in his first 100 days*. Economic Policy Institute. https://www.epi.org/publication/100-days-100-ways-trump-hurt-workers/.

19. National Labor Relations Board. (2025). *National Labor Relations Act*. https://www.nlrb.gov/guidance/key-reference-materials/national-labor-relations-act.

20. McNicholas, C., Sanders, S., Bivens, J., Poydock, M., & Costa, D. (2025, April 25). *100 ways Trump has hurt workers in his first 100 days*. Economic Policy Institute. https://www.epi.org/publication/100-days-100-ways-trump-hurt-workers/.

21. The White House. (2025a, January 20). *Ending radical and wasteful government DEI programs and preferencing*. https://www.whitehouse.gov/presidential-actions/2025/01/ending-radical-and-wasteful-government-dei-programs-and-preferencing/.

22. Kern, R. (2025, April 9). Project 2025 wanted to hobble the federal workforce. DOGE has hastily done that, and more. *Government Executive*. https://www.govexec.com/transition/2025/04/project-2025-wanted-hobble-federal-workforce-doge-has-hastily-done-and-more/404390/.

23. Wagner, E. (2025a, January 28). Trump reportedly will offer 'buyouts' to all 2 million federal workers. *Government Executive*. https://www.govexec.com/workforce/2025/01/trump-reportedly-will-offer-buyouts-all-2-million-federal-workers/402571/.

24. Hsu, A. (2025b, June 6). *Officially, 59,000 federal jobs are gone under Trump. There's more to the picture*. All Things Considered, NPR. https://www.npr.org/2025/06/04/nx-s1-5421277/trump-federal-workers-layoffs-doge.

25. Kern, R. (2025, April 9). Project 2025 wanted to hobble the federal workforce. DOGE has hastily done that, and more. *Government Executive*. https://www.govexec.com/transition/2025/04/project-2025-wanted-hobble-federal-workforce-doge-has-hastily-done-and-more/404390/.

26. The White House. (2025b, February 11). *Implementing the President's "Department of Government Efficiency" workforce optimization initiative*. https://www.whitehouse.gov/presidential-actions/2025/02/implementing-the-presidents-department-of-government-efficiency-workforce-optimization-initiative/.

27. *Government Executive*. (2025, February 27). *RIF watch: See which agencies are laying off federal workers*. Retrieved July 23 from https://www.govexec.com/workforce/2025/02/rif-watch-see-which-agencies-are-laying-federal-workers/403342/.

28. Turner, C., & Mehta, J. (2025, March 12). *U.S. Education Department says it is cutting nearly half of all staff*. Morning Edition, NPR. https://www.npr.org/2025/03/11/nx-s1-5324746/trump-education-department-layoffs-closure-reorganization.

29. Kern, R. (2025, April 9). Project 2025 wanted to hobble the federal workforce. DOGE has hastily done that, and more. *Government Executive*. https://www.govexec.com/transition/2025/04/project-2025-wanted-hobble-federal-workforce-doge-has-hastily-done-and-more/404390/.

30. Berger, S., & Leibenluft, J. (2025, May 2). *Trump administration's mass layoffs of federal workers are illegal*. Center on Budget and Policy Priorities. Retrieved June 24, 2025, from https://www.cbpp.org/research/federal-budget/trump-administrations-mass-layoffs-of-federal-workers-are-illegal.

31. The White House. (2025d). *Fact sheet: President Donald J. Trump creates new federal employee category to enhance accountability*. https://www.whitehouse.gov/fact-sheets/2025/04/fact-sheet-president-donald-j-trump-creates-new-federal-employee-category-to-enhance-accountability/.

32. Sullivan, E. (2025, June 10). In Trump's 'patriotic' hiring plan, experts see a politicized federal work force. *The New York Times*. https://www.nytimes.com/2025/06/10/us/politics/trumps-politicized-federal-work-force.html.

33. Hsu, A. (2025b, June 6). *Officially, 59,000 federal jobs are gone under Trump. There's more to the picture*. All Things Considered, NPR. https://www.npr.org/2025/06/04/nx-s1-5421277/trump-federal-workers-layoffs-doge.

34. Wagner, E. (2025b, March 14). Union sues DHS to protect TSA screeners'collective bargaining rights. *Government Executive*. https://www.govexec.com/workforce/2025/03/union-sues-dhs-protect-tsa-screeners-collectivebargaining-rights/403781/.

35. Hsu, A. (2025a, March 28). *Trump signs order ending union bargaining rights for wide swaths of federal employees*. Weekend Edition, NPR. https://www.npr.org/2025/03/28/nx-s1-5343474/trump-collective-bargaining-unions-federal-employees.

36. AFL-CIO. (2025, June 25). *AFL-CIO president applauds district court ruling to block Trump's union-busting of federal workers* [Press release]. AFL-CIO. https://aflcio.org/press/releases/afl-cio-president-applauds-district-court-ruling-block-trumps-union-busting-federal.

37. The White House. (2025c, March 27). *Fact sheet: President Donald J. Trump exempts agencies with national security missions from federal collective bargaining requirements*. https://www.whitehouse.gov/fact-sheets/2025/03/fact-sheet-president-donald-j-trump-exempts-agencies-with-national-security-missions-from-federal-collective-bargaining-requirements/.

38. Foley, R. (2025, April 24). *Largest federal employee union, a leading Trump opponent, to lay off more than half of staff*. Associated Press. https://apnews.com/article/afge-federal-union-trump-cuts-layoffs-downsizing-53c0a1491cc5af65278fbd16b8cfb 6b5.

39. Kunzelman, M. (2025, March 6). *Federal judge reinstates labor board member fired by President Donald Trump*. Associated Press. https://apnews.com/article/nlrb-member-gwynne-wilcox-trump-2029dbf4945ef4 9f8f2cf3d4733f966d.

40. Eidelson, J. (2025, January 31). *The email firing two NLRB leaders cites conflicts with Trump agenda*. Bloomberg News. https://www.bloomberg.com/news/newsletters/2025-01-31/trump-email-firing-nlrb-leaders-cites-views-similar-to-elon-musk-s-on-labor.

41. Maye, A., & Wilson, V. (2025, May 27). *Trump is making it easier for employers to discriminate*. Economic Policy Institute, Federal Policy Watch. https://www.epi.org/policywatch/targeting-elimination-of-federal-mediation-and-conciliation-service/.

42. Purifoy, P., & Rozen, C. (2025, February 14). *Trump to lay off federal workers after paralyzing labor panels*. Bloomberg Law Convergence. https://myconvergence.bna.com/ContentItem/ArticlePublic/263233364000000003/298944?itemGuid=b4f14fef-d221-4cbb-9c99-7b96a557a9d7.

43. Shapiro, C. (2025, July 30). *When the majority disagrees on the shadow docket*. SCOTUSblog. https://www.scotusblog.com/2025/07/when-the-majority-disagrees-on-the-shadow-docket/.

44. Kruzel, J. (2025, May 22). *US Supreme Court lets Trump keep labor board members sidelined for now*. Reuters. https://www.reuters.com/world/us/us-supreme-court-lets-trump-keep-labor-board-members-sidelined-now-2025-05-22/.

45. Clark, S. (2025, April 29). How Donald Trump's first 100 days went 'beyond' Project 2025. *Newsweek*. https://www.newsweek.com/donald-trump-first-100-days-beyond-project-2025-2064981.

46. *McMahon* v. *New York, et al.* 06 U.S. ____ (2025).

47. Iafolla, R. (2025, August 19). *SpaceX keeps labor board case frozen with Fifth Circuit win*. Bloomberg Law. https://news.bloomberglaw.com/daily-labor-report/spacex-keeps-labor-board-case-frozen-with-fifth-circuit-victory.

48. Katta, A. (2025, August 20). *Tracking attacks on the NLRB: Fifth Circuit finds NLRB removal protections unconstitutional*. OnLabor. https://onlabor.org/tracking-attacks-on-the-nlrb-fifth-circuit-finds-nlrb-removal-protections-unconstitutional/.

49. Mascarenhas, L. (2025, June 10). *Who is David Huerta, the California labor leader who was arrested in Los Angeles*. CNN. https://www.cnn.com/2025/06/10/us/david-huerta-seiu-union-leader.

50. *The Communicator*. (2025). *In their own words: Members share experiences on SEIU's Justice Journey* (Vol. 43, No. 6). New York State Public Employees Federation. https://communicator.pef.org/issue/volume-43-no-6/in-their-own-words-members-share-experiences-on-seius-justice-journey/.

51. Schlitz, H. (2025, October 10). *Chicago ICE raids, National Guard troops prompt new lesson plans: 'Know your rights.'* Reuters. https://www.reuters.com/legal/government/chicago-ice-raids-national-guard-troops-prompt-new-school-leaflets-know-your-2025-10-10/.

52. Daly, A. (2025, October 9). 'Hands Off NYC' coalition forms to resist potential Trump crackdown on city. *amNewYork*. https://www.amny.com/new-york/hands-off-nyc-coalition-forms-resist-trump-crackdown/.

53. Hsu, A. (2025c, October 7). *Why some federal workers aren't scared by the threat of shutdown layoffs*. National Public Radio. https://www.npr.org/2025/10/07/nx-s1-5563872/government-shutdown-federal-workers-layoffs-rifs.

54. Hsu, A. (2025d, October 10). *'I'm done being afraid': How the shutdown has led federal workers to speak out*. Morning Edition, NPR. https://www.npr.org/2025/10/10/nx-s1-5565228/government-shutdown-federal-employees-congress.

55. Estreicher, S., Roger King, G., & Sherwyn, D. (2025, June 25). *Dealing with the likely demise of Humphrey's executor*. OnLabor. https://onlabor.org/dealing-with-the-likely-demise-of-humphreys-executor/.

8

THE FAILED PRESIDENCY OF DONALD TRUMP: THE DEATH OF DEMOCRACY IN THREE ACTS

Douglas Kellner

University of California, Los Angeles (UCLA), USA

In 2024, Donald Trump's campaign claimed that he would rebuild the American economy, bring the Russia–Ukraine and Israel–Palestine wars to a halt, and "Make America Great Again." Instead, he and his co-campaigner, Elon Musk, initiated an assault on the US democracy, created a foreign policy and tariff wars that alienated the USA from its closest allies, and aligned his presidency with global dictators. The economy increasingly works only for the wealthy, major wars continue unabated (even those where ceasefires were agreed to), and America seems far from "Great." As 2025 came to an end, many agreed that Trump's second term represents a failed presidency, not only in its inability to address issues of unaffordable and inaccessible health care, skyrocketing housing and food costs, and unabated climate change – but also one that severely subverted the very root of the nation's democracy – the Rule of Law – leaving the US Constitution itself in crisis.

Meanwhile, the Epstein scandal has undermined Trump's presidency as victims of Epstein's sex trafficking – as well as media outlets, politicians, and citizens across the political spectrum – all demand to know Trump's knowledge of, and involvement in, Epstein's horrors. For months, House Speaker, Mike Johnson, did Trump's bidding by sending Congress home during a recent government shutdown to avoid discussing the bill that eventually forced the release of all investigative and court materials comprising the so-named "Epstein files." Once the legislature reopened in November 2025, persistent demands pressured them to vote on the bill. Support was so strong that, not only did the House pass it overwhelmingly, but the Senate did so by acclamation. Even Trump was compelled to sign it.[1]

Throughout Trump 2.0, the Epstein scandal, Trump's tariff wars, and the Musk/Trump assaults on democracy have further divided the country. But these dynamics also delegitimized Trump's presidency and weakened the US position in the world to a degree unprecedented in the last century. How did this all happen?

ACT 1: 100 DAYS OF TRUMP AND MUSK DISMANTLING DEMOCRACY

Initially, Elon Musk served as a kind of co-president with Trump, hovering about at official Cabinet meetings and appearing regularly in Oval Office interviews and photo-ops. Together, they pushed a corporate capitalist and the US imperialist agenda.[i] But their subsequent war on government institutions, laws, and personnel was unprecedented. Musk represents a high-tech, corporate oligarch elite. Trump, a failure in business and as 45th president, has always yearned to be in such elite company – paling around with the most powerful figures in the world – ever since he left Queens for Manhattan in the 1980s.[ii] With Musk's help, Trump sought to join – and

---

[i] For my trilogy on the Bush-Cheney Gang, see Kellner (2001,[2] 2003,[3] 2005[4]).

[ii] On Trump's history and background, see Blair (2000),[5] who documents Trump's early years in real estate with his father, Fred Trump, in Queens and Brooklyn, and Trump's desire to make it big in Manhattan. On Trump's triumphs and failures in Manhattan real estate, the collapse of his gambling casino failures in Atlantic City, and how Trump's businesses all went into bankruptcy, with his father Fred bailing him out

lead – a global oligarchy. He would finally receive the status and respect he thought he deserved.

The Musk–Trump "co-presidency" created a psychodrama in which they both engaged in vendettas *against* democracy. Musk, a child of South African apartheid, sought revenge for Afrikaners who lost white power and autocracy.[6] He also wanted to dismantle the US government agencies empowered to regulate (and sue) his companies and Big Tech in general.[iii] Trump, too, had personal vendettas fueled by grievances against the Department of Justice[7] (DOJ), other agencies, and individuals he perceived as "enemies" from his first term.

Through the Department of Government Efficiency (DOGE) and Trump's control over the DOJ, these autocrats found initial success – especially in their ability to skirt the Constitution and democratic principles to dismantle federal agencies, particularly the United States Agency for International Development (USAID). Yet their individual megalomania and contrasting personalities had many anticipating an eventual break-up. This separation occurred in late May as Musk left Washington after public disagreements with Trump. He didn't leave without a parting shot, though, tweeting that Trump's name would be found prominently in the Epstein files. He was right.[iv]

In the following section, I document the Trump/Musk autocracy, beginning with Trump's 90-plus-minute spectacle signing over 40 executive orders (EOs) on day one. I will also sketch how Musk rose to the co-presidency and his impact running DOGE in Trump 2.0.

---

for hundreds of millions of dollar losses, see O'Brien (2015, 2016, new edition).[8] On Trump's three presidential runs and his two administrations, where Trump has created chaos, upheavals, and failures that he exhibited in his businesses, making Donald J. Trump a loser unparalleled in the US business and politics, see Kellner (2016,[9] 2017,[10] 2025[11]).

[iii] Musk has had many run-ins with the US Justice System during his business career, and one of his grounds for joining Trump's administration was to cancel or nullify the many court cases that threatened him. See Lipton et al. (2025).[12] On Musk's early life in South Africa, see the biography by Walter Isaacson (2023).[13]

[iv] Later, it was found that there were also embarrassing references to Musk in the Epstein files; see Robins-Early (2026).[14]

From EOs to a War on Democracy

In his 2024 campaign, Trump promised that he would carry out mass deportations of the US immigrants, slash government spending, and shut down agencies exhibiting fraud and waste. Hours after his inauguration, he entered the Oval Office and, in a bizarre, televised spectacle, he signed dozens of EOs, almost all of them fulfilling Project 2025 – what had been billed as the radical right's blueprint for dismantling democracy in America.[15,v]

On "day one," Trump granted clemency to the January 6, 2021, insurrectionists charged and convicted of assaulting the Capitol, beating police officers, and attempting to impede the transfer of power to a duly elected new President. The mob's violent insurrection resulted in five deaths, hundreds of injuries, and wrecked the US Capitol building.[16] Shockingly, one of the self-proclaimed "Law and Order" President's first acts freed the most violent US insurrectionists since the Civil War.[17]

An outspoken critic of wind-based and solar energy, Trump also ordered a 60-day pause on approval for all "renewable energy development" on public lands.[18] He also withdrew the USA (again, as he did in Trump 1.0) from the Paris Climate Agreement, reasserting that climate change was a hoax. Next, showing his readiness to violate the Constitution and playing to his racist, anti-immigrant base, Trump moved to end birthright citizenship. Since birthright citizenship is a right enshrined in the Constitution, a judge immediately challenged Trump's action as a violation of the 14th Amendment.[19]

Trump then restored the federal death penalty and renamed the Gulf of Mexico the "Gulf of America," in a perverse synthesis of Trump's egomania and "America First" obsession. These complex dynamics that combined his penchant for rebranding to an insatiable need for "winning" would lead Trump to ponder taking over Greenland, Panama, and even Canada.[20] With his next EO, Trump set off a firestorm of controversy, demanding an end to diversity, equity, and inclusion (DEI) efforts. Federal agencies were ordered to place all DEI staff on paid administrative leave –

---

[v] On Project 25, as constructed by the Right-wing Heritage Foundation, see ACLU (2025b).[21]

effective immediately – and to make plans for staff reductions by the end of the day on January 31. EO14151 titled "Ending Radical and Wasteful Government DEI Programs and Preferencing" also resulted in books, films, and other materials being banned from federal agency and military libraries.

Other Trump executive actions were equally objectionable, such as pardoning the creator of "Silk Road," a dark web marketplace where illicit drugs and other goods were sold. Some EOs were simply petty and nasty, such as canceling flights for refugees already approved to travel to the USA (14163). Others, however, were of major impact, such as EO14287, which immediately sent 1,500 US troops to the southern border and threatened to prosecute local officials who obstructed immigration enforcement. This order included: sweeps of immigrant communities by federal troops; rounding up immigrants indiscriminately, regardless of their citizenship; and putting them in deportation camps, thus creating chaos in immigrant communities.

Trump also threatened to withhold money from cities that did not cooperate with his immigration crackdown. Playing off his MAGA base's anti-trans sentiment, Trump required trans-women to be housed in prisons for men, ordered federal prisons to house transgender women in men's facilities, and halted medical treatments related to gender transition, although a judge blocked this order.[22] Day one of Trump 2.0 was a busy day, which displayed the frantic presidency attacking democracy and the state, and putting his own dark stamp on the presidency.

Soon afterwards, Trump would ask a federal judge to drop corruption charges against New York Mayor Eric Adams in return for the Mayor's help in supporting Immigration and Customs Enforcement (ICE) raids in New York City. This judicial strong-arming set off a flurry of resignations in the DOJ, as did other presidential demands for prosecuting perceived enemies and doing "extra-legal" favors for friends. Trump's presidency quickly became characterized as a protracted struggle between authoritarianism and the preservation of the US democracy and the rule of law. But the nation had never elected a convicted felon as President before.

The Strange Alliance of Donald Trump and Elon Musk

Historically, Musk had supported Democratic Party and liberal candidates, but in the 2023 Republican presidential primaries, he supported Florida Senator Ron DeSantis with huge campaign contributions. He also contributed to Robert F. Kennedy Jr and Vivek Ramaswamy's primary runs before eventually backing the winner, Donald Trump. After announcing his outright support for Trump in 2024, Musk campaigned exuberantly, promoting numerous conspiracy theories and falsehoods about Democrats, election fraud, and immigration, and often appeared on stage with Trump. Musk eventually contributed over $288 million to the campaign.[23]

Following Trump's victory, Musk moved into Mar-a-Lago and spent weeks planning the transition with the new President and his closest advisors. Day after day, Musk would appear on camera with Trump, first at Mar-a-Lago and then in the Oval Office, at Cabinet Meetings, and other official activities. While Trump signed EOs on day one, Musk greeted a large MAGA victory celebration with what appeared to be a fascist salute (Musk has denied this intent, but the image became a meme in the media world). Trump immediately made Musk head of DOGE, where he began slashing government budgets, personnel, and even whole agencies in the name of efficiency and "common sense." Cuts centered on some age-old conservative irritants like the Department of Education, Environmental Protection Agency (EPA), Internal Revenue Service (IRS), the Consumer Financial Protection Bureau (CFPB), and the Department of Energy. Trump also went after the DOJ, which he perceived as "anti-Trump" dating back to his first administration. Musk specifically targeted agencies that had regulatory power over his businesses – some of which had ongoing lawsuits against his companies already in the courts.[24]

Trump–Musk's controversial moves to dismantle the USAID also set off a storm of controversy.[25] This agency is independent of the federal government and is responsible for administering civilian foreign aid and development assistance around the world. Established in 1961 by John Fitzgerald Kennedy (JFK), USAID unites several foreign assistance organizations and programs – global health, disaster, and poverty relief, etc. – all under one agency.[26] It was also a particularly popular and effective arm of US foreign policy as it demonstrated both US power and compassion during the Cold War. Defunding USAID sparked a showdown with Democrats who blasted the effort as illegal and vowed a court fight. When Democrats sought to enter the USAID headquarters, federal officers blocked them from even getting into the lobby. The shutdown dramatized the massive power Musk was wielding over Washington, D.C. He then boasted in a tweet: "Spent the weekend feeding USAID into the woodchipper."[27]

The Trump White House also shielded DOGE from public records requests, declaring the documents Musk's office handled were presidential records. That designation could insulate them from public records requests under the Freedom of Information Act, as well as most judicial intervention, until at least 2034. While halting work at the CFPB, Trump/Musk also cut staff and funding for the Security Exchange Commission's enforcement and regulation activities, allowing their own cryptocurrency holdings to grow exponentially without oversight.[28]

Aside from policies that increased Trump/Musk's personal wealth,[29] many staff and agency reductions degraded the nation's infrastructure and its ability to serve important public welfare and democratic functions. From air traffic control and transportation safety to disaster relief and national security, Americans became increasingly *less* safe under Trump 2.0. The results of these cuts and the questionable processes followed to operationalize them led to many judicial injunctions and restraints – orders that have been simply ignored by Trump 2.0.[30] Similarly, cuts to almost every important foreign policy budget had an even more foreboding global impact. Aside from USAID, cuts to many United Nations programs cast uncertainty on the US leadership role in global politics. Recent illegal military actions against Venezuela and in Nigeria have only created more concern about the US willingness to break international law and violate our own military's rules for engagement.

Musk/Trump Violate Basic Principles of US Democracy

So much of DOGE's work was not only done in secret but required access to confidential treasury records (from citizens and corporations) and other agency information and platforms supporting government paychecks, tax refunds, and Social Security funds. On February 8, 2025, Judge Paul Engelmayer paused DOGE's access to "sensitive" records, claiming their incursion carried a high risk of improper disclosure, theft, or simply hacking sites to prevent the distribution of government payments. In a *New York Times* op-ed penned by five former Treasury secretaries, the authors wrote: "The nation's payment system has historically been operated by a very small group of nonpartisan career civil servants," an administrative norm upended by DOGE's "political actors [who] have not been subject to the same rigorous ethics rules as civil servants."[31]

The battle between the Trump–Musk Gang and the Law continued on February 10, 2025, as Musk again sought access to the US Treasury but was blocked again by a federal judge.[32] Musk also targeted the CFPB that day. When agency workers entered their offices that morning, they received an internal memo from the Office of Management and Budget Director (and Project 2025 architect) Russell Vought, terminating their employment. As *Rolling Stone* reported:

> *One of Vought's first official acts was to seize the reins as acting director at CFPB, the agency designed by Congress to safeguard Americans from the predatory practices of Wall Street and other financial malefactors. The brainchild of Senator Elizabeth Warren, the CFPB is one of the few agencies in Washington whose mission is to protect individual Americans against corporate power .... [They] routinely order large corporations to refund money to duped and abused consumers. To insulate CFPB from partisan reprisal, it is funded by the Federal Reserve, meaning that a hostile congressional majority can't zero out its budget.*[33]

Project 2025 recommended abolishing the bureau – calling it "utterly unaccountable" – but as of the beginning of 2026, it remains intact, but on life support.[34]

In a span of hours on February 10, government workers received notices that DOGE had forced out officials responsible for government ethics and whistleblower complaints. The government fired more than a dozen inspector generals tasked with rooting out waste, fraud, corruption, and abuse at government agencies.[35]

As Musk departed soon after the first 100 days were over (more about this below), democratic principles and Constitutional protections lay in shambles. But Trump had only just begun to dismantle global trade and foreign policy.

ACT TWO: A BEAUTIFUL WORLD, A BEAUTIFUL WORD, AND A WONDERFUL SECRET

Throughout his campaign, Trump promised an aggressive, "America First" administration, which generally signifies an isolationist policy focused on domestic issues. Yet Trump has tried to expand the US sphere of influence, threatening to take back the Panama Canal, annex Greenland, and turn Canada into the 51st state.[vi] Trump started threatening Venezuela in September 2025, going so far as to blow up 30 boats and kill over 100 people. Initially, he claimed these strikes constituted part of the "war on drugs," but later admitted his goal was regime change. Trump hoped to regain land and resources once held by US oil companies prior to Hugo Chavez's nationalization of Venezuelan industries in the early 2000s. Accordingly, Trump tweeted that Venezuela was

> *completely surrounded by the largest Armada ever assembled in the history of South America ... until such time as they return to the United States of America all of the oil, land and other assets that they stole from us.*[36]

In early January, Trump's military arrested President, Nicolas Maduro – who now sits in a Brooklyn, NY, prison – and declared himself "acting president" of the country.

While Trump and his "Department of War" subordinate, Pete Hegseth, deploy military might to demand global respect and openly ignore national and international laws and rules of engagement, the

---

[vi] Trump's threats to take over Canada came as Canadian Prime Minister Justin Trudeau was in crisis and he stepped down, enabling Liberal Party leader Mark Carney to take over as Prime Minister, calling an election and easily winning over the favored conservative candidate. Carney vigorously stood up to Trump, telling him Canada would not give up its sovereignty, thus winning support for Carney as a protector of Canada's independence. See Zurcher (2025).[37]

administration's major global impact has been to instigate economic upheavals everywhere. Throughout the campaign, Trump promoted his America First economic platform based on what he called a "beautiful word – tariffs." The lynchpin of his economic policies, huge tariffs on over 100 countries, led the stock market to whipsaw and the national economy to contract by 0.3% on an annualized rate in the first quarter of Trump 2.0. Erratic policy decisions, including abrupt and volatile tariff changes, mass federal workforce layoffs, and the longest government shutdown in history eroded economic expectations to the lowest rate in almost 13 years.[38]

Almost immediately following what Trump called "Tariff Liberation Day" (April 2, 2025), states, corporations, small businesses, and trade organizations sued him in court. Opponents claimed Trump could not unilaterally declare these tariffs either through EO or by using the International Emergency Economic Powers Act. While the Supreme Court has yet to decide on Trump's appeal of lower court rulings *against* his tariff policy, Trump continues to destabilize trade relations and traditional alliances while personally absconding with billions of dollars from side deals with foreign dictators. And while he grades his economy as an "A+++++," inflation remains high, job creation is negligible, unemployment is up, manufacturing is down, the consumer price index is up, and overall consumer confidence levels continue to tank. Apparently, the beauty of words like "tariff" is in the ear of the beholder.

The Trump/Epstein Scandal

During the summer of 2025, the MAGA base and many of its major media influencers clamored for the release of the Epstein files, which Trump had promised to make public. Despite the possibility that such files could expose claims of Trump's knowledge of or complicity in Epstein's criminal enterprise, most MAGA people believed Democrats would be hurt the most.

The controversy also opened space for the women victimized by Epstein's crimes; they organized a very successful pressure campaign to force government action. Increasing attention was paid to

Epstein's *first* arrest in Palm Beach, Florida, where federal officials identified 36 girls as possible victims.[39] Epstein was convicted in 2008, but as part of a controversial plea deal – arranged by the then US Attorney, Alex Acosta – he served only 13 months (mostly with extensive work release). Acosta would later be rewarded by Trump 1.0 with a position as Labor Secretary, despite little experience. When Epstein was arrested on new and extensive charges in 2019, Acosta immediately resigned from the Cabinet.[vii] The Epstein/Acosta "deal of the century" was quickly unraveling.[viii]

Awaiting trial in a Manhattan prison, Epstein allegedly committed suicide – although three minutes of missing footage from Epstein's cell camera gave rise to conspiracy theories about murders and secret societies.[ix] During Epstein's and his co-conspirator Ghislaine Maxwell's trials, information arose, including client lists with names of Wall Street moguls, major politicians, British royalty like Prince Andrew, Epstein's own lawyer Alan Derschowitz, and, inevitably, Donald Trump.[40] Increasing information, photos, and videos shared between Epstein and Trump fueled beliefs that the

---

[vii] For an excellent account of the Epstein case, his business endeavors, his cronies, and the sex scandal concerning the trafficking of underage girls, see Brown (2021). Julie K. Brown had been reporting on the Epstein case for years for the *Miami Herald*, tracking down some of the girls that Epstein exploited, and documenting how the legal system had turned a blind eye to Epstein's exploits, providing documented testimony and evidence that helped lead to his arrest and trials that finally brought him to justice, while exposing some of the powerful people and the corrupt system that protected him. I shall draw on this and several other major books on Epstein that I shall cite in the following Epstein study.

[viii] For more details and documentation on the Epstein trials and Acosta affair, see Levine (2020)[41] Edwards and Henderson (2020),[42] and Patterson and Connolly (2020).[43] I also recommend the two documentaries released on Netflix, *Jeffrey Epstein: Filthy Rich* (2020), based on Patterson and Connolly's (2020) book, and *Ghislaine Maxwell: Filthy Rich* (2022), that is not based on Patterson and Connolly's book. On Maxwell, see Cawthorne (2021).[44]

[ix] There are many credible media sources on the story, including Dhruv Mehrotra (2025a).[45] A later *Wired* analysis of the Epstein prison video provides an even more detailed analysis and documentation of the video. See Mehrotra (2025b).[46] Some Epstein scholars, like Edwards and Henderson (2020) do not believe Epstein was murdered, while Brown (2021) sorts out the arguments for suicide versus murder.

President *was* implicated in the files. While promising to release the files as nominee, he blocked their release as President.

Meanwhile, stories resurfaced documenting Trump and Epstein's relationship. In 2002, Trump told *New York Magazine*: "I've known Jeff for fifteen years. Terrific guy. He's a lot of fun to be with. It is even said that he likes beautiful women as much as I do, and many of them are on the younger side."[47,x] Michael Wolff, a veteran journalist and author of books on Trump[48] wrote, "Jeffrey Epstein ...Trump and Tom Barrack [a close business and political ally of Trump] were a 1980s and '90s set of nightlife Musketeers ... (Epstein, who remained close to Barrack, had been whitewashed out of the Trump biography)" (Wolff, 2018, p. 28).[49]

This Epstein scandal exploded on July 17, 2025, when the *Wall Street Journal* published a story recounting a commemorative book assembled for Epstein's 50th birthday which included a note appearing to carry Trump's signature.[50] Trump has denied writing the letter, threatened to sue the *Wall Street Journal*, and referred to the whole affair as a hoax.[xi]

The story exploded in the media as the Trump administration played cat and mouse with legislators who demanded the files full release. Media outlets called for the President to explain persistent false claims and flimsy denials.[51] Each break in the story came complete with newly exposed accusations and more women were emboldened to speak out about their sexual abuse by Epstein and co-conspirators. Despite almost two decades of trying to get their story heard, suddenly, not an evening on cable news passes without victims being interviewed and calling for pressure on Congress to force the full release of the files.

The rapidly growing and diverse support for transparency led the House of Representatives to initiate a "discharge petition" to consider a bill forcing the DOJ to turn over all the Epstein files. Eventually, pressure mounted and Trump had to "allow" Republicans to vote in favor. After numerous delays, the House voted 427-1 in favor of the legislation. The Senate passed it by acclamation, and

---

[x] Listen to the Jeffrey Epstein Tapes.[52]

[xi] See Falconer (2025).[53] *The Wall Street Journal (WSJ)* moved to dismiss the case, which is now in legal limbo. See Hill (2025).[54]

the President signed it only days later, despite adamantly maintaining the files were a "Democratic Hoax." Meanwhile, Trump's former personal attorney and DOJ Assistant Attorney General, Todd Blanch, moved Ghislaine Maxwell (then serving 20 years for aiding Epstein's sex trafficking ring) to new prison accommodations at a minimum-security facility in Texas. In return, she would maintain her silence on Trump and Epstein while possibly winning a pardon for her crimes.[55]

Yet the Epstein scandal would not die down. In fact, outrage grew over Maxwell's transfer and other perks that included special food, a puppy for company, and after-hours access to exercise areas and special accommodations for her lawyers and visitors.[56] As 2025 ended, Trump 2.0 could be accurately characterized as a corrupt, anti-democratic enterprise, dismantling piece-by-piece Constitutional provisions, processes, and protections for most Americans while using authoritarian power to enhance his own profiteering and protect himself from past and present crimes.

ACT THREE: FIGHTING BACK – RECLAIMING AND REENVISIONING DEMOCRACY

The Trump/Musk break-up may have been predictable – an inherently fragile partnership. Yet one main reason Musk left D.C. to run his businesses arose from the tremendous resistance organized against him. Activists consistently picketed and demonstrated at Tesla dealerships and SpaceX facilities. These actions culminated in the March 28th, 2025, Global Day of Action led by the "Tesla Takedown" campaign. Acts of vandalism and sabotage against Tesla vehicles, dealerships, and charging stations intensified in the Spring of 2025 as protestors called on Musk to resign. Tesla sales decreased 13% in the USA, revenue from sales dropped over 20%; European sales fell almost 40%, and overall profits dropped 70% in the first quarter of 2023. Massive resistance to Musk's efforts showed the power of protest early on in Trump 2.0.[57]

In many honorable ways, parts of the legal profession stood up to Trump and his administration. The *New York Times* published "The Recklessness Itself Sends a Message: 35 Legal Experts Assess

Trump's Return." The piece provided portraits of judges and legal experts who have heroically resisted Trump 2.0's attacks on the rule of law and the Constitution.[58] Trump EOs threatened major law firms with loss of security clearance, terminating government contracts, and even barring attorneys from entering government buildings. While some firms capitulated, most did not. Perkins Coie – one of the largest D.C. firms – sued Trump for his threats and overreach, soon followed by over 500 other firms that filed briefs in their support. During the first 100 days, the American Civil Liberties Union (ACLU) filed 53 cases against the Trump administration, "seeking emergency relief in 38 of these cases, winning at least some form of preliminary or temporary order in 27 cases."[59]

Over 250 lawsuits involving Trump 2.0 have reached the courts – the vast majority of which are efforts to challenge the legality of EO's and other administrative initiatives related to freedom of speech, violations of due process and Constitutional provisions, executive branch overreach, and dozens of other efforts to carry out military strikes, deploy military and National Guard in US cities, and obstruct the legislative branch from doing their jobs. From the ACLU to Teachers Unions, from State Attorneys General to immigrant rights groups, media companies and businesses large and small, no other Presidential administration has faced such a breadth and depth of legal resistance in the US history.

Like the direct-action protests against Musk and Tesla, perhaps the most effective resistance has come from the streets where millions have marched in major cities and small towns and hamlets across the USA.[xii] While some have simply called for "NO KINGS," referencing general discontent for authoritarian, anti-democratic rule, others have been more targeted against closing government agencies, dismantling the EPA, turning health and human services into an anti-science misinformation pit, and cutting billions of dollars from education for poor and disabled youth.

[xii] Many news outlets have reported on myriad anti-Trump 2.0 protests over the past year. Most notable has been Rachel Maddow's persistent coverage of cities and towns – big and small – openly protesting the president's policies and actions. See Maddow (2025).[60]

Yet the most notable direct-action tactics and displays have been in response to ICE and attempts at mass deportation. Hundreds of organizations around the country have started rapid response teams to inform communities of ICE's presence. Groups train immigrant workers and community supporters about their rights and legal forms of protest. Stories and evidence are now legion of citizens obstructing ICE raids and efforts to arrest and detain innocent people and separate families. Hundreds of cities have witnessed daily demonstrations at detention centers where clergy, legislators, and activists increase the pressure on ICE and the administration to retreat.

Meanwhile, Trump's popularity recedes as the protests, scandals, and his political and economic overreach expose his frailty and his inadequacy.[61] ICE brutality and Department of Homeland Security incompetence have made Trump's immigration policies increasingly unpopular. Only one-third of Americans support Trump's handling of the economy, and 2025 ended with the lowest consumer confidence rating since the peak of Covid-19 inflation. Warring Conservative and MAGA factions, along with growing questions about Trump's own physical and mental capacities, forebode an eventual reckoning with the country.[xiii] He's even faced his first major defeat in the Supreme Court as justices ruled against his deployment of National Guard troops to Chicago. As year one of Trump 2.0 ends, his failing presidency is clearer than ever. But his demise may be a boon for the future of democracy.

NOTES

1. Schermele, Z., Wire, S. D., Chambers, F., Mansfield, E., Morin, R., & Loria, M. (2025, November 18). Epstein files updates: Senate unanimously agrees to release records, Trump to sign deal. *USA TODAY*. Retrieved November 22, 2025, from https://www.usatoday.com/story/news/politics/2025/11/18/epstein-files-trump-congress-live-updates/87317643007/.

[xiii] On Trump's declining mental ability, see Houghtaling (2026).[62] The polling also shows wide majorities disapprove of almost every Trump policy and action; see Quinnipiac University Polling (2025).

2. Kellner, D. (2001). *Grand theft 2000. Media spectacle and a stolen election*. Rowman and Littlefield.

3. Kellner, D. (2003). *From September 11 to terror war: The dangers of the Bush legacy*. Rowman and Littlefield.

4. Kellner, D. (2005). *Media spectacle and the crisis of democracy*. Paradigm Press

5. Blair, G. (2000). *The Trumps. Three generations that built an empire*. Simon and Schuster.

6. Jacobs, R. (2025). Culture, Christianity, and the Afrikaner blues. *CounterPunch* https://openurl.ebsco.com/EPDB%3Agcd%3A15%3A27954783/detailv2?sid=ebsco%3Aplink%3Ascholar&id=ebsco%3Agcd%3A183873529&crl=c&link_origin=www.google.com.

7. U.S. Department of Justice. (2016). *Report on the investigation into Russian interference in the 2016 presidential election*. Retrieved July 22, 2025, from https://www.justice.gov/archives/sco/file/1373816/dl?inline=.

8. O'Brien, T. L. (2015). *The art of being the Donald*. Grand Central Publishing (2005; 2016 new edition).

9. Kellner, D. (2016). *American nightmare: Donald Trump, media spectacle, and authoritarian populism*. Sense Publishers.

10. Kellner, D. (2017). *The American horror show: Election 2016 and the ascent of Donald J. Trump*. Sense Publishers.

11. Kellner, D. (2025). *Media spectacle in the 21st century: From the stolen election of 2000 to the Trump horror show*. Springer Nature.

12. Lipton, E., Fahrenthold, D., Krolik, A., & Grind, K. (2025, October 20). U.S. agencies fund, and fight with, Elon Musk. A Trump presidency could give him power over them. Elon Musk, the richest man in the world, will be a major political player no matter who wins the presidential election. *New York Times* Retrieved May 7, 2025, from https://www.nytimes.com/2024/10/20/us/politics/elon-musk-federal-agencies-contracts.html.

13. Isaacson, W. (2023). *Elon Musk*. Simon & Schuster.

14. Robins-Early, N. (2026, January 30). Elon Musk had more extensive ties to Epstein than previously known, emails show. Newly released files from DoJ show the pair making plans in 2012 and 2013 for the Tesla CEO to visit Epstein's island. *The Guardian*. Retrieved February 16, 2026, from https://www.theguardian.com/technology/2026/jan/30/elon-musk-epstein-files-island-visits.

15. Yourish, K., Rabinowitz, E., Wu, A., Gamio, L., Kavi, A., & Kim, M. (2025, July 20). All of the Trump administration's major moves in the first 30 days. *New York Times*. https://www.nytimes.com/interactive/2025/us/trump-agenda-2025.html.

16. American Oversight. (2023, September 26). *The January 6 attack on the U.S. Capitol. The heavily armed, Trump-incited mob attack of Jan. 6, 2021, was an attack not just on the U.S. Capitol building, but also on democracy and the rule of law*. American Oversight. Retrieved February 17, 2025, from https://americanoversight.org/investigation/the-january-6-attack-on-the-u-s-capitol/.

17. Dreisbach, T., Johnson, C., Shapiro, A., & Woerkom, B. V. (2025, January 21). *Trump gave pardons to hundreds of violent Jan. 6 rioters. Here's what they did*. NPR, All Things Considered. Retrieved February 18, 2025, from https://www.npr.org/2025/01/21/nx-s1-5268919/trump-issues-jan-6-pardons-attack-capitol-clemency.

18. Eisenson, M. (2025, May 5). *100 days of Trump 2.0: Renewable energy siting and permitting*. Sabine Center for Climate Change Law. Retrieved November 28, 2025, from https://blogs.law.columbia.edu/climatechange/2025/05/05/100-days-of-trump-2-0-renewable-energy.

19. ACLU. (2025a, February 10). *Federal court blocks Trump birthright citizenship executive order. Case: New Hampshire Indonesian Community Support V. Donald J. Trump. Affiliates: ACLU of New Hampshire, ACLU of Massachusetts, ACLU of Maine*. ACKU. Retrieved February 18, 2025, from https://www.aclu.org/press-releases/federal-court-blocks-trump-birthright-citizenship-executive-order.

20. Lee, B. X. (2019). *The dangerous case of Donald Trump: 37 psychiatrists and mental health experts assess a president-updated and expanded with new essays*. Thomas Dunne Books.

21. ACLU. (2025b). *Project 25 explained*. Retrieved July 19, 2025, from https://www.aclu.org/project-2025-explained.

22. Dewan, S. (2025, February 4). Judge blocks Trump effort to move trans women to men's prisons. A temporary restraining order blocked the administration from transferring transgender women and from ending gender-transition treatment for prisoners. *New York Times*. Retrieved February 18, 2025, from https://www.nytimes.com/2025/02/04/us/trans-women-prisons-executive-order-ruling.html.

23. Thadani, T., Morse, C. E., & Reston, M. (2025, January 31). Elon Musk donated $288 million in 2024 election, final tally shows. The official count of Musk's donations further cemented him as the country's largest – and most prominent – donor. *Washington Post*. Retrieved February 16, 2025, from https://www.washingtonpost.com/politics/2025/01/31/elon-musk-trump-donor-2024-election/.

24. Lipton, E., & Grind, K. (2025, February 11). Elon Musk's business empire scores benefits under Trump shake-up. Elon Musk controls six companies, including Tesla. Mr. Musk's companies secured $13 billion in Federal contracts over the past five years. *New York Times*. Retrieved February 11, 2025, from Https://Www.Nytimes.Com/2025/02/11/Us/Politics/Elon-Musk-Companies-Conflicts.Html.

25. American Oversight. (2025, February 27). *Donald Trump and Elon Musk's illegal dismantling of USAID*. American Oversight. Retrieved May 8, 2025, from https://americanoversight.org/investigation/donald-trump-and-elon-musks-illegal-dismantling-of-usaid/.

26. Roy, D. (2025, February 7). *What is USAID and why is it at risk?* Council for Foreign Relations. Retrieved May 8, 2025, from https://www.cfr.org/article/what-usaid-and-why-it-risk.

27. Lautman, O. (2025, February 3). *Trump tyranny tracker: Day 15*. Trump Tyranny Tracker. Retrieved May 8, 2025, from https://trumptyrannytracker.substack.com/p/trump-tyranny-tracker-day-15.

28. Goldstein, M., & Silver-Greenberg, J. (2025). How Trump is gutting oversight of business. *The New York Times*, February 15, B1.

29. Stone, P. (2025, June 17).‘ I have never seen such open corruption’: Trump’s crypto deals and loosening of rules shock observers. *The Guardian* https://www.theguardian.com/us-news/2025/jun/17/trump-crypto-memecoin-corruption.

30. Montague, Z. (2025, March 18). Musk’s role in dismantling aid agency likely violated constitution, judge finds. *New York Times* https://www.nytimes.com/2025/03/18/us/politics/elon-musk-usaid-doge-unconstitutional.html.

31. Rubin, R. E., Summers, L. H., Geithner, T. F., Lew, J. J., & Yellen, J. L. (2025, February 10). Five former treasury secretaries: Our democracy is under siege. *New York Times*. Retrieved February 11, 2025, from https://www.nytimes.com/2025/02/10/opinion/treasure-secretaries-doge-musk.html.

32. McDougald, P. (2025, February 10). *Feb. 10: DOGE comes for the treasury*. The Scroll. Retrieved February 11, 2025, from https://thedailyscroll.substack.com/p/feb-10-doge-comes-for-the-treasury.

33. Dickinson, T., & Perez, A. (2025, February 10). Inside Trump and Musk’s war on the Consumer Financial Protection Bureau. Taking cops off the beat could be America’s loss, and Trump and Musk’s personal gain. *Rolling Stone*. Retrieved February 16, 2025, from https://www.rollingstone.com/politics/politics-features/trump-musk-cfpb-consumer-financial-protection-bureau-1235262743/.

34. Riquier, A. (2025, January 10). Billions of dollars for millions of Americans: Why ‘delete the CFPB’ might not fly. *USA Today*. https://www.usatoday.com/story/money/2025/01/10/delete-cfpb-elon-musk-consumer-financial-protection-bureau/77597930007/.

35. Tucker, E., Price, M. L., & Miller, Z. (2025). *With firings and lax enforcement, Trump moving to dismantle government’s public integrity guardrails*. Associated Press. Retrieved February 11, 2025, from https://apnews.com/article/trump-inspectors-general-firing-justice-department.

36. Smith, C. (2025, December 23). The real reason Trump keeps ranting about Venezuelan oil. *Vanity Fair* https://www.vanityfair.com/news/story/donald-trump-venezuela-oil?srsltid=AfmBOoopsmBF0_Ubhugo0_hp8aSMQnjDpML7esFWLtK8JpMCP7sIfe1t.

37. Zurcher, A. (2025, April 28). *Trump made Carney's turnaround victory possible.* BBC News. Retrieved May 7, 2025, from https://www.bbc.com/news/articles/c5ypz7yx73wo.

38. Horsley, S. (2025, April 30). *The U.S. economy shrinks as Trump's tariffs spark recession fears.* NPR. Retrieved May 8, 2025, from https://www.npr.org/2025/04/30/nx-s1-5380204/trump-economy-gdp-tariffs-recession-consumers.

39. Brown, J. K. (2021). *Perversion of justice: The Jeffrey Epstein story.* HarperCollins. Retrieved July 19, 2025, from https://www.google.com/books/edition/_/UovoDwAAQBAJ?hl=en&gbpv=1.

40. Brown, J. K. (2021). *Perversion of justice: The Jeffrey Epstein story.* HarperCollins. Retrieved July 19, 2025, from https://www.google.com/books/edition/_/UovoDwAAQBAJ?hl=en&gbpv=1.

41. Levine, L. (2020). *The spider: Inside the criminal web of Jeffrey Epstein and Ghislaine Maxwell.* Crown.

42. Edwards, B. J., & Henderson, B. (2020). *Relentless pursuit: My fight for the victims of Jeffrey Epstein.* Simon & Schuster.

43. Patterson, J., & Connolly, J. (2020). *Filthy Rich: The shocking true story of Jeffrey Epstein.* Little, Brown and Company.

44. Cawthorne, N. (2021). *Ghislaine Maxwell. The fall of America's most notorious socialite.* Gibson Square.

45. Mehrotra, D. (2025a, July 11). Metadata shows the FBI's 'raw' Jeffrey Epstein prison video was likely modified. *Wired.* Retrieved July 21, 2025, from https://www.wired.com/story/metadata-shows-the-dojs-raw-jeffreyepstein-prison-video-was-likely-modified/.

46. Mehrotra, D. (2025b, July 22). The FBI's Jeffrey Epstein prison video had nearly 3 minutes cut out. Metadata from the "raw" Epstein prison video shows approximately 2 minutes and 53 seconds were removed from one of two stitched-together clips. The cut starts right at the 'missing minute.' *Wired.* Retrieved July 23, 2025, from https://www.wired.com/story/the-fbis-jeffrey-epstein-prison-video-had-nearly-3-minutes-cut-out/.

47. Landon, T., Jr. (2002, October 28). Jeffrey Epstein: International moneyman of mystery. 'Terrific guy,' Donald Trump booms from a

speakerphone. 'He's a lot of fun to be with.' *New York Magazine*. Retrieved July 19, 2025, from https://nymag.com/nymetro/news/people/n_7912/.

48. Wolff, M. (2018). *Fire & fury: Inside the Trump White House*. Henry Holt; Wolff, M. (2019). *Siege: Trump under fire*. Henry Holt; Wolff, M. (2021). *Too famous the rich, the powerful, the wishful, the notorious, the damned*. Henry Holt.

49. The three Trump books by Michael Wolff, who was interviewing Epstein for a book on his life, provide provocative but controversial material on the Trump–Epstein relationship.

50. Safdar, K., & Palazzolo, J. (2025, July 17). Jeffrey Epstein's friends sent him bawdy letters for a 50th birthday album. One was from Donald Trump. The leather-bound book was compiled by Ghislaine Maxwell. The president says the letter 'is a fake thing.' *Wall Street Journal*. Retrieved July 18, 2025, from https://www.wsj.com/politics/trump-jeffrey-epstein-birthday-letter-we-have-certain-things-in-common-f918d796.

51. Lowell, H., & Helmore, E. (2025, July 17). Trump requests release of Epstein grand jury transcripts amid report of 'bawdy' birthday note. President directs Pam Bondi to seek release of testimony from sex-trafficking case and threatens to sue *Wall Street Journal*. *The Guardian*. Retrieved July 18, 2025 from https://www.theguardian.com/us-news/2025/jul/17/trump epstein-grand-jury-testimony-wall-street-journal.

52. Jeffrey Epstein Tapes: "I Was Donald Trump's Closest Friend," The Daily Beast. Retrieved July 20, 2025, from thedailybeast.com/listen-to-the-jeffrey-epstein-tapes-i-was-donald-trumps-closest-friend.

53. Falconer, R. (2025, July 17). *Trump threatens to sue WSJ for story alleging racy letter to Epstein*. Axios. Retrieved July 19, 2025, from https://www.axios.com/2025/07/18/trump-epstein-wsj-murdoch-sue-letter.

54. Hill, J. (2025, September 22). WSJ moves to dismiss Trump's $10B lawsuit over alleged letter in Epstein birthday book. The motion contends that the paper's article about the letter is true. *The Wall Street Journal*. Retrieved November 23, 2025, from https://abcnews.go.com/US/wsj-moves-dismiss-trumps-10b-lawsuit-alleged-letter/story?id=125830250.

55. Ferguson, M. (2025, September 9). *Ghislaine Maxwell lawyer makes stunning quid pro quo confession.* The New Republic.

56. Sullivan, M. (2025). The Maxwell prison transfer is just another element of the many-ringed circus act that is American politics these days. *The Guardian.* Retrieved November 23, 2025, from https://www.theguardian.com/commentisfree/2025/aug/20/ghislaine-maxwell-prison-transfer-epstein.

57. Altchek, A. (2025). Protesters are taking a victory lap after Tesla's dismal earnings – and taking aim at Musk's other companies. *Business Insider;* Petrow-Cohen, C. (2025, April 22). Tesla profit falls in the wake of brand controversy and tariffs. *Los Angeles Times* https://www.businessinsider.com/tesla-protesters-celebrate-bad-earnings-call-2025-4.

58. New York Times Opinion. (2025) The 'Recklessness itself sends a message': 35 legal experts assess Trump's return. *New York Times.* Retrieved July 26, 2025, from https://www.nytimes.com/2025/04/28/opinion/trump-constitution-rule-of-law.html.

59. Wang, C. (2025, April 30). *We are defending freedom in the courts – and still winning. With 53 lawsuits filed against the Trump administration and counting, we will not surrender our freedoms to a lawless executive branch.* Retrieved May 7, 2025, from https://www.aclu.org/news/civil-liberties/we-are-defending-freedom-in-the-courts-and-still-winning.

60. Maddow, R. (2025, December 2). *Anti-Trump protests sweep the country as his approval rating sinks to new lows.* MaddowBlog. https://www.ms.now/rachel-maddow-show/maddowblog/trump-approval-rating-protests-healthcare-redistricting-immigration-raids.

61. Quinnipiac University Polling. (2025, July 16). *63% of voters disapprove of the Trump administration's handling of the Jeffrey Epstein files, Quinnipiac University national poll finds.* Retrieved July 31, 2025, from https://poll.qu.edu/poll-release?releaseid=3928.

62. Houghtaling, E.Q. (2026, January 21). *Ex-ally warns Trump's decline is "significant" after disastrous speech. Former White House lawyer Ty Cobb said Donald Trump's cognitive decline is "palpable."* The New Republic. Retrieved February 16, 2026, from https://newrepublic.com/post/205441/trump-white-house-giant-epstein-birthday-letter-dc.

9

ASSAULTING OUR ENVIRONMENT AND THE CLIMATE: TRUMP 2.0, OIL-IGARCHY, AND THE POLLUTER-INDUSTRIAL COMPLEX

Daniel Faber

Northeastern University, USA

THE SECOND COMING OF AN AUTHORITARIAN: TRUMP 2.0

Donald J. Trump is once again President of the United States, and the results are proving to be disastrous. Trump is unleashing a relentless assault on the hard-fought policy achievements of the ecology, climate justice (CJ), and environmental justice (EJ) movements (as well as all other progressive social movements). The outcome of these battles will no doubt reshape the fabric of American life and the environment for years to come. Here we see the second coming of a Right-wing populist who exhibits the traits of an authoritarian, richly supported by a slew of conservative billionaires, high tech capital, and major corporate polluters (especially Big Oil). Trump openly touts a reactionary ethno-capitalist vision committed to "Make America Great Again" (MAGA). Many of these dynamics are discussed in other chapters of this collection.

One way to understand this convergence is to consider Trumpism the merger of four distinct political agendas into a type of a new authoritarianism unique to American history. These agendas include: (1) a pro-corporate neoliberal economic program committed to the deregulation of industry, tax cuts for the rich, and the defunding and dismantling of the federal government; (2) a hawkish foreign policy committed to the use of gunboat diplomacy for the purpose of acquiring foreign resources and assets for the US capital, as seen in military actions against Iran and Venezuela and the threats leveled against Denmark and Greenland, Colombia, Panama, Cuba, Canada, and other nations; (3) a Right-wing economic populism (tariffs on foreign capital) meant to appeal to working class whites suffering the impacts of neoliberal trade policy; and (4) a highly militant neoconservative social policy agenda devoted to the rollback of diversity, equity, and inclusion (DEI) programs, immigrant rights, racial and social justice, liberal educational institutions, and other enemies in the culture wars.

Trump's political rhetoric and actions are designed to stoke the flames of racism, bigotry, misogyny, and anti-immigrant sentiments among the Christian nationalists and other reactionary forces that make up his MAGA base. His peculiar brand of xenophobic authoritarian populism favors monoculturalism over multiculturalism; national self-interest over international cooperation and development aid; closed borders over the free flow of people, ideas, labor, and capital; and traditionalism over progressive and liberal social values. As stated by the social scientists Ronald Inglehart and Pippa Norris, Trump's political discourses have always been designed to stir up a "potent mix of racial resentment, intolerance of multiculturalism, nationalistic isolationism, nostalgia for past glories, mistrust of outsiders, traditional misogyny and sexism, the appeal of forceful strong-man leadership, attack-dog politics, and racial and anti-Muslim animus."[1] In short, Trumpism is nothing less than an attack on the guardrails of America's liberal democracy itself.[2]

This danger is now on full display, as seen in systematic efforts that seek to marginalize, discipline, and control dissenting social groups and oppositional politics.[3] Following the playbook outlined in the influential Heritage Foundation's Project 2025 conservative agenda and Trump's policy manifesto Agenda47, the rights of women, people of color, and the lesbian, gay, bisexual, transgender, and queer people are being targeted. Millions of immigrants and undocumented workers from the Global South face the daily threat of arrest and mass deportations at the hands of the US government. Trump is also extending the US support for the Israeli government's brutal and illegal war on the Palestinian people in Gaza and beyond.[4]

And as the human and ecological harms associated with Trumpism spur resistance among the American people (such as the "No Kings "protests), his administration has intensified the use of repressive tactics of social control. Journalist Michael Tomasky recently revealed that just three days before the killing of Renee Good in Minneapolis by an US Immigration and Customs Enforcement (ICE) agent, Homeland Security put out a press release celebrating the successes of ICE's "wartime recruitment" campaign that resulted in the hiring of 22,000 new ICE agents. The recruitment social media post that Department of Homeland Security (DHS) placed in August for this campaign stated: "Serve your country! Defend your culture! No undergraduate degree required."[5] To protect our freedoms, including our right to live in a safe and clean environment, requires us to directly confront Trump's assault on American democracy. This will be no easy task.

WHY TRUMP WON – ANOTHER VIEW OF THE FORETOLD MESS

So, how did this happen? How can we make sense of this election? Bonilla-Silva's chronicle of the "foretold mess," another chapter in this collection, is spot on. Here, we would only drill down (pun intended) to focus on Trump's ascendency as a byproduct of neoliberal capitalism and corporate-led globalization. Under the North American Free Trade Agreement (NAFTA) and other trade arrangements brokered by both Republicans and neoliberal Democratic presidents such as Presidents Bill Clinton and Barack Obama, the industrial heartland of America has suffered from decades of severe job losses and economic crises stemming from the deindustrialization and the relocation of the US-based manufacturing to

Mexico, China, and the Global South. In this respect, the neoliberal wing of the Democratic Party functioned to advance the interests of corporate America and transnational capital at the economic expense of millions of working-class and the middle-class Americans. NAFTA especially devastated blue-collar communities in the industrial heartland in the 1990s and into the new millennium. The corresponding job losses for the industrial working class in the "Rust Belt" resulted in declining living standards and a deep resentment toward corporate Democrats.[6]

In the 21st century, such resentment has only intensified. The increased mobility of capital, technological innovation and automation (including the adoption of artificial intelligence), deindustrialization and the shift toward lower-paying service jobs, and the imposition of temporary contract work (instead of full-time permanent work) are all undermining the workers' ability to secure and maintain full-time employment status, higher (or any) wages, and better (or any) benefits to which they are traditionally accustomed. The decreasing power of unions to address these dynamics has been presented earlier in Rhomberg's chapter on labor under Trump 2.0. Precarious employment is becoming the new normality for many US workers as they move in and out of temporary jobs that offer little opportunity for social mobility and fulfillment. Once largely restricted to women, African Americans, and Latinos, ever-larger segments of white working-class males, college graduates, and the salaried are also becoming part of the new precariat.[7] High inflation rates and health care costs are adding insult to injury. In the 2024 presidential election, both Joe Biden and Kamala Harris failed to adequately address the most important concern of both working- and middle-class Americans – the high cost of living.[i] It cost them the White House.

Trump's Right-wing populism appealed to many disaffected white working-class families and brought them into the Republican fold in 2024. He seized upon their economic anxieties and

---

[i] See the Pew Research Center survey of American voters conducted in September of 2024. Eight in ten registered voters (81 percent) said that the economy and inflation were very important to their vote in the 2024 presidential election. https://www.pewresearch.org/politics/2024/09/09/issues-and-the-2024-election/.

anger and redirected them toward affirmative action and people of color. He villainized immigrants for taking jobs and hard-earned tax dollars away from American-born workers. Trump railed against the corporate media and the corrupt "elite establishments" in both parties, openly ridiculing both Democratic and Republican challengers along the way. He positioned himself as a voice of working people and promised to take on plutocracy by "draining the swamp" of lobbyists and special interests in Washington, D.C. He identified the failings of American capitalism as deriving from "bad" trade deals negotiated by "inept" politicians that gave away manufacturing jobs to "opportunistic" foreign governments. Trump promised to utilize his bargaining skills as a businessman to bring back good paying jobs and "MAGA." And he promised to restore prosperity to the American economy by rolling back "costly" government programs, environmental regulations, and action on climate change. In short, he pledged to spearhead an all-out assault on environmental protection – as a key element to restore economic growth, jobs, and higher corporate profits.

THE NEW OIL-IGARCHY: TRUMP AND THE POLLUTER-INDUSTRIAL COMPLEX

As was the case during his first administration, Trump is keeping to this pledge, unleashing a full-frontal assault on the EJ, CJ, environmental, and climate change movements. This offense is being carried out in full partnership with the most environmentally destructive sectors of American business. In fact, under President Trump, one could say that the executive branch of the federal government (as well as most of Congress and the Supreme Court) is now colonized by what I term *the polluter-industrial complex* (PIC).[8]

The PIC is a sophisticated political infrastructure made up of corporate polluters, their trade associations, and allied think tanks, research centers, policy institutes, foundations, academic institutions and training programs, media and judicial watchdogs, public relations firms, corporate lobbying groups, and fake "citizen-based" (or *astroturf*) organizations that function as corporate front groups. The policy institutes are either: (1) large multi-issue organizations (such as the Heritage Foundation or Competitive Enterprise Institute) committed to a variety of conservative causes (including anti-environmentalism); or (2) more specifically anti-environmental organizations focused on climate denialism and delay (such as the Heartland Institute). Most of the identifiable funding for the PIC policy infrastructure comes from large corporate polluters, corporate and conservative family foundations, and dark money sources such as donors trust and the donors capital fund. These are donor advised funds (DAFs) that conceal the identity of contributors. From 2003 to 2018, $9.77 billion in donations was channeled to some 128 PIC-related organizations working against climate change legislation. Out of this $9.77 billion total in support, $2.65 billion came from 3,787 private foundations in the form of grants. Just 10 percent of these grant makers, which include the oil-related Charles Koch Institute and Foundation and ExxonMobil Foundation, accounted for 94 percent of these grants. Many of the largest and most powerful of these foundations were started and/or strongly supported by the oil and gas industry and other corporate polluters, and now play a highly influential role in the Trump administration.[9]

In recent years, the income of these 128 PIC-related organizations has averaged around $800 million a year. Some 74 percent of all their donations came from completely unidentified sources.[10] These "well-oiled" contributions provide the resources for one of the most expensive corporate propaganda campaigns in history: climate change denialism and delay. As such, the PIC operates as a power bloc, an organizational alliance representing those sectors of industry that stand to profit from a dismantling of environmental regulations. These industries include petro-chemical companies and agribusiness firms seeking to relax rules governing the use of pesticides and other chemicals; timber and mining interests looking to open up protected areas to resource exploitation; tobacco companies seeking to weaken public health standards; and railroads, auto manufacturers, and big utilities seeking exemptions for clean air regulations, etc. Looking to beat back regulatory controls on greenhouse gas emissions and greatly expand the production of fossil fuels, the oil, coal, and gas industries are at the top of the list.

Together, they constitute some of the most politically powerful and profitable corporations on the planet.[11]

The PIC functions to roll back and/or prevent environmental regulations, EJ programs, public health and safety measures, and climate change legislation. The PIC is especially committed to merchandising "climate denialism and delay" vis-à-vis corporate propaganda campaigns designed to sow the seeds of doubt among the public, media, and policy makers, claiming that climate change is not real, and/or that it poses no threat to the country or the world.[12] They have helped to spread targeted voter disinformation, draft repressive voting suppression strategies, and work to weaken labor unions. To achieve this goal, the PIC funnels resources to government officials who are leading the legislative charge against voting rights, as well as environmental regulation, and/or meaningful climate change legislation.[13] The America First Policy Institute (AFPI) has developed a particularly close working relationship with the Trump administration in advancing a pro-fossil fuel agenda. As noted by Public Citizen and the Revolving Door Project, AFPI also receives generous financial support from the fossil fuel industry, including the Texas oil billionaire Tim Dunn. Grounded more explicitly in the Christian far right, Dunn and other oil billionaires are challenging the traditional supremacy of Koch Brothers-sponsored organizations within the PIC. Koch Industries is one of the largest privately held oil services companies in the world and perhaps the most significant funder (and organizer) of the conservative movement in America.[14]

As a type of "oil-igarchy," the PIC is working in close partnership with the Trump administration to reshape public opinion on the need for environmental protection, to provide policy recommendations and political strategies to administration officials, to recruit and train personnel to serve in the administration, and to mobilize core constituencies to the anti-environmental cause.[15] It also serves to apply sustained political pressure on the media, colleges and universities, the federal judiciary, foundations and state funding agencies, scientific organizations, and other social institutions. The interconnected organizations that make up this network are united in their demands for neoliberal economic policies designed to deregulate and reprivatize the economy – to "free" the marketplace of costly environmental regulations and climate change programs detrimental to their corporate interests.

In the United States, the corporate-sponsored think tanks and policy institutes within the PIC play a particularly important role in moving international, national, and state public policy priorities to the Right and against the planet. In contrast to lobbying efforts by individual companies or specific trade associations, PIC-related policy planning institutions serve as the place where various owners and chief executive officers (CEOs) of corporate America come together to develop coordinated political strategies. Enlisting the services of academic advisors, conservative intellectuals, scientists and lawyers, and other "technical" experts, these PIC-related think tanks bring together the inner circles of top CEOs to serve as a leadership group, what C. Wright Mills and G. William Domhoff termed "the power elite," on behalf of American capital.[16] As a result, there are extensive interlocking members among the Boards, trustees, directors, and other key positions in large polluting corporations, and their attending think tanks, foundations, research centers, policy planning groups, and federal advisory committees.[17]

Since first running for office, Trump has gained the support of the PIC by doing their political bidding. As President from 2016 to 2020, Trump officially reversed, revoked, or otherwise rolled back more than 100 major environmental rules.[18] Under Trump 2.0, we now see an even more devastating assault. Politico reports that the oil and gas industry is now literally writing drafts of executive orders camera ready for Trump's signature.[19] In the first 100 days of his second administration, Trump initiated more attacks on the environment than during his entire first term – some 145 actions aimed at undoing rules to protect our air, water, and the climate.[20] In fact, since the Trump administration took office in January 2025, it has taken or proposed at least 400 actions that directly threaten the environment, climate, and human health. And the administration seems to be just getting started.[ii]

[ii] For a systematic accounting of the Trump's administration's efforts rollback federal government environmental protection initiatives, I highly recommend the tracking tool "White House Watch" conducted by the Natural Resources Defense Council at https://www.nrdc.org/resources/white-house-watch-tracking-attacks -our-environment-health.

This is not unexpected. After all, "drill, baby, drill" has served as the mantra for Trump's campaigns for many years. But Trump has now taken it to new extremes. In an "energy round table" dinner on April 11th of 2024 (hosted at Mar-a-Lago), Trump blatantly told a group of 20 top oil executives and lobbyists that they should donate $1 billion to his 2024 presidential campaign. If elected, he would roll back environmental rules that he said hampered their industry. As reported by Ed Pilkington of *The Guardian*, Trump specifically promised "on the first day" to end the Biden administration's freeze on liquid natural gas (LNG) export permits. He also promised to auction off more leases to drill in the Gulf of Mexico, to reverse restrictions on oil and gas development in the Alaskan Arctic, to remove Biden's "mandate" on electric vehicles, and to attack wind power as a source of energy. Attendees at the meeting included executives from Chevron, Continental Resources, Exxon, Occidental Petroleum, EQT Corporation, and the American Petroleum Institute. The CEOs from Venture Global and Cheniere Energy, companies that would benefit directly from the repeal of the LNG regulation, also attended.[21]

Critics of this meeting charged that Trump was arranging a *quid pro quo* exchange of campaign money for public policy favors. The oil industry's response? According to campaign finance records, soon after Trump made his solicitation, Continental Resources donated $1 million to Make America Great, Inc., a super political action committee (PAC) supporting Trump's reelection effort (Harold Hamm, Executive Chairman of Continental Resources, helped to co-organize the event).[22] This was just the tip of the melting iceberg. Eventually, the oil and gas industry would spend hundreds of millions of dollars to elect Trump and other Republicans.[23] According to a recent report by Climate Power, Big Oil alone spent a total $450 million to win "influence" with Donald Trump and Republicans throughout the 2024 election cycle and 118th Congress. This funding included $96 million in direct donations to support Trump's presidential campaign and "super PACs" and $243 million on lobbying. Some $80 million was spent on advertising to support Trump, the Republican Party, and their anti-environmental policies.[24] In all, the oil and gas industry provided some

$151 million in what is called "outside spending" to PACs during the election period.[25] The private oil giant Koch Industries and their political machinery were the top oil and gas spender in the 2024 election; 44 current Trump administration officials come from these same Koch-backed groups.[26]

Those figures only tell part of the story. Individual oil barons lavished millions of dollars of their own money on the Trump campaign. This included the likes of Kelcy Warren (CEO of Energy Transfer), Timothy Dunn (CEO of the oil firm CrownQuest), and Harold Hamm (Continental Resources).[27] Timothy Dunn, who contributed $5 million through his company to a Trump super PAC, helped to start and fund the AFPI, a Right-wing think tank that has helped to shape the anti-climate change policy agenda for the Trump administration.[iii] Furthermore, according to the Brennan Center, record levels of "dark money" made the 2024 federal election cycle, "one of the most secretive since the Supreme Court's *Citizens United* decision in 2010." Dark money groups poured more than $1.9 billion into the 2024 election cycle, nearly double the prior record of $1 billion donated in 2020.[28] Dark money is especially insidious because it permits billionaires and corporate polluters to anonymously inject money into political activities and issue campaigns not "directly" related to an election. And they are not legally required to reveal their donors.[29]

Since the 2024 election, the PIC continues to funnel money to Trump-related organizations. According to the US Federal Election Commission, oil and gas interests alone donated over $19 million to Trump's inauguration fund, with Chevron being the largest contributor.[30] Meanwhile, Trump's main super PAC has received millions more, including $25 million from Energy Transfer Partners and its CEO Kelcy Warren.[31] It is worth noting here that on the first day of his second term, Trump rescinded President Biden's executive order blocking the permit for Energy Transfer's controversial Keystone XL pipeline despite their history as an ecologically bad actor. Energy Transfer has a long list of enforcement actions

---

[iii] For more information on Timothy Dunn, go to the Climate Criminals website at https://www.climatecriminals.org/timothy-dunn.

against it and accepted "criminal responsibility" for dozens of charges filed by the state of Pennsylvania over the contamination of water supplies.[32]

THE FOXES ARE NOW IN CHARGE OF THE HENHOUSE: CORPORATE POLLUTERS CAPTURE THE STATE

Trump is drawing heavily upon the PIC infrastructure to make key appointments to his administration and is elevating a slew of corporate polluters to positions of power within the federal government. The hegemony of the PIC in the United States is now on full display. According to Public Citizen, some 111 people deemed "fossil fuel insiders and renewable energy opponents" now staff the Environmental Protection Agency (EPA), Department of Interior, Department of Energy (DOE), and five other major agencies or departments of the government responsible for energy, environmental, and climate policy.[33] The list includes the corporate lawyers and the staffers from PIC-related think tanks directly tied to Trump's dirty energy agenda. It also includes 43 people who were directly employed by the coal, oil, or gas industries. Twenty-nine other officials are from polluters whose business interests are tied up with fossil fuels, such as chemicals, automaking, mining, and utility companies.

Under Trump, the corporate foxes allied with the oil and gas industry are now in charge of the government henhouse. As described by Public Citizen and the Revolving Door Project below,[34] these figures include:

1. Lee Zeldin, EPA Administrator: As a former Republican Congressman from New York, Zeldin had a track record of anti-environmental votes. Since heading up the EPA, Zeldin had some 3,700 EPA staff were terminated, crippling the agency's ability to fulfill its mission. Zeldin also terminated EPA's EJ, DEI arms, and scientific research office. On March 25, 2025, Zeldin announced a rollback of 31 key regulations originally designed to protect the environment, human health, and stem climate change. Zeldin stated, "Today is the greatest day of deregulation our nation has ever seen. We are driving a

dagger straight into the heart of the climate change religion to ... unleash American energy ... and more."[35]

2. David Fotouhi, the Deputy Administrator at the EPA: Fotouhi is a former lawyer at Gibson Dunn, a corporate law firm that has represented numerous oil and gas clients, including the American Petroleum Institute, Energy Transfer, Enbridge, and ConocoPhillips. There, he focused on securing environmental regulatory rollbacks and defending his corporate clients accused of violating environmental laws.

3. Chris Wright, DOE Secretary: Wright is the former CEO of the gas fracking company Liberty Energy. Several Liberty Energy personnel have been brought in by Wright to work at DOE. Before joining the Trump administration, Liberty Energy and its subsidiaries were regularly cited for workplace safety and environmental violations. He is a leader in the administration's attack on renewable energy and climate science.

4. Doug Burgum, Secretary of the Interior: A long-time friend of the oil industry, Burgum signed four bills as governor of North Dakota, increasing penalties against the Indigenous and environmental protesters of the Dakota Access Pipeline. Burgum now chairs Trump's National Energy Dominance Council, a multi-agency coordination group focused on speeding up the development of fossil fuel projects. Burgum also signed a series of secretarial orders intended to open publicly owned lands and waters across America to the fossil fuel and mining industries, and to roll back national monument designations for some of America's most pristine landscapes.

5. Brooke Rollins, US Department of Agriculture (USDA) Secretary: Under his leadership, the USDA, which manages more than 190 million acres of public lands via the US Forest Service, has spent the last six months scrubbing all mentions of the climate crisis from its website, expanding timber production, and other rollbacks. Rollins was part of the AFPI and the Texas Public Policy Foundation (TPPF), a project of Tim

Dunn, the former CEO of Texas oil company CrownQuest Operating, which he sold to Occidental Petroleum. Rollin's husband, Mark Rollins, is the president of both Hillwood Energy (a drilling company) and HKN Energy. TPPF's funders have included the Koch Industries, ExxonMobil, State Farm Insurance and R.J. Reynolds.

The list goes on and on.

TRUMP'S ATTACK ON THE ENVIRONMENT: PRIVILEGING POLLUTERS OVER PEOPLE AND THE PLANET

Since coming back into office, President Trump has wasted no time in launching a breathtaking assault on the planet, overhauling government agencies, axing climate-related programs, and gutting environmental rules. On his first day in office, Trump falsely declared a "national energy emergency" (EO4156), making the absurd claim that the Biden administration's focus on wind and solar power had created an energy crisis. He then signed a dizzying array of executive actions aimed at dramatically expanding fossil fuel production, including drilling in the pristine Arctic National Wildlife Refuge (EO14154). He also eliminated Biden's climate and clean energy policies, including rules intended to make vehicles more fuel-efficient and less polluting. He also issued a presidential memorandum halting approvals, permits, leases, and loans for both offshore and onshore wind projects.[36] He eliminated a climate jobs training program and scrubbed mentions of climate change from some federal agency websites. Trump then used the myth of an "energy crisis" to promote more coal production as a solution, setting up the National Energy Dominance Council to carry out this agenda. Eleven days later – on January 31, 2025 – Trump issued an executive order requiring federal agencies to eliminate 10 existing regulations for each new one implemented (EO14192).

Since then, the administration has taken one step after another to implement a neoliberal agenda committed to: (1) the privatization of federal resources and selling off public lands to the fossil fuel industry and mining interests; (2) the weakening and elimination of rules and regulations designed to protect the environment and promote EJ; (3) reducing the enforcement of key environmental laws, including the budgets and staff of key environmental agencies; and (4) the elimination of programs and policies that support renewable energy and clean production technologies. In fact, the administration has continually issued illegal stop-work orders for some offshore wind projects that were already under construction.[37]

During his first 100 days, Trump also had the Republican-dominated Congress pass the One Big Beautiful Bill Act (OBBBA), widely acknowledged as one of the most regressive and anti-environmental pieces of legislation ever adopted by the federal government. The Act provided massive giveaways to the fossil fuel industry, which, in part, were paid for by devastating cuts to climate change projects, EJ programs, Supplemental Nutrition Assistance Program (SNAP), Medicaid, and clean energy initiatives. At the time of the Act's passage, Mike Sommers, president of the American Petroleum Institute, said the bill "includes almost all of our priorities."[38]

In total, OBBBBA opened 200 million acres of federal land for fossil fuel and mining industry development, while slashing royalty payments and other fees. The law also eliminates processes for public comment on proposed projects. A recent report by Oil Change International finds that the OBBBA grants tens of billions of dollars in new subsidies to the oil and gas industry over the next decade. Prior to OBBBA passage, the administration had previously committed nearly $40 billion in new federal subsidies for oil, gas, and coal over the coming decade. The OBBBA adds another $30.8 billion *a year* in taxpayer dollars to these preexisting subsidies. As a result, the US government will provide a total of $34.8 billion annually in subsidies directly to the fossil fuel industry.[39]

Climate Change

Perhaps some of the more appalling actions of the administration have been around climate change. On the first day of 2.0, Trump issued EO14162, withdrawing the United States from the Paris Agreement, a treaty adopted by some 196 parties in 2015 that outlines plans for combating climate change and adapting to its impacts (the Order took effect on January 27, 2026). Then on

January 7, 2026, Trump signed a subsequent Memorandum pulling the United States out of the UN Framework Convention on Climate Change (UNFCCC). The convention was ratified in a 92-0 Senate vote in 1992 and provides the bedrock structure through which the United States and other countries negotiate limits on greenhouse gas emissions outlined in the 2015 Paris Agreement. Every nation in the world is party to the UNFCCC now except the United States. Trump's memorandum also withdraws the United States from over 60 other treaties and organizations, including the top United Nations scientific body, the Intergovernmental Panel on Climate Change. It also includes the Green Climate Fund, an international organization that finances climate mitigation efforts in the Global South. The results of this action will eventually prove devastating to the climate. The United States is now poised to be the first country to ever withdraw from the UNFCCC and become the only nation in the world not party to the main international agreement aimed at addressing the climate crisis. As stated by the *New York Times*, this was a "finger in the eye of the billions of people, including Americans, suffering [the]... dangerous and cost effects of a warming planet."[40]

These actions were not unexpected. Since coming into office, Trump has continuously sought to publicly undermine the widely accepted science around climate change. The administration even recruited notorious climate skeptics to form a "Climate Working Group." They produced a 2025 DOE report titled "A Critical Review of Impacts of Greenhouse Gas Emissions on the U.S. Climate," that derided what it termed "exaggerated projects of future warming." The authors included Stephen Koonin, a former chief scientist at the oil company BP.[41] Derided by actual climate change experts as full of misinformation, the DOE uses the report to justify overturning a key legal finding that forms the basis of virtually all US climate regulations – the 2009 Endangerment Finding.[42] On January 30, 2026, the US federal judge William G. Young ruled that the Climate Working Group was formed unlawfully, and that its secretive operation to challenge climate science was illegal.[43]

The Endangerment Finding was established under the Clean Air Act and concludes that greenhouse gas (GHG) emissions threaten the public's health and welfare, therefore enabling the government to regulate them. It's the basis of virtually all climate regulations in the United States. More specifically, it provides both a scientific and legal rationale for the government to regulate GHGs under the Clean Air Act. EPA Administrator Lee Zeldin is attempting to overturn the Endangerment Finding, effectively removing the basis for most climate regulations. The consequences of this action could prove devastating.[44] As stated by the American Lung Association, "... if the Endangerment Finding is undermined, the health and future of millions of Americans will be put at risk."[45] The Trump administration has already granted Clean Air Act exemptions to dozens of fossil fuel-burning power plants, delaying their need to reduce emissions of mercury and other air toxins that endanger public health.[46]

Environmental Injustice

In the United States, communities that lack *control capacity* over political-economic power structures are typically made up of racial and ethnic minorities, as well as lower-income segments of the white working class. However, it is typically America's undocumented immigrants, Chicano farmers, Indigenous peoples, and residents of low-income communities of color who are *selectively victimized* to the greatest extent by environmental health abuses. As part of the country's *subaltern* experiencing multiple forms of political domination, economic exploitation, and cultural oppression, the environment for them is effectively a life-and-death issue. The resulting environmental injustices take the form of noxious industrial pollutants and hazardous waste sites being situated in poor African-American communities in the rural South, or undocumented Mexican workers laboring in the pesticide-soaked agricultural fields of California, Texas, and Florida.[47] In short, the concentration of environmental and health hazards among the subaltern is creating ecological sacrifice zones – areas where it is simply dangerous to breathe the air or take a drink of water.[48] As such, ecological sacrifice zones serve as locations where capital can ignore compliance with environmental regulations.

Trump is now actively gutting federal EJ policies and programs meant to serve these communities. He has revoked all existing

EJ-related orders, including President Clinton's Executive Order on EJ, which, for more than 30 years, required federal agencies to consider how their decisions would address the disproportionate environmental burdens based on race and class. He has completely shuttered the EPA's EJ arm and closed all 10 of the EPA's regional EJ offices. He has also rescinded Biden's executive orders to address environmental injustice, laid off hundreds of EJ-related federal workers, and amputated the Justice40 initiative, which dedicated 40 percent of the benefits from federal investments in housing and clean energy to EJ communities. He also attempted to cancel almost every single one of the EPA's 800 grants to address pollution in EJ communities, as well as $3 billion in funding for some 350 Environmental and CJ Grant programs.[49] Trump 2.0 has also overseen the removal of multiple online climate and EJ datasets and webtools, including both the Council on Environmental Quality's Climate and EJ Screening Tool and EPA's EJScreen, an interactive environmental justice mapping tool that allowed the public to analyze the impact of specific pollutants in local communities.[50]

The results of Trump's attack on EJ programs and policies will no doubt prove to be devastating to the health and well-being of Black, Brown, Asian-American, and Indigenous communities for years to come. In the United States, the weight of the ecological burden upon a community is dependent upon the balance of power between capital, the state, and social movements responding to the demands of the people for a clean environment. Trump has greatly shifted power now toward corporate polluters. Following the path of least political resistance will mean that corporate polluters and government agencies will increasingly target the most marginalized communities in society for the siting of ecologically hazardous industrial facilities, toxic waste sites, and destructive forms of natural resource extraction and energy development. The less political power a community of people possesses; the fewer resources (time, money, education) they have to defend themselves from potential threats. The Union of Concerned Scientists has already released an interactive map, "Dirty Air, Dirty Deeds," which details how President Trump's legally dubious Clean Air Act exemptions for polluting facilities will increase cancer risks in communities already overburdened by pollution, climate, health, and social stressors nationwide.[51]

Toxic Chemicals and Pollution

Trump has also moved swiftly to eliminate many other critical environmental and public health policies. In the area of chemicals policy, the result of these actions will be to expose the American people to ever more dangerous levels of pollutants and toxic chemicals – to "Make America Poisoned Again"[52] and make a mockery of his pledge to "Make America Healthy Again." Trump offered two-year exemptions to Clean Air Act pollution standards for over a third of all domestic coal plants, chemical manufacturers, coke ovens, commercial sterilizers, and highly toxic facilities. The administration also no longer estimates the monetary value of lives saved from two of the deadliest air pollutants – fine particulate matter (PM2.5) and ozone. That means that the EPA will only count costs to business when considering new regulations, despite causing over tens of thousands of premature deaths every year.[53] This is an astounding transformation of EPA policy in favor of industry.

The administration has also narrowed the definition of waterways protected under the Clean Water Act and announced plans to weaken standards for the disposal of toxic heavy metals (like arsenic, lead, and mercury) from coal plants. The EPA is now moving to rescind various federal regulations on per- and polyfluoroalkyl substances (PFAS), a family of highly persistent "forever chemicals" linked to cancer and a host of developmental issues. Furthermore, the agency is moving to weaken rules for containing hazardous chemical risks to the public under the Toxic Substances Control Act (TSCA).[iv]

Finally, Trump is also proposing a series of very harmful changes to the EPA's risk evaluation for formaldehyde, a widespread and highly toxic carcinogen, under the Toxic Substances Control Act (TSCA). According to the EPA, formaldehyde is responsible for greater cancer risks than any other toxic air pollutant nationwide. Yet the Agency has proposed deleting almost all mention of cancer from the formaldehyde risk evaluation. The administration is additionally developing plans to weaken or eliminate environmental safeguards that will result in the increased emissions of at least 13-cancer-causing pollutants. As stated by a recent Center for

[iv] For a concise summary, see Dharna Noor and Milman (2026).[54]

American Progress report, "canceling these life-saving pollution limits would enhance polluters' profits at a strikingly high cost to Americans ... by causing roughly 200,000 early deaths across the United States in the next 25 years."[55]

TOWARD A JUST AND SUSTAINABLE FUTURE

There are many other areas where the Trump administration is assaulting the environment. In January of 2026, Trump's National Oceanic and Atmospheric Administration (NOAA) finalized a new rule allowing companies to apply for permits to engage in the deep mining of the ocean floor. Studies show that the mining of the seabed for minerals and other resources would be devastating to the ecosystems of the ocean.[56] The Trump administration has also introduced new plans to roll back provisions of the Endangered Species Act and to dismantle other critical wildlife protections.[57] To advance the construction of new data centers beneficial to the high-tech industry, the administration has also opened up a deregulatory floodgate for clean water regulations and fast-tracking approval of new hazardous chemicals (including those known as "forever chemicals" that never break down in the environment, and are particularly dangerous to human health).[58] And the list goes on and on.

For those of us engaged in the struggle for environmental protection and CJ, this new reality is demoralizing. However, we must remember that the contradictions created by Trump's energy, environmental, and economic policies are numerous and likely to reveal themselves in short order. In fact, Trump's political base is already beginning to fracture, and his popularity is collapsing.[59] Meanwhile, the resistance to Trumpism continues to grow. New coalitions of EJ advocates, labor, climate change, and environmental activists are coming together to offer more comprehensive approaches to problem-solving the ecological crisis. These approaches include the adoption of the precautionary approach over risk management of toxic chemicals, pollution prevention over pollution control strategies, a renewable energy economy over a fossil fuel economy, a "just transition" and a "superfund" for workers displaced out of polluting industries, environmental regulations, and a Green New Deal that offers jobs to disadvantaged workers and marginalized communities. These new coalitions are now engaged in the struggle for a more transformative environmental politics and a restoration of American democracy. Important victories are being won all over the country at the state and local level, and the momentum of the movement is growing. Rather than retreating into despair, we must see Trumpism as an opportunity to organize and mobilize our forces, and to create a powerful vision of a just and sustainable future– one that will inspire all of us to take up the banner to build a new society committed to social and environmental justice for all Americans.

NOTES

1. Inglehart, R. F., & Norris, P. (2016). *Trump, Brexit, and the rise of populism: Economic have-nots and cultural backlash* [Faculty Research Working Papers Series RWP16-026, pp. 1–59]. Harvard University.

2. Levitsky, S., & Ziblatt, D. (2018). *How democracies die*. Broadway Books.

3. Bruff, I., & Tansel, C. B. (2019). Authoritarian neoliberalism: Trajectories of knowledge production and praxis. *Globalizations*, *16*(3), 233–244. https://doi.org/10.1080/14747731.2018.1502497.

4. United Nations General Assembly. (2024, September 18). General Assembly overwhelmingly adopts historic text demanding Israel end its unlawful presence, policies in Occupied Palestinian Territory within one year. https://press.un.org/en/2024/ga12626.doc.htm.

5. Michael, T. (2026, January 9). *In ICE's own words, it's "wartime" in America*. The New Republic. https://newrepublic.com/post/205122/ice-recruitment-wartime-america-renee-good.

6. Faber, D. (2024). Trump's election victory, the climate crisis, and the working class: What does this mean for the future? *Capitalism, Nature, Socialism*, *35*(4), 1–18.

7. Standing, G. (2016). *The precariat: The new dangerous class*. Bloomsbury.

8. Faber, D. (2008). *Capitalizing on environmental injustice: The polluter-industrial complex in the age of globalization*. Rowman & Littlefield.

9. Brulle, R. J., Hall, G., Loy, L., & Schell-Smith, K. (2021). Obstructing action: Foundation funding and US climate change counter-movement

organizations. *Climatic Change*, *166*(17), 2–7. https://doooi.org/10.1007/s10584-021-03117-w; Brulle, R. J. (2022). Advocating inaction: A historical analysis of the global climate coalition. *Environmental Politics*, *32*(2), 185–206. https://doi.org/10.1080/09644016.2022.2058815.

10. Brulle, R. J., Hall, G., Loy, L., & Schell-Smith, K. (2021). Obstructing action: Foundation funding and US climate change counter-movement organizations. *Climatic Change*, *166*(17), 2–7. https://doi.org/10.1007/s10584-021-03117-w.

11. Faber, D. (2008). *Capitalizing on environmental injustice: The polluter-industrial complex in the age of globalization*. Rowman & Littlefield.

12. Oreskes, N., & Conway, E. M. (2012). *Merchants of doubt: How a handful of scientists obscured the truth on issues from tobacco smoke to global warming*. Bloomsbury.

13. Faber, D., Vestergaard, K., Schlegel, N., & Spector, C. (2022). *Voter suppression, climate justice, and the polluter-industrial complex: How the corporate assault on American democracy and the climate are connected* (pp. 1–62). Global Center for Climate Justice.

14. Rosenthal, T. A. (2025). *Trump's polluter playground: 100+ Fossil fuel insiders & far-right ideologues prop up dirty energy, plunder public lands, and thwart wind & solar* (pp. 1–43). Revolving Door Project and Public Citizen.

15. Faber, D. (2023). American oil-igarchy: How the corporate assault on liberal democracy and the climate are connected. *Capitalism, Nature, Socialism*, *34*(3), 1–21.

16. Domhoff, G. W. (2022). *Who rules America? The corporate rich, White Nationalist Republicans, and inclusionary Democrats in the 2020s*. Routledge.

17. Moore, G., Sobieraj, S., Whit, J. A., Mayorova, O., & Beaulieu, D. (2002). Elite interlocks in three US sectors: Nonprofit, corporate, and government. *Social Science Quarterly*, *83*, 726–744.

18. Popovich, N., Albeck-Ripka L., & Pierre-Louis, K. (2021, January 20). The Trump administration rolled back more than 100 environmental rules: Here's the full list. *New York Times*. https://www.nytimes.com/interactive/2020/climate/trump-environment-rollbacks-list.html.

19. Lefebvre, B. (2024, May 8). *A little bold and gross: Oil industry writes executive orders for Trump to sign*. Politico. https://www.politico.com/news/2024/05/08/oil-industry-orders-trump-day-one-00156705.

20. Milman, O. (2025, May 1). Trump has launched more attacks on the environment in 100 days than his entire first term. *The Guardian*. https://www.theguardian.com/environment/2025/may/01/trump-air-climate-pollution-regulation-100-days.

21. Ed Pilkington, E. (2024, May 9). Trump promised to scrap climate laws if US oil bosses donated $1bn – report: Trump promised to 20 executives at Mar-a-Lago dinner to increase oil drilling and reverse pollution rules among other pitches. *The Guardian*. https://www.theguardian.com/us-news/article/2024/may/09/trump-oil-ceo-donation.

22. U.S. House of Representatives Press Release. (2024, September 10). *In new bicameral letters, democratics demand big oil executives comply with investigation into Trump's attempt to sell official actions for $1 billion*. House Committee on Oversight and Government Reform. https://oversightdemocrats.house.gov/news/press-releases/new-bicameral-letters-democrats-demand-big-oil-executives-comply-investigation.

23. Noor, D. (2025, January 23). Big oil spent $445m in last election cycle to influence Trump and Congress, report says. *The Guardian*. https://www.theguardian.com/us-news/2025/jan/23/big-oil-445m-trump-congress.

24. Climate Power. (2025). *Big oil spent $450 million to influence Trump and the 119th Congress* [Oil and Gas Influence Report PROG 2025-01-07 [DR]]. https://climatepower.us/research-polling/big-oil-spent-450-million-to-influence-trump-the-119th-congress/.

25. Kirk, M. (2025, January 3). *The fossil fuel industry spent $219 million to elect the new U.S. government*. Climate Connections. https://yaleclimateconnections.org/2025/01/the-fossil-fuel-industry-spent-219-million-to-elect-the-new-u-s-government/.

26. Whitehouse, S. (2018, June 28). *Trump is in the back pocket of billionaires*. U.S. Senate Office of Sheldon Whitehouse. https://www.whitehouse.senate.gov/op-eds/trump-is-in-the-back-pocket-of-billionaires/.

27. Milman, O. (2024, October 18). Trump gets record donations from big oil but far less than $1bn he wanted. *The Guardian*. https://www.theguardian.com/us-news/2024/oct/18/election-trump-oil-gas-fundraising.

28. Massoglia, A. (2025, May 7). *Dark money hit a record high of $1.9 billion in 2024 federal races*. Brennan Center for Justice. https://www.brennancenter.org/our-work/research-reports/dark-money-hit-record-high-19-billion-2024-federal-races#:~:text=Dark%20money%20groups%2C%20nonprofits%20and,of%20%241%20billion%20in%202020.

29. Kaufman, L. (2023, June 20). *Unmasking dark money: How fossil fuel interests can undermine clean energy progress*. Kleinman Center for Energy Policy. https://kleinmanenergy.upenn.edu/commentary/blog/unmasking-dark-money-how-fossil-fuel-interests-can-undermine-clean-energy-progress/.

30. Noor, D. (2025, July 10). Trump inaugural fund received $19m from fossil fuel industry, analysis shows. *The Guardian*. https://www.theguardian.com/us-news/2025/jul/10/trump-inaugural-fund-fossil-fuel-industry.

31. Bacskai, O. (2025, September 15). *Fossil fuel industry donors see major returns in Trump's policy*. Brennan Center. https://www.brennancenter.org/our-work/analysis-opinion/fossil-fuel-industry-donors-see-major-returns-trumps-policies.

32. Phillips, S. (2022, August 5). *Energy Transfer held criminally responsible for damage from Mariner East pipeline construction*. The Allegheny Front. https://www.alleghenyfront.org/energy-transfer-held-criminally-responsible-for-damage-from-mariner-east-pipeline-pennsylvania/.

33. Rosenthal, T. A., & Alan Zibel, A. (2025, October). *Trump's polluter playground: Fossil fuel insiders & ideologies prop up dirty energy & derail clean power*. Public Citizen and the Revolving Door Project. https://www.citizen.org/article/trumps-polluter-playground/.

34. Rosenthal, T.A., & Alan Zibel, A. (2025, October). *Trump's polluter playground: Fossil fuel insiders & ideologies prop up dirty energy & derail clean power*. Public Citizen and the Revolving Door Project. https://www.citizen.org/article/trumps-polluter-playground/.

35. EPA Press Office. (2025, March 12). *EPA launches biggest deregulatory action in U.S. history* (pp. 1–4). Environmental Protection Agency. https://www.epa.gov/newsreleases/epa-launches-biggest-deregulatory-action-us-history.

36. Trump, D. J. (2025, January 29). *Temporary withdrawal of all areas on the outer continental shelf from offshore wind leasing and*

review of the Federal government's leasing and permitting practices for wind projects [Presidential Memorandum, Federal Register Document No. 2025-01966]. https://www.federalregister.gov/documents/2025/01/29/2025-01966/temporary-withdrawal-of-all-areas-on-the-outer-continental-shelf-from-offshore-wind-leasing-and.

37. Tamborrino, K. (2025, September 4). *States, companies sue Trump administration over wind farm stop-work order*. Politico https://www.politico.com/news/2025/09/04/orsted-revolution-wind-trump-administration-00543607.

38. Hughes, A. (2025, September 8). *The energy sector has spend hundreds of millions of dollars on lobbying this year: Watchdogs say that's only half the story*. Inside Climate News. https://insideclimatenews.org/news/08092025/energy-sector-lobbying-spending/.

39. Rees, C., Koplow, D., Rosenbluth, A., & Stockman, L. (2025, September). *Paying for climate chaos: U.S. federal subsidies to fossil fuel production* (pp. 1–29). Oil Change International. https://oilchange.org/wp-content/uploads/2025/09/paying-for-climate-chaos.pdf.

40. Sengupta, S., & Friedman, L. (2026, January 8). Trump withdraws from 66 international organizations, says they 'no longer serve American interests'. *New York Times*. https://www.nytimes.com/2026/01/07/us/politics/trump-withdraw-un-organizations.html.

41. Christy, J., Curry, J., Koonin, S., McKitrick, R., & Spencer, R. (2025, July 23). *A critical review of impacts of greenhouse gas emissions on the U.S. climate* (pp. 1–140). The Climate Working Group, U.S. Department of Energy.

42. Milman, O., & Noor, D. (2025, September 2). Trump team's contentious climate report 'makes a mockery of science', experts say. *The Guardian*. https://www.theguardian.com/us-news/2025/sep/02/trump-administration-climate-report.

43. Varona, R. A. (2026, January 30). *DOE-created climate panel was unlawful, judge rules*. Law360. https://www.law360.com/articles/2436567/doe-created-climate-panel-was-unlawful-judge-rules.

44. Jenks, C., Kranz, E., & Dewey, S. (2025, August 12). *EPA's proposal to eliminate the endangerment finding and motor vehicle greenhouse gas regulations*. Environmental & Energy Law Program, Harvard Law School. https://eelp.law.harvard.edu/epas-proposal-to-eliminate-the-endangerment-finding-and-motor-vehicle-greenhouse-gas-regulations/.

45. ALA Editorial Staff. (2025, November 5). *Ignoring greenhouse gasses emissions endangers us all*. American Lung Association. https://www.lung.org/blog/greenhouse-gas-endangerment.

46. Walke, J., & Levin, A. (2025, May 1). *Trump proclamation exempts nation's dirtiest coal plants from Mercury & Air Toxics Standards*. Natural Resources Defense Council. https://www.nrdc.org/media/trump-proclamation-exempts-nations-dirtiest-coal-plants-mercury-air-toxics-standards-mats.

47. Bullard, R. D. (1994). *Dumping in Dixie: Race, class, and environmental quality*. Westview Press; Faber, D. (2020). Poisoning the world for profit. Petro-chemical capital and the global pesticide crisis. *Capitalism, Nature, Socialism*, *31*(4), 1–17. https://doi.org/10.1080/10455752.2020.1829794.

48. Lerner, S. (2010). *Sacrifice zones: The front lines of toxic chemical exposure in the United States*. MIT Press.

49. Beard, J., Jr, & DiFelice, M. (2025, September 24). *How Trump's attacks on environmental justice will cost lives*. Food and Water Watch. https://www.foodandwaterwatch.org/2025/09/24/trumps-attacks-on-environmental-justice/.

50. Ludwig, M. (2025, April 19). *EPA deletes pollution tracking tools as it offers exemptions to polluter*. Truthout. https://truthout.org/articles/epa-deletes-pollution-tracking-tools-as-it-offers-exemptions-to-polluters/.

51. UCS Bulletin. (2025, December 8). *Dirty air, dirty deeds: Trump administration shuts out public input, increases toxic air pollution*. Union of Concerned Scientists. https://www.ucs.org/resources/dirty-air-dirty-deeds.

52. Pollychroniou, C. J. (2025, November 18). *Trump's environmental policy is determined to 'Make America Poisoned Again.'* Truthout. https://truthout.org/articles/trumps-environmental-policy-is-determined-to-make-america-poisoned-again/?utm_source=Truthout&utm_campaign=bc6f98fb77-EMAIL_CAMPAIGN_2025_11_18_10_06&utm_medium=email&utm_term=0_bbb541a1db-bc6f98fb77-650131333.

53. Zhang, S. (2026, January 12). *EPA no longer considering lives saved in pollution rule, only cost to business*. Truthout. https://truthout.org/articles/epa-no-longer-considering-lives-saved-in-pollution-rules-only-cost-to-business/?utm_source=Truthout&utm_campaign=46bb7fc5ce-EMAIL_CAMPAIGN_2026_01_13_10_05&utm_medium=email&utm_term=0_bbb541a1db-46bb7fc5ce-650131333.

54. Dharna Noor, D., & Milman, O. (2026, January 30). How Trump's EPA rollbacks could harm our air and water – and worsen global heating. *The Guardian*. https://www.theguardian.com/environment/2026/jan/30/trump-epa-rollbacks-air-water-climate.

55. Kelly, C., Branks, L., & Rosenthal, J. (2025, September 15). *The Trump administration's attack on environmental protections will increase cancer-causing pollution*. Center for American Progress. https://www.americanprogress.org/article/the-trump-administrations-attack-on-environmental-protections-will-increase-cancer-causing-pollution/.

56. Mulkey, S. K. (2026, January 31). New U.S. rule aims to speed up mining of the Seafloor. *New York Times*. https://www.rsn.org/001/new-us-rule-aims-to-speed-up-mining-of-the-seafloor.html.

57. Canon, G. (2025, November 20). Trump officials reveal plan to roll back regulations in Endangered Species Act. *The Guardian*. https://www.theguardian.com/us-news/2025/nov/20/trump-endangered-species-act.

58. Taft, M. (2025, December 7). *The Trump administration's data center push could open the door for new forever chemicals*. Grist. https://grist.org/accountability/the-trump-administrations-data-center-push-could-open-the-door-for-new-forever-chemicals/.

59. Hartig, H., & Kiley, J. (2026, January 29). *Confidence in Trump dips, and fewer now say they support his policies and plans*. Pew Research Center. https://www.pewresearch.org/politics/2026/01/29/confidence-in-trump-dips-and-fewer-now-say-they-support-his-policies-and-plans/.

10

QUEER RAGE: THE FIGHT AGAINST THE TRUMP REGIME'S VIOLENT AGENDA TO ERASE TRANS AND QUEER PEOPLE

Baker A. Rogers

Georgia Southern University, USA

This volume considers the current political crisis caused by Trump's neo-fascist movement. The Trump regime has attacked, demonized, and discredited social science (and science more generally). Why? Because social scientists could be most effective in criticizing Make America Great Again violence and Trump's authoritarianism. Nevertheless, as this volume suggests, sociologists have a poor track record of holding powers accountable, often leaving this task to our more vulnerable colleagues in the humanities, or those with boots on the ground like social workers, social service providers, and activists. Critical social scientific analysis is usually siloed in academic journals (often behind paywalls) and books that most people never read.[i]

[i] Did you know about half of Americans did not read a single book last year?

As a Sociologist with a Master of Social Work degree, I believe my ethical duty requires that I stand up to Trump and his regime's brutal attacks on minoritized communities. As Desmond Tutu stated, "If you are neutral in situations of injustice, you have chosen the side of the oppressor."[1] My personal and professional ethics make me an activist by default. Many scholars with the knowledge to understand Trump's harmful impact might remain silent and scared, inactive, or just aloof. Elitism has also plagued academia, and we see many faculty and college administrators choosing complacency, apathy, or even capitulation in response to attacks on the academy and beyond.

To be perfectly clear, fear at this moment is understandable. But often fear leaves the most vulnerable people unprotected as they do the political work necessary to protect themselves. If you are trans or queer, or part of any targeted group in this country, you must first take care of yourself. Survival can be a powerful form of resistance. This chapter is not a diatribe against those simply trying to stay safe. But it is a diatribe against an elitist academy that too often bends to the will of bullies who now run this country.

This chapter focuses on the harm directed at queer and trans people in the USA. This violence and bigotry emanate from the revocation of rights, direct attacks in the media, and attempts to delegitimize gender and sexuality studies in education. It is impossible to examine all the harm Trump has caused queer and trans people in just one chapter. The general scope of damage and cruelty achieved by cuts to health care, education, and social services, as well as restricting abortion, due process, and other human rights, harms everyone, not just queer and trans people.

Yet, Trump 2.0 has carried out over 400[ii] direct attacks against trans and queer people. For an extensive (yet not comprehensive) list of these attacks, see the Appendix to this chapter. Trump has

---

[ii] For a full list and timeline of Trump's vicious attacks on queer and trans people, GLAAD has a great resource, the Trump Accountability Tracker, where they have a timeline of the 433 (as of December 26, 2025) attacks against lesbian, gay, bisexual, and transgender (LGBT) people he has made during both terms in office so far. https://glaad.org/trump-accountability-tracker/. At the rate Trump is going, this number will continue to rise substantially over the next three plus years.

tried to redefine sex and gender (in ways that ignore the biological reality that intersex and trans people exist), and changed policies and laws that irrevocably hurt queer and trans people. As many chapters in the book have discussed, Trump has employed "executive lawlessness" by using executive orders (EOs) and directing a willfully ignorant Republican Congress and a Trump-stacked Supreme Court to further restrict basic human rights.

Day one of Trump 2.0 featured powerful attacks on trans and queer people:

- *Order 14168,* "Defending Women from Gender Ideology Extremism and Restoring Biological Truth to the Federal Government," required the federal government to recognize only two immutable sexes: male and female.
- *Order 14148*, "Initial Rescissions of Harmful Executive Orders and Actions," revoking multiple Biden-era policies that addressed discrimination based on gender identity or sexual orientation.
- *Order 14151,* "Ending Radical and Wasteful Government Diversity, Equity, and Inclusion (DEI) Programs and Preferencing" ended DEI programs across the federal government, putting staff on immediate administrative leave and leading to the banning of any books and materials even tangentially related to race, gender, or lesbian, gay, bisexual, transgender, and queer (LGBTQ) subjects from federal agencies, as well as eliminating LGBTQ and human immunodeficiency virus (HIV) focused content and resources from the White House website and other key federal agency sites.

Writing this chapter and watching the chaos unfold daily, I know I cannot truly capture this moment in history briefly or easily. I go back and forth about what to write because the hellscape is so totally overwhelming. But, as I slog through the hundreds of atrocities directed at trans and queer people in the last year, I wonder why we have to say any of this at all? How deep is the hole in someone's head or heart that they are unaware or unmoved by the immense pain and trauma Trump has unleashed? Part of the resistance, however, is documenting and analyzing the present to adequately condemn, resist, and change it for the future.

THE IMPORTANCE OF SYMBOLIC VIOLENCE

On December 1, 2025, Trump initiated a new firestorm by withdrawing all funds for World AIDS Day, failing to recognize this global event for the first time since 1988. This symbolic violence clearly communicates the current regime's ability to ignore the humanity of queer people. But such governmental ignorance and abuse are not new.

In 1993, the *San Francisco Chronicle* published a photo taken by Eric Luse of the San Francisco Gay Men's Chorus. It depicted a large choral group standing in rows in an auditorium. While most individuals appear in dark clothing, a small number are wearing white. The people in white are the surviving members of the original Chorus.

All the men in black represent chorus members lost to Acquired Immunodeficiency Syndrome (AIDS) by 1993. *Only* seven members survived that long because the political agenda in the 1980s and 1990s did not take the AIDS crisis seriously. To many in the Gay Rights movement, the Reagan/Bush administrations did not see gay people as human.[2] For an illustration of this historical period, see *My Government Means to Kill Me,* by Rasheed Newson.

In January 2025, EO 14183 banned transgender people from military service, claiming "gender dysphoria" to be "inconsistent" with "troop readiness, lethality, cohesion, honesty, humility, uniformity, and integrity" – falsely linking trans identities to violence. A federal judge later called the EO "unsupported, dramatic and facially unfair exclusionary policy."[3] On December 9, 2025, the military asked the Fourth Circuit Court to let it disqualify applicants who are HIV-positive. They argued that HIV-positive service members pose significant financial and logistical burdens on the military.[4] These policies simultaneously demonize LGBT people as risky for military service and too violent to be trusted.

USING MURDER TO FALSELY JUSTIFY HATE

On August 27, 2025, a 23-year-old trans woman committed a mass shooting at a Catholic Church in Minneapolis. Based on this incident, the US Department of Justice (DOJ) considered restricting trans Americans' Second Amendment right to own firearms. Such a policy would require declaring trans people mentally "defective" (an argument also made to ban trans people from the military). Such diagnostic stigmatization has been officially and professionally discredited since 1973, when the American Psychological Association removed homosexuality as a "disorder" from the *Diagnostic and Statistical Manual of Mental Disorders*. To be clear about guns, out of almost 5,800 mass shootings since 2013, only *five* were confirmed trans shooters (less than 0.1% of mass shooters in the USA).[5]

Soon after this discussion, on September 10, Charlie Kirk, anti-queer conservative media personality and co-founder of Turning Point USA (TPUSA),[iii] was assassinated during a debate at Utah Valley University. Immediately following the assassination, on September 11, the *Wall Street Journal* published a leaked memo that *falsely* claimed the shell casings found near the scene of Kirk's murder were engraved with expressions of "transgender and anti-fascist ideology."[6] The next day, the DOJ removed a study from its website detailing that far-right extremists have killed more Americans than any other domestic terrorist group. As Nico Dialesandro of Uncloseted Media put it, "Trump has weaponized the assassination of Charlie Kirk to put an even bigger target on trans Americans."[7]

Charlie Kirk's assassination was also used to censure academics who oppose hate against queer and trans people. On September 15, Joshua Bregy, an assistant professor in the Department of Environmental Engineering and Earth Sciences, was one of three employees at Clemson University fired for social media posts critical of Kirk after he was killed.[iv] Bregy's post included some of Kirk's own words about gun violence in the USA. Faculty across the country have initiated dozens of lawsuits (from K–12 through colleges)

[iii] Until his death, Kirk served as the executive director of TPUSA, the organization also behind the professorwatchlist.org.

[iv] You can learn more about this ongoing case here: https://www.aclusc.org/cases/bregy-v-clemson/.

claiming they were fired for public comments about Kirk and his assassination. Just as Dolgon (Chapter 6 in this book) argues that anti-semitism has been weaponized by Trump to attack and silence university critics of Israel in specific (and white nationalism and imperialism in general), criticism of Kirk and TPUSA has helped operationalize the Trump administration's anti-trans and queer positions and policies.

CLASSIFYING TRANS AND QUEER PEOPLE AS TERRORISTS IN ORDER TO ELIMINATE US

If we've learned anything since September 11, 2001, it is that when we label a group as a terrorist threat, all bets are off. Anyone who is part of the dehumanized "terrorist" group – even people who simply "look like them" – is fair game for elimination. In *One Day, Everyone Will Have Always Been Against This*, Omar El Akkad[8] explains:

> *One of the most damaging, longest-lasting consequences of the War on Terror years is an utter obliteration of the obvious moral case for nonviolence. The argument that violence in any form debases us and marks the instant failure of all involved is much more difficult to make when the state regularly engages in or approves of wholesale violence against civilians and combatants alike. Instead, the case for nonviolence becomes, in the ugliest way, pragmatic: the state wants violence, because in that playing field it maintains every advantage, from bigger guns to total immunity to the privilege of perpetual victimhood.*

As Akkad, an Egyptian-American author and journalist, explained, the USA has used the term "terrorism" almost exclusively for Brown people to justify violence against them. To me, Trump's policies demonstrate what Akkad calls the "diaphanousness" definition or transparent nature of terrorism. Following 9-11, the term "domestic terrorist" appeared more regularly in policy discussions and in the media, but primarily applied to Brown people.

In September 2025, the Trump regime began labeling trans people as "terrorists," too.[9] Since then, the regime has deployed the term more freely, raising the likelihood of government violence against trans and queer people, as demonstrated in research by Michael Cobb.[10] At a September 15 press conference, Brian Glenn, a far-right content creator, asked Trump to remove Pride flags from public spaces. Glenn labeled these symbols as "transtifa" flags and explained that labeling trans people as domestic terrorists would make removing Pride flags much easier. Trump responded that he had no problem removing all Pride flags from Washington, D.C. streets.[11]

Three days later, on September 18, two national security officials reported that the Federal Bureau of Investigation (FBI) was considering classifying trans people as a subcategory within its new "domestic extremism" threat model – a model originally used to classify now pardoned January 6 rioters.[12] In fact, the FBI and Department of Homeland Security (DHS) term "domestic violent extremism" as applied to trans people recasts social and political activism, both by limiting trans people's constitutional protections of free speech, expression, and assembly, and also spreading paranoia and fear, further legitimizing violence against trans activists.

Discussing his own early adulthood, Akkad (p. 138) explained:

> *There has been no greater totem of fear in the Western World than "the terrorist." So overwhelming is this construction that not only has it justified – without question or consequence – one of the largest state-sponsored killing sprees in modern history [Gaza], but has imposed onto entire swaths of people a binary experience.*

On September 22, White House Press Secretary, Karoline Leavitt, said the government was investigating why trans people are turning to "domestic terrorism." The claim of domestic terrorism is demonstrably false, but evidence does show that trans people are *far* more likely to be *victims* of crime than perpetrators.[13] But using the term "terrorist" accomplishes Trump's ideological effort to criminalize trans people. Terrorists are rhetorically subhuman, justifying exclusion and even elimination from society. Based on the regime's constant practice of "newspeak" (George Orwell's *1984* term for fake news), trans people do not even exist.

Very quickly, we may be approaching the "last stages of genocide" for trans and queer people in the USA. The 10 Stage Model of Genocide (developed by Gregory Stanton, professor and founder of *Genocide Watch*) warns about the dangers of demonization and othering. *Stage 7* includes a national leader and plans to target groups with language that dehumanizes them. According to *Operation Broken Silence*,[14] those in power "often use euphemisms to cloak their intentions, such as referring to their goals as ... 'counter-terrorism.'" But this stage entails operationalizing such demonization – using the term "terrorist" – to mobilize arms and publics against intended targets. "They build armies, buy weapons, and train their troops and militias." This process can be seen on the US Immigration and Custom's Enforcement (ICE) own home screen, where Trump is recruiting a new army and mobilizing the National Guard to threaten cities around the country.

These actions produce more fear, which Akkad (p. 131) calls a

> *precondition of existence within a system whose currency of justification is fear .... The exchange rate is very real .... It isn't the rationality or evidence of the fear that matters, but rather its purchasing power. He concludes that fear "buys everything .... It moves armies, obliterates thousands."*

Dialesandro writes that starting in August, the Trump regime began testing out a new phrase to intensify people's fear of trans people, reporting that Trump said that Democrats want "transgender for everybody." He goes on to say that Trump has used the phrase "so many times that we couldn't include every reference," just in the last 100 days. Trump's administration continues to use similar phrases and false claims to demean queer and trans people across all positions and places of power. It is a rhetorical strategy intended to induce anger and fear.

As a harrowing comparison, the National Center for LGBTQ Rights[v] explains:

> *At the turn of the 20th century, despite the German Criminal Code banning homosexuality, Germany had a thriving LGBTQ community. In Berlin alone, there were over one hundred queer bars, cafes, clubs, and organizations. Queer publications were plentiful and LGBTQ activists fought for a more equitable society.*
>
> *However, as the Nazis rose to power, hostility towards LGBTQ people – especially gay men – increased, as they considered homosexuals to be a detriment to their goals of an 'Aryan' race. While lesbians were also persecuted, queer men were targeted in greater numbers as men held more positions of power at the time.*
>
> *Throughout the Holocaust, it's estimated that upwards of 15,000 gay men were sent to concentration camps. Inside the camps, they were forced to wear a pink inverted triangle on their uniforms – clearly marking them as LGBTQ. The symbol indicated to everyone in the prison that the wearer was "bottom tier" – and often the wearers would receive harsher treatment. Sadly, 60% of gay men sent to concentration camps were killed.*

FASCISM AND END-STAGE CAPITALISM

Do not let the recent electoral victories, the release of some of the Epstein files, and the Supreme Court's decision *not* to rehear marriage equality (but it will likely be back in 2026) fool you. While they do threaten the strength of Trump's authoritarian regime, the stages of genocide predict these "political processes, such as peace accords that threaten the dominance of the ruling group through elections or prosecution IN THE COURTS for corruption, may

[v] https://www.nclrights.org/the-significance-of-the-pink-triangle/

actually trigger genocide." Furthermore, small wins have been shown to appease the base and *reduce* pushbacks against fascism. These wins may only benefit a small, and generally less vulnerable, group of oppressed people, leaving the most marginalized further harmed and forgotten.

Truly proactive strategies and tactics against the attempted erasure of marginalized groups might include congressional challenges such as arms restrictions, defunding ICE, and other limitations on the government's use of force, but such actions may no longer be possible. On November 20, six Congressional Democrats, military veterans, reminded current soldiers not to follow unlawful orders. Trump responded with death threats. He wrote that the members of Congress who released this statement should be arrested for "seditious behavior ... punishable by death."[15] Department of Defense (DOD) Secretary Pete Hegseth is currently pursuing charges, but on February 12, 2026, District Judge Richard J. Leon barred Hegseth from enforcing a censure against Kelly. Hegseth has vowed to pursue them.[16]

> *Many of us like to ask ourselves, "What would I do if I was alive during slavery? Or the Jim Crow South? Or apartheid? What would I do if my country was committing genocide?"*
>
> *The answer is, you're doing it. Right now.*
>
> – *Aaron Bushnell*[17]

This historical moment *is* a decisive turning point for our country and the world. Future generations will study this period and examine where people stood when faced with fascism, evil, death, and destruction. In my opinion, our best hope lies in strategies of mutual aid that return to the basic principles of the dignity and worth of all people. Our nonprofits can't save us – most have been defunded or rendered ineffective (or worse, co-opted by the regime). Charity won't work – the oppression is far too widespread (as we saw clearly when Trump let Supplemental Nutrition Assistance Program (SNAP) benefits lapse for the first time since they were enacted in 1964). Billionaires control most resources. Only by dismantling that domination can the rest of us survive. Almost two centuries ago, Marx and Engels declared that working people had "nothing to lose but their chains. They have a world to win."[18] Marx could never have imagined the wealth disparities today. Iequality.org reports:

> *The bottom half of households in America – 66 million of them – had $4.1 trillion all together at the end of 2024. The 905 billionaires in the U.S. hold a combined $7.8 trillion in wealth, according to Forbes data from September 29, 2025. This alarming narrowing of wealth has given those at the very top political influence and power that undermines our democracy.*[vi]

End-stage capitalism is the most accurate characterization of the current economic and social reality. It describes the advanced phase of capitalism, characterized by globalization, corporate domination, widespread commodification, the dismantling of liberal democracies, and the rise of totalitarian regimes. During end-stage capitalism, wealth inequality expands, environmental destruction intensifies, and every aspect of life is commoditized for private profits. This stage also demands increased authoritarianism to protect the wealthy few from the increasingly demonized and outcast masses. Targeting trans people also increases as an attendant ideological arm of such fascist mobilization.

A REFLECTIVE NOTE ON QUEER RAGE AND RESISTANCE

In my research over the past decade, I have moved away from studying *the hate directed toward queer people* to the joy experienced *by* queer people – "Queer Joy."[19] My search for *queer joy* brought *me* more joy than I knew I was capable of. It led me to open a queer bookstore in South Carolina (the only one in the state, no surprise). It led me to stake out a literal queer space in the place I call home. The store and the community we have created brought me, and many other people across the city, the state, and the world, a place to experience and create queer joy. I strongly believe that

---

[vi] https://inequality.org/article/billionaire-wealth-concentration-is-even-worse-than-you-imagine/

joy is a form of rebellion, especially for those of us whose joy is being stolen. Finding spaces and times for queer joy is vital for surviving this hate.

At the same time, I must turn my focus back to the hate directed toward queer people and "queer rage" because this is not a time to celebrate what is happening in this country. All parts of this corrupt system work together and must be stopped together. We do not have time or space to find contentment in minor victories. While celebrating our wins is an important part of the process, we *must* stay focused on the prize – a different kind of society that doesn't leave a few with *FAR* more than most, and doesn't leave large communities of its citizens fearing for their lives.

It is time for *queer rage*. Discussing queer rage in the context of college campuses, Freeman and Bailey[20] use the Stonewall Riots and ACT UP as examples of the power and importance of rage. Especially on college campuses, civility and "professionalism" are used to quiet anger, but Freemen and Baily show how "anger from the margins is a necessary corrective to power abuses." They explain:

> *In the face of pressures to put others at ease, it is more essential than ever to reclaim the integrity and validity of queer rage .... There is something to be learned from angry queer and trans folks about harnessing shame and grief in ways that are authentic as well as politically and pedagogically useful.*

We, along with so many others (many discussed in more detail in this volume), have been dehumanized and classified as a terrorist threat.[21] I wear my upside-down pink triangle proudly tattooed on my right forearm. It is both ironic and declaratory – no one else will brand me! I am telling the oppressors who I am; my people will not go quietly. This is part of my queer rage.

Furthermore, we need this rage to be felt by all, not only trans and queer people. We cannot do this alone; no minoritized community can. We need cis people and straight people to feel this rage, too. The key to this is human empathy and decency. We need you to rage against Trump and this corrupt system, and most importantly, what is being done to your fellow humans.

Akkad (p. 148) claims that an unbridgeable chasm has developed where one side of humanity fears mostly instability and disorder and hopes mostly for a return to normalcy. The other side, he continues, "having witnessed the horror, is simply unable to continue as before ... any society whose functioning demands ignoring carnage on this scale for the sake of artificial normalcy is by definition sociopathic." He concludes that raging against this normalcy may be portrayed as extremism, but in fact it is the very definition of sanity – what is abnormal is to accept it.

Things do seem to be bad and getting worse daily. Our only hope is to condemn, resist, and confront an oppressive system if we are to stall the current march toward fascism and increasing body counts as described in the Introduction to this collection. It is a time for *rage*! It is time for us to choose what side of history we want to be on and act!

Is there any good news? We have seen some minor victories for queer and trans rights in the USA toward the end of 2025, and predictions that Democrats will do well in the November 2026 midterm elections may also be helpful. (Although many argue Democrats are part of the problem, not the solution, they comprise a segment of people seeking normalcy, not an end to the madness.) The one positive dynamic that brings me hope is that it appears people are finally starting to collaborate and mobilize to resist Trump. People are fighting back against the system by boycotting. We are seeing the beginnings of a resistance that has the potential to bring about real social change if we keep our momentum.

So many of the problems I've described can seem overwhelming, and our actions small in comparison. But the people of Minnesota have proven otherwise. So, while it feels like small efforts are futile, they are not! We all must continue chipping away at our small areas of resistance to bring down a much larger, corrupt system set to destroy us. Do whatever you can do. If you are privileged and still relatively safe today, use that power! If you are not, do what you can to contribute to the efforts safely. If you need some ideas on how to fight back, check out 198 methods of nonviolent action from Dr Gene Sharp's *The Politics of Nonviolent Action*.[vii]

[vii] https://www.aeinstein.org/198-methods-of-nonviolent-action

Like Akkad, we should all return to the words of queer Palestinian poet, Rasha Abdulhadi. They remind us how important active resistance at any and every level can be. They write, "Wherever you are, whatever sand you can throw on the gears of genocide, do it now. If it's a handful, throw it. If it's a fingernail full, scrape it out and throw. Get in the way however you can."[22] Show up to school boards and town councils, to ICE detention centers, and No Kings rallies in the streets. The biggest threat to all vulnerable people is apathy. The growth and infestation of fascism requires apathy to fester as it mobilizes ideological and military forces. But all forms of resistance can derail Trump's regime and foretell a different future. The system intends to dehumanize us and wear us down to a point that we can't, or don't, resist. But as Ruth Bader Ginsburg said, "When injustice becomes law, resistance becomes duty."[23] It is my duty, and yours, to defy apathy and combat the oppression of all people. Like many great social justice warriors before us have echoed, "Nobody's free until we are all free." Right now, it may be hard to see a future at all. But if we want a future for ourselves, our children, and future generations, we have to tap into our queer rage and throw sand whenever and wherever we can.

APPENDIX: TRUMP 2.0 VIOLENCE TOWARD TRANS AND QUEER PEOPLE ... SO FAR[viii]

ERASING TRANS AND QUEER PEOPLE FROM EDUCATION AND SPORTS

1-31 The Department of Education (DOE) told K–12 schools/colleges that it would reinstate policies from Trump's first term, limiting schools' responsibility in sexual misconduct cases, and provided more extensive rights to students accused of sexual harassment/assault. And, reversed the Biden administration's broadening of Title IX law, which held that harassment/exclusion based on sexual orientation and gender identity is a form of discrimination.

4-4 DOE and DOJ created a new Title IX Special Investigations Team focused on preventing trans women/girls from women's/girls' sports teams and restrooms.

4-28 Announced that the University of Pennsylvania had violated sex discrimination laws by allowing a trans woman to participate in women's sports. The DOE said it would require the university to strip records from trans swimmer Lia Thomas and demanded it send letters of apology to other female athletes who were discriminated against.

5-27 Ordered local authorities to prevent a trans athlete from competing in the California state track and field finals, and warned that federal funding to California could be withheld if they do not comply with his directive.

6-3 DOJ threatened action over California's policy allowing trans athletes in girls' sports, and Trump promised "large scale fines." A letter from Harmeet Dhillon of the Justice Department's civil rights division falsely and baselessly claims "Scientific evidence shows that upsetting the historical status quo and forcing girls to compete against males would deprive them of athletic opportunities and benefits because of their sex."

[viii] Remember, this is not a comprehensive list. Refer to the Trump Accountability tracker: https://glaad.org/trump-accountability-tracker for more information on each example laid out in the Appendix.

6-26 US Department of Health and Human Services (DHHS) announced the investigation of a Minnesota state policy that allows trans students to participate in sports, after accusations that a high school softball team won a championship with a trans player.

7-9 DOJ announced a lawsuit against California's DOE and the California Interscholastic Federation, which oversees state high school sports, for declining to comply with Trump administration demands to ban trans athletes from women's/girls' sports. California's policy to prohibit discrimination in schools based on gender identity has been in place since 2013.

7-11 Released court records document how the Trump administration pulled 600 books from Department of Defense (DD) schools that include themes of racial justice and LGBTQ identities.

7-21 The US Olympic and Paralympic Committee changed its eligibility rules to ban trans women from competing in women's sports, claiming an "obligation to comply with federal expectations" from an EO. This contradicts the International Olympic Committee's (IOC) guidelines for trans inclusion.

7-25 Launched an investigation into the Oregon DOE, alleging that the state violates civil rights law by allowing trans girls to participate in girls' school sports.

7-29 DOJ issued a memo to federal agencies threatening funding if agencies support DEI.

7-29 Brown University announces a settlement that restores $510 million in funding illegally frozen, agreeing to adhere to a ban on the participation of trans athletes in intercollegiate sports and to not provide gender affirmation healthcare to minors.

8-8 DHS announced a visa policy that will ban trans women from traveling to the USA to compete in professional sports.

8-26 Administration warned the US states and territories that they will lose federal funding for sex education unless they "remove all references to gender ideology."

8-27 Told the US states and territories that they will lose federal funding for their sex education programs if they do not remove references to trans people.

8-28 DOE ordered Denver Public Schools to replace gender-neutral restrooms with sex-designated facilities within 10 days or lose federal funding.

9-9 Texas A&M University fired a professor, Melissa McCoul (and the department head and dean) over course instruction related to gender identity.

9-16 The University of California, Los Angeles (UCLA) faculty and workers' unions sued Trump for freezing $584 million in research grants, arguing it violates academic freedom and constitutional rights. The freeze follows a DOJ letter demanding that UCLA end gender-affirming care for minors, ban trans athletes, and align policies with anti-DEI directives.

9-17 DOE threatened to withhold $15 million in federal funding for New York City's magnet schools if they refused to remove their trans-inclusive policies.

10-3 Education Secretary sent a nine-page proposal to nine universities demanding they ban trans-inclusive facilities, define sex by "reproductive function," and limit race, gender, or identity factors in admissions.

10-10 Announced sweeping layoffs to the DOE, cutting roles that oversee civil rights, grants, and disability services.

12-1 Northwestern University is the sixth school to reach a deal with the Trump administration, which claimed allegations of unlawful discrimination, race-based admissions, and fostering a hostile educational environment for Jewish students. Requires Northwestern to pay $75 million to the US government over several years; in turn, the administration will restore nearly $800 million in Congressionally appropriated federal research funding.

ELIMINATING TRANS AND QUEER HEALTHCARE

2-10 EO signed to target gender-affirming medical care for trans youth (using inaccurate and inflammatory graphic language).

2-18 Added a baseless disclaimer to the top of government websites for the Federal Drug Administration (FDA), Center for Disease Control (CDC), and DHHS after a federal judge ordered that webpages that contained vital information about trans people and other marginalized groups be reinstated. The header read:

> *Any information on this page promoting gender ideology is extremely inaccurate and disconnected from the immutable biological reality that there are two sexes, male and female ... The Trump Administration rejects gender ideology and condemns the harms it causes to children by*

> *promoting their chemical and surgical mutilation, and to women, by depriving them of their dignity, safety, well-being, and opportunities. This page does not reflect biological reality, and therefore the Administration and this Department reject it.*

3-4 Took more than $800 million in research into the health of LGBTQ people.

3-14 Department of Veteran's Affairs (DVA) rescinded Directive 1341, a policy ensuring trans, nonbinary, and intersex veterans receive respectful, clinically appropriate health care, including access to hormone therapy, mental health support, and the ability to use VA facilities in accordance with their gender identity.

4-4 Targeted trans health care in a proclamation declaring April National Child Abuse Prevention Month, calling trans health care a form of child abuse.

5-28 Centers for Medicare and Medicaid Services (CMS) sent letters to hospitals that provide trans care services to children demanding data on their quality standards and finances. CMS Administrator Oz's statement falsely claimed: "These are irreversible, high-risk procedures being conducted on vulnerable children, often at taxpayer expense."

6-3 FBI began Pride month by asking citizens to report doctors, hospitals, and clinics that offer gender-affirming surgeries to minors, claiming that those procedures amount to child mutilation. In social media posts, the FBI spokesperson asked for tips on "any hospitals or clinics who break the law and mutilate children under the guise of 'gender affirming care.'"

7-11 DOJ announced that it has issued subpoenas to more than 20 doctors and health clinics providing trans-affirming care.

7-17 Terminated a part of the 988 suicide and crisis lifeline dedicated to LGBTQ+ youth.

7-18 Hospitals across the USA announced rollbacks and bans on gender-affirming care for trans youth, to comply with the DOJ investigation into these providers.

8-20 Subpoenas from the DOJ were made public, showing officials are seeking patients' private medical records at hospitals treating LGBTQ youth.

8-21 The Supreme Court of the United States (SCOTUS) upheld an order that directed National Institutes of Health (NHS) to cut funding for more than 1,700 grants focusing on HIV/AIDS and its impact on minority groups, including LGBTQ people and people of color.

9-3 After a settlement requiring the administration to restore health and science information to federal websites, DHHS remains "committed to its mission of removing radical gender and DEI ideology from federal programs." The reversal follows an EO meant to eliminate the term "gender" from policies and delete public health pages about pregnancy risks, opioid addiction, and HIV.

9-8 Three military families sued the DOD over a ban on trans health care.

9-9 Announced removing gender-affirming care from the health care services covered under the Federal Employees Health Benefits (FEHB) Program beginning in 2026.

9-9 Federal judge blocks the administration's attempt to subpoena medical records of trans minors at Boston Children's Hospital.

9-17 CDC issued new "priorities" that declare biological sex is "unchangeable," and seek to "protect children" by deprioritizing programs offering trans health care.

9-20 CDC removed or restricted access to nearly two dozen webpages from their website, many relating to LGBTQ health care.

9-7 DOJ attorney suggested SCOTUS overturn Colorado's ban on conversion therapy for minors.

10 15 Health Resources and Services Administration (HRSA), an agency under DHHS Secretary Robert F. Kennedy, announced a new goal of "stopping medical and surgical gender-affirming care for adolescents" and threatened to revoke Federally Qualified Health Centers (FQHC) status from medical centers found to violate these new guidelines.

10-27 A lawsuit from UCLA shows that the Trump administration attempted to intimidate and defund the school unless its affiliated hospitals halt health care for transgender youth, which is supported by every major medical association, as well as stop allowing transgender women to participate in sports in accordance with state law.

10-30 National Public Radio (NPR) shared draft text of two proposed rules by DHHS that would heavily restrict trans health care; one prohibits Medicaid reimbursement for gender-affirming care for people under 18, and another blocks all Medicare and Medicaid funding for hospitals that provide the care to minors.

11-19 DHHS released the final version of a report criticizing health care for trans youth.

12-18 DHHS announced actions to bar hospitals from performing gender-affirming care for trans children by prohibiting Federal Medicaid/ CHIP Funds from covering gender-affirming care for youth and blocking all Medicaid and Medicare funding for any services at hospitals that provide pediatric gender-affirming care.

LIMITING TRANS AND QUEER PEOPLE'S ABILITY TO MOVE FREELY AND ESCAPE VIOLENCE

2-4 Applications for the gender-neutral "X" marker on US passports were frozen.

2-10 Removed "T" [from LGBT Travelers] from the State Department travel advisory website.

5-5 Federal Bureau of Justice Statistics (BJS) removed all references to gender or gender identity from at least four federal surveys, making it nearly impossible to monitor crimes and violence against trans people.

6-17 White House (WH) spokesperson denounced a federal judge's ruling allowing trans and intersex people to obtain passports consistent with their gender identity, saying it is "yet another attempt by a rogue judge to thwart President Trump's agenda and push radical gender ideology that defies biological truth."

6-18 Chair of the Equal Employment Opportunity Commission (EEOC) acknowledged that trans workers are protected under civil rights laws but defended her decision to drop lawsuits on their behalf, saying her agency is not independent and must comply with Trump's orders.

9-19 Trump petitioned SCOTUS to let him enforce a passport policy for trans and nonbinary people that requires male or female sex designations based on birth certificates.

11-6 SCOTUS allowed Trump's administration to enforce a policy blocking trans and nonbinary people from choosing passport sex markers that align with their gender identity, including changing the policy allowing an "X" in place of a gender identity on passports.

11-17 The State Department made unannounced changes to its website to threaten invalidation of passports for transgender, nonbinary, and intersex Americans.

12-4 DOJ instructed inspectors to stop evaluating prisons and jails using standards designed to protect transgender, intersex, and gender-non-conforming people from sexual violence.

ERASING TRANS AND QUEER PEOPLE FROM THE ARTS AND MEDIA

2-14 The National Park Service (NPS) removed the word "transgender" from the Stonewall Monument website.

4-15 Request Congress rescind $1.1 billion in (already appropriated) federal funding from the Corporation for Public Broadcasting (CPB), which contributes to NPR and Public Broadcasting Service (PBS); specifically criticized PBS for airing programs featuring trans characters.

6-4 Trump does not acknowledge Pride Month.

6-12 Trump does not acknowledge the Pulse Nightclub mass shooting, and the Transportation Secretary sends a letter to governors introducing a "safety initiative" seeking consistent markings on roads, specifically targeting rainbow crosswalks.

7-9 DOD deadline for all trans military personnel to "voluntarily separate."

7-11 Removed references to bisexuality from the Stonewall Monument website.

7-24 Artist Amy Sherald canceled her show at the Smithsonian after being asked to remove a painting of a trans woman as the Statue of Liberty; she would have been the first contemporary Black artist to have a solo exhibition at the Smithsonian.

8-12 Ordered a "comprehensive" review and investigation into the Smithsonian to determine whether it conforms to the administration's standards, including an exhibit at the Smithsonian National Museum of American History (NMAH) featuring trans athletes.

9-24 Withheld $1.25 million in Congressionally approved funds from 20 projects serving LGBTQ and underrepresented communities.

12-1 Trump does not acknowledge World AIDS Day.

SLANDERING AND DEMONIZING TRANS AND QUEER PEOPLE TO EVOKE FEAR:

1-27 EO directed the Secretary of Defense to reinstate a ban on trans people serving in the military, which prohibits trans people from enlisting, currently serving transgender personnel from transitioning, and ends the use of authentic pronouns.

8-29 DHHS Secretary Robert F. Kennedy Jr told Fox News that studies were being conducted on a possible link between medications "for gender transitions" and violence.

9-1 In response to last month's mass shooting in Minneapolis, the DOJ is considering limiting trans Americans' Second Amendment right to possess firearms.

9-13 Leaked memo from the Bureau of Alcohol, Tobacco, Firearms, and Explosives (ATF) falsely claimed shell casings were engraved with "transgender ideology" near the scene where activist Charlie Kirk was murdered.

10-25 The United States Department of Agriculture (USDA) posts the following notice:

> *Senate Democrats have now voted 12 times to not fund the food stamp program, also known as the Supplemental Nutrition Assistance Program (SNAP). Bottom line, the well has run dry. At this time, there will be no benefits issued on November 1. We are approaching an inflection point for Senate Democrats. They can continue to hold out for healthcare for illegal aliens and gender mutilation procedures, or reopen the government so mothers, babies, and the most vulnerable among us can receive critical nutrition assistance.*

11-2 In an interview on 60 Minutes, Trump repeatedly misgendered trans women and accused Democrats of promoting "transgender for everybody."

11-10 Trump ddministration sued for denying early retirement benefits to trans members of the US Air Force, amid the administration's ongoing efforts to remove transgender service members from the military.

11-20 A class action lawsuit has been filed against the Trump administration, challenging its policy banning transgender and intersex federal employees from being able to use the restroom consistent with who they are.

11-21 The British Broadcasting Association (BBC) reported that the Trump administration is preparing to formally accuse countries that support race and gender diversity policies of "infringing on human rights."

CLASSIFYING TRANS AND QUEER PEOPLE AS TERRORISTS TO ELIMINATE THEM

9-18 Two National Security Officials (NSO) tell journalist Klippenstein that the FBI is weighing whether to classify trans people as a subcategory within its new "domestic extremism" threat model that was originally used to classify January 6 rioters.

9-22 WH Press Secretary said the administration is investigating the many reasons that trans people are turning to "domestic terrorism."

NOTES

1. Brown, R. (1984). *Unexpected news: Reading the Bible with third world eyes*. Westminster John Knox Press.

2. Castiglia, C., & Reed, C. (2011). *If memory serves: Gay men, AIDS, and the promise of the queer past*. University of Minnesota Press.

3. Charalambous, P. (2025, March 28). *"Unfair exclusionary policy": 2nd judge blocks Trump's transgender military ban in scathing ruling*. ABC News. https://abcnews.com/US/unfair-exclusionary-policy-2nd-judge-blocks-trumps-transgender/story?id=120255260.

4. Dodson, J. (2025, December 9). *Military asks Fourth Circuit to let it disqualify applicants with HIV*. Courthouse News Service. https://www.courthousenews.com/military-asks-fourth-circuit-to-let-it-disqualify-applicants-with-hiv/.

5. White House Fact Sheet. (2025, January 27). https://www.factcheck.org/2025/09/few-mass-shooters-have-been-transgender/.

6. Carnell, H., Mitchell, S., & Pauly, M. (2025, September 12). A timeline of right-wing attempts to blame trans people for Charlie Kirk's murder. *Mother Jones*. https://www.motherjones.com/politics/2025/09/charlie-kirk-shooter-trans-ideology-false/.

7. DiAlesandro, N. (2025, November 17). *Days 201–300: Every anti-LGBTQIA+ move the Trump administration has made*. Uncloseted Media. https://www.unclosetedmedia.com/p/days-201-300-every-anti-lgbtq-move.

8. Akkad, O. E. (2025). *One day, everyone will have always been against this* (p. 138). Knopf/Penguin Random House.

9. Webster, L. (2025, December 23). *We must not look away: The escalating targeting of trans people*. Center for Constitutional Rights: The Blog.

10. Cobb, M. (2006). *God hates fags: The rhetorics of religious violence* (Vol. 20). NYU Press.

11. Heatherman, M. (2025, September 17). Fox News Alum, Brian Glenn, prods Trump to remove LGBTQ+ flags in D.C. – Suggests using 'Transtifa' designation. *Go Magazine*. https://gomag.com/article/fox-news-alum-brian-glenn-prods-trump-to-remove-trans-flags-in-d-c-suggests-using-transtifa-designation/.

12. Reed, E. (2025, September 20). *New memo reveals push for FBI to designate trans advocacy as violent extremism*. Truthout. https://truthout.org/articles/new-memo-reveals-push-for-fbi-to-designate-trans-advocacy-as-violent-extremism/.

13. Baćak, V. (2023, October). Looking back: Victimization of transgender persons and the criminal legal system. *American Journal of Public Health*, *113*(10), 1043–1045.

14. Operation Broken Silence. (2025, October 3). *The 10 stages of genocide*. https://operationbrokensilence.org/blog/the-10-stages-of-genocide.

15. Mayes-Osterman, C. (2025, November 20). Trump accuses six Democratic lawmakers of 'seditious behavior, punishable by death.' *USA TODAY*. https://www.usatoday.com/story/news/politics/2025/11/20/trump-accuses-democrats-seditious-behavior/87370773007/.

16. Rizzo, S. (2026, February 12). Judge rejects Hegseth bid to punish Mark Kelley. *Washington Post*. https://www.washingtonpost.com/national-security/2026/02/12/mark-kelly-hegseth-censure-ruling/.

17. Gessen, M. (2024, February 28). Aaron Bushnell's act of political despair. *The New Yorker*. https://www.newyorker.com/news/our-columnists/aaron-bushnells-act-of-political-despair.

18. Engels, F., & Marx, K. (2004). *The communist manifesto* (Vol. 13, Chapter 4). Penguin.

19. Rogers, B. A. (2021). Researching while queer: A research note about a genderqueer lesbian conducting qualitative research in the Southeastern United States. *International Journal of Social Research Methodology, 24*(1), 31–37.

20. Freeman, S. K., & Bailey, C. (2021). Queered outrage: Reclaiming anger amid facile calls for campus civility. *AAUP Journal of Academic Freedom, 12*.

21. McCoy, R. (2025, September 19). *The FBI is coming for trans people: According to a new report, the Federal Bureau of Investigation is planning on labeling all trans people "violent extremists."* The New Republic. https://newrepublic.com/post/200688/fbi-coming-trans-people-kash-patel-charlie-kirk.

22. Abdulhadi, R. (n.d.). Contributor profile. *The Offing Magazine*. https://theoffingmag.com/contributor/rasha-abdulhadi/.

23. Moyers, B. (2020, February 14). *Transcript: Justice Ruth Bader Ginsburg in conversation with Bill Moyers*. Bill Moyers Collection, Library of Congress. https://billmoyers.com/story/transcript-justice-ruth-bader-ginsburg-in-conversation-with-bill-moyers/.

EPILOGUE: WE ARE ALL MINNESOTANS NOW

Corey Dolgon

Stonehill College, USA

> *There is no doubt that the fate of every revolution at a certain point is decided by a break in the disposition of the army .... Thus in the streets and squares, by the bridges, at the barrack gates, is waged a ceaseless struggle – now dramatic, now unnoticeable – but always a desperate struggle, for the heart of the soldier.*
>
> *Leon Trotsky, History of the Russian Revolution, 1930*

In July 2025, the *Atlantic* magazine published an article on declining morale among Immigration and Customs Enforcement (ICE) agents. The reporter, Nick Miroff, explained that, despite Trump's and Noem's and Miller's vaunted claims, "The reality of Trump's mass-deportation campaign is far less glamorous." Miroff continued:

> *Officers and agents have spent much of the past five months clocking weekends and waking up at 4 a.m. for predawn raids. Their top leaders have been ousted or demoted, and their supervisors – themselves under threat of being fired – are pressuring them to make more and more arrests to meet quotas .... Having insisted for years that capturing criminals is its priority, ICE is now shelving major criminal investigations to prioritize civil*

> *immigration arrests, "grabbing asylum seekers at their courthouse hearings, handcuffing mothers as their U.S. citizen children cry, chasing day laborers through Home Depot parking lots." As angry onlookers attempt to shame ICE officers with obscenities and activists try to dox them, officers are retreating further behind masks and tactical gear. "It's miserable," one career ICE official told me. He called the job "mission impossible."*

Current and former agents complained about not doing the jobs they initially signed up for. "No drug cases, no human trafficking, no child exploitation …. It's infuriating," said one agent. A former ICE investigator claimed, "Morale is in the crapper …. Even those that are gung ho about the mission aren't happy with how they are being asked to execute it – the quotas and the shift to the low-hanging fruit to make the numbers." Miroff wrote that a longtime ICE employee was "thinking about quitting rather than having to continue 'arresting gardeners.'"[1]

While ICE agents are far from a mass revolt, the inability of established officers to meet the 3,000 detainees-a-day quota and the growing staff dissatisfaction and departures inspired a massive hiring program complete with big bonuses, fewer requirements and qualifications, and expedited (and inadequate according to most experts) training. Career officials who complained have been pushed out of leadership roles. Miroff reports, "Other employees have decided to quit." Attorney Adam Boyd resigned from ICE's legal department last Summer and told Miroff that he left because the mission was no longer about protecting the homeland from threats: "It became a contest of how many deportations could be reported to Stephen Miller by December." Boyd concluded: "We still need good attorneys at ICE. There are drug traffickers and national-security threats and human-rights violators in our country who need to be dealt with. But we are now focusing on numbers over all else."[2]

It may be unrealistic to imagine mass defections at ICE anytime soon, but the people of Minnesota demonstrated that not only could mass resistance be organized (protestors by the thousands had already shown up in Los Angeles, Chicago, Portland, Oregon and even Lewiston, Maine), but they proved it could prevail. The struggle demanded intense commitment and creativity, and an affinity for the below zero temperatures. The counter resistance from ICE was brutal and even created martyrs with the murders of Renee Good and Alex Pretti. But daily demonstrations and blocking ICE vehicles and headquarters; blowing whistles to warn neighbors that ICE agents were in the vicinity of mutual aid operations to care for the needs of immigrants afraid to leave their homes; loud midnight protests outside hotels where ICE agents tried to sleep and boycotts of local businesses that supplied ICE rental cars or collaborated with raids and investigations all worked to force border czar, Tom Homan, to end the surge. As a Museum of Protest research report concludes:

> *What made Minnesota different wasn't the size of the protests – though 50,000 to 100,000 people marching in negative 16-degree weather is remarkable. It was how labor unions, faith leaders, immigrant rights advocates, and community organizers pressured the government in many different ways at once: mass street protests, economic disruption through business closures, civil disobedience by clergy members, political pressure from state and local leaders, and ongoing organizing that showed the resistance wouldn't end.*[3]

What Minnesotans did can be a blueprint to oppose the Trump administration in ways that *Project 2025* was a blueprint for American Thuggery.

In fact, anti-ICE work continues to be cutting-edge as small towns and big cities are now fighting back and winning against Department of Homeland Security attempts to build immigration detention centers in their communities. From Kansas City, MO to Salt Lake City, UT; from Orange County, NY to Hutchins, TX; from Howard County, MD to Marshall County, MS, people are demonstrating to stop ICE detention centers. They are going to local town and city councils to speak out and pressure public officials to stop the sales of facilities. Groups are even demonstrating in front of business and property owners, whose warehouses are targeted for ICE facilities, threatening boycotts. Town after town is winning these battles, making it increasingly difficult for ICE to do its business and meet Miller's and Noem's quotas.[4]

The news is not always positive. The inability of Democrats to extend Medicare subsidies meant that around 22 million people on the Affordable Care Act had their insurance premiums more than doubled.[5] Verbal attacks on immigrants of color and lesbian, gay, bisexual, transgender, and queer people continue.[6] Trump has moved two major aircraft carriers with multiple warships and dozens of fighter planes into the persian gulf. Thousands of troops were prepared for what appeared to be an imminent strike.[7] And as Daniel Faber predicted in Chapter 9 of this volume, Trump repealed the Environmental Protection Agency's "endangerment finding," which allowed widespread regulation of greenhouse gases. Maintaining his belief that climate change is a hoax, Trump claimed this act will be the "single greatest deregulatory act in U.S. history."[8]

We enter the second year of Trump 2.0, unavoidably aware of serious and existential threats to our health and democracy. The zone remains flooded and the atrocities committed by a president in search of a totalitarian regime continue. But Minnesotans may have shown us the way. Organized and mobilized citizens across the country are stepping up and standing out to set limits on administrative overreach and *Project 2025* policies that enact violence and tyranny on workers, citizens, students, and families. Even the Supreme Court found the will to rule against Trump's tariffs and send his economic policies back to the chalkboard. His initial reaction was a public tirade besmirching the character and intellect of the six justices who ruled against him, and then used Section 122 of the Trade Act of 1974 to announce a 10% global tariff on all countries.[9]

The struggle for our future is inevitable but not without hope. The 2026 mid-term elections may be the next step in this conflict as Trump has expressed his desire to nationalize elections in 15 states he believes are vital to maintaining a Republican majority in Congress.[10] Federal Bureau of Investigation officials have commandeered Georgia ballot boxes from 2020, and the Department of Justice is intensifying calls for agents and officers at polling places around the country to stop rampant "voter fraud." No evidence of such fraud exists or has existed for decades, but as a red herring, it makes Trump's strategy to intimidate voters and have Republican officials take over ballot boxes and counting procedures in the hope of stealing the election. If he succeeds, there may be no more doubt about the extent to which the United States has become a tyranny. But if the people succeed in stopping his plans, we may not only protect democratic institutions and civil rights in general, but we may build from our new hard-won experiences in civic and democratic engagement the ability to forge a new vision and commitment to democracy and justice for all.

NOTES

1. MIroff, N. (2025, July 10). Trump loves ICE. Its workforce has never been so miserable. *The Atlantic*. https://www.theatlantic.com/politics/archive/2025/07/trump-ice-morale-immigration/683477/

2. Miroff, N. (2025, July 10). Trump loves ice. Its workforce has never been so miserable. *The Atlantic*. https://www.theatlantic.com/politics/archive/2025/07/trump-ice-morale-immigration/683477/ Holloway, K. (2026, January 27). Whom is ICE really recruiting? *The Nation*. https://www.washingtonpost.com/ripple/2026/01/27/ice-recruitment-white-supremacists/ Harwell, D. (2025, December 31). ICE plans $100 million dollar 'wartime' recruitment push targeting gun shows, military fans for hires. *The Washington Post*. https://www.washingtonpost.com/technology/2025/12/31/ice-wartime-recruitment-push/

3. Museum of Protest. (2026, February 13). *How Minnesota's multi-front strategy pressured ICE to withdraw. Museum of Protest On-Line*. https://museumofprotest.org/news/how-minnesotas-multi-front-strategy-pressured-ice-to-withdraw/

4. Calacal, C. (2026, February 12). *Kansas city developers halt sale of warehouse for ICE detention center as public pressure mounts*. KCUR News. https://www.kcur.org/news/2026-02-12/kansas-city-developers-halt-sale-of-warehouse-for-ice-detention-center-as-public-pressure-mounts Cann, C. (2026, February 5). Will that warehouse become an ICE detention center? Locals push back. *USA TODAY*. https://www.usatoday.com/story/news/nation/2026/02/05/ice-warehouse-communities-push-back/88495305007/ Traster, T. (2026, February 14). Public officials across Hudson Valley unite in opposition to ICE detention center in village of Chester in Orange County. *Rockland County Business Journal*. https://rcbizjournal.com/2026/02/14/

orange-county-executive-says-former-warehouse-in-chester-sold-to-ice-waiting-for-deed-to-be-filed-to-take-legal-action/ Santana, A. (2026, February 5). Howard County bans private immigration detention centers. *Baltimore Sun*; Pittman, A. (2026, February 6). *Byhalia ICE facility plans ditched amid Mississippi opposition, Wicker says*. Mississippi Free Press. https://www.baltimoresun.com/2026/02/05/howard-county-bans-immigration-detention-centers/

5. Appleby, J. (2026, February 10). Obamacare sign-ups drop, but the extent won't be clear for months. *KFF News*. https://kffhealthnews.org/health-care-costs/affordable-care-act-aca-obamacare- sign-ups-subsidies-higher-premiums/

6. Markey, E. (2026, February 11). *As Trump administration continues cruel attacks on transgender community, Markey and Jayapal reintroduce Transgender Bill of Rights*. Senator Ed Markey Press Release. https://www.markey.senate.gov/news/press-releases/as-trump-administration-continues-cruel-attacks-on-transgender-community-markey-and-jayapal-reintroduce-transgender-bill-of-rights

7. Lamothe, D., George, S., & Ledur, J. (2026, February 19). Trump appears ready to attack Iran as U.S. strike force takes shape. *Washington Post*. https://www.msn.com/en-us/news/world/trump-appears-ready-to-attack-iran-as-us-strike-force-takes-shape/ar-AA1WGK9v

8. Friedman, L. (2026, February 12). Trump administration erases the government's power to fight climate change. *New York Times*. https://www.nytimes.com/2026/02/12/climate/trump-epa-greenhouse-gases-climate-change.html

9. CBS News. (2026). *Supreme Court rules most Trump tariffs illegal in major setback for economic agenda*. Retrieved March 13, 2026, from https://www.cbsnews.com/news/supreme-court-tariffs-decision-trump/.

10. Green, E., Gold, M., & Jimison, R. (2026, February 5). Trump repeats call to 'nationalize' elections, as White House walks it back. *New York Times*. https://www.nytimes.com/2026/02/03/us/politics/trump-save-act-elections.html Galston, W. (2026, February 11). *Does President Trump have the authority to 'nationalize' voting?* Brookings Institute. https://www.brookings.edu/articles/does-president-trump-have-the-authority-to-nationalize-voting/

ABOUT THE EDITOR

Corey Dolgon is a sociologist, professor, musician, author, organizer and activist. He is the Co-founder and Co-director of the European Union-sponsored Summer Action Research Camp and has served as President of the Society for the Study of Social Problems and the Association for Humanist Sociology. He has published numerous books, including the award-winning *End of the Hamptons: Scenes from the Class Struggle in America's Paradise* (2005) and *Kill It to Save It: An Autopsy of Capitalism's Triumph over Democracy* (2015). He has also edited many anthologies, most recently, *The Oxford University Press Handbook of Sociology for Social Justice* (2024). He has also toured around the globe with his "singing lecture" on folksongs and social movements.

ABOUT THE CONTRIBUTORS

Onwubiko Agozino is a Professor of Sociology and Africana Studies at Virginia Tech, Blacksburg, VA, USA. He is ranked as one of the top criminologists in the world today by www.AcademicInfluence.com, and he is the author of the following books – *Community Policing in Nigeria* (co-authored, FDP and VTP, 2021); *Routledge Handbook on Africana Criminologies* (co-edited, 2020); *Critical, Creative and Centered Scholar-Activism* (2016, FDP); *Counter-Colonial Criminology* (2003); *Pan African Issues in Crime and Justice* (co-edited, 2004, 2017); and *Black Women and the Criminal Justice System* (1997, 2018). He was also Director-Producer of *IE: Inclusive Excellence*, selected for the Open Vision Film Festival, 2021; and *Shouters and the Control Freak Empire*, winner of the Best International Short Documentary prize, Columbia Gorge Film Festival, USA, 2011. He was appointed Professor Extreaordinasrius by the University of South Africa, 2021–2024 and he won the Excellence in Outreach and International Initiatives from the College of Liberal Arts and Human Sciences, Virginia Tech, 2021. He was the Founding Editor-in-Chief of the *African Journal of Criminology and Justice Studies* from 2005 to 2022. He has been a Visiting Fellow at the University of Auckland, New Zealand, and Flinders University, Australia. He is the Secretary of the Association of Black Sociologists, USA.

Deborah Billings is a social scientist who has worked for 30 years to integrate social science and public health approaches to address issues of equity, justice, human rights, and access in reproductive, sexual, and maternal and child health. She led global research collaborations with partners based in health systems, community based organizations, academic institutions, and nongovernmental organizations, with a focus on community-based action, participatory action, qualitative, and implementation research strategies. Her work with Ipas on abortion access around the world informs her ongoing work, including co-producing three documentaries about abortion access in Mexico and the USA. She is an Adjunct Associate Professor and Senior Research Associate at the University of South Carolina, Senior Advisor for Group Care Global, and activist.

Eduardo Bonilla-Silva is the James B. Duke Distinguished Professor of Sociology at Duke University. He is a "race scholar" who has written on racial theory, methodology, and substantive racial matters in the USA. He is known for his 1997 article, "Rethinking Racism: Toward a Structural Interpretation," as well as his book, *Racism Without Racists: Color Blind Racism and the Persistence of Racial Inequality in America*. His intellectual and political praxis has always been guided by Marx's 11th Thesis on Feuerbach, "Philosophers have only *interpreted* the world, in various ways; the point, however, is to *change* it."

Saphronia Carson is a PhD student in the Department of Women's, Gender, and Sexuality Studies at Emory University. She completed her Master's in Sociology in 2023 at the University of Central Florida, where her research revolved around studying the racialized and white supremacist logics structuring conservative anti-abortion movements in the USA. Her current research is focused on women of color reproductive justice movements in Atlanta, Georgia, and the ways in which they enable an expansive theory of power and resistance.

Katrinell M. Davis is a Professor of Sociology and Director of African American Studies at Florida State University. Her research focuses on how racial, gender, and class inequities shape access to quality neighborhood resources and impact marginalized communities. She is the author of *Hard Work is Not Enough* and *Tainted Tap*, which examine workplace inequalities and the Flint water crisis, respectively.

Daniel Faber is Professor of Sociology at Northeastern University. He is a Co-founder and Senior Research Fellow at the Global Center for Climate Justice, and serves as the Co-editor-in-Chief of the journal *Capitalism, Nature, Socialism*. He served as the Director of the Northeastern Environmental Justice Research Collaborative from 1999 to 2024. His research is focused on the areas of political economy and crisis theory, environmental sociology and policy, climate justice, social movements, classical and contemporary social theory, environmental justice, philanthropy, Central America and underdevelopment, and globalization.

Selene M. Gomez is a scholar and practitioner whose work bridges rigorous research and civic engagement. She holds a Doctorate in Political Behavior and Public Policy, with a focus on voter access, representation, and state-level variation in democratic institutions. Her research examines the intersections of election law, political participation, racialization, and structural racism, examining how institutional design and policy regimes shape unequal access to democratic participation. Drawing on large-scale survey data and multilevel analysis, she advances scholarship on structural inequity within the US democracy. In addition to her academic work, she operationalizes her research through executive leadership of national voter education initiatives, transforming empirical analysis into large-scale strategies that expand voter access, strengthen institutional capacity, and safeguard democratic participation.

Douglas Kellner taught for 25 years in the Department of Education and Information Studies at the University of California, Los Angeles and has had guest professorships throughout the USA, Europe, and Asia. He is author of many books on social theory, politics, history, and culture, including *Media Culture* and *Media Spectacle*; a trilogy of books on postmodern theory with Steve Best; and most recently *Media Spectacle in the 21st Century: From the Stolen Election of 2000 to the Trump Horror Show*, 2025; *Re-Visioning Education: Cultural Studies, Critical Media and Digital Literacies, and Democracy*, 2024; *Critical Theory and Pedagogy. Towards The Reconstruction of Education*, 2023; and *Technology and Democracy: Toward A Critical Theory of Digital Technologies, Technopolitics, and Technocapitalism*, 2021.

Chris Rhomberg is Professor of Sociology at Fordham University in New York City. He has published internationally on historical and contemporary issues in American labor, including strikes, collective bargaining and labor law, workers in media and in low-wage industries, and current economic and political junctures in the USA, including unions and rising political authoritarianism and state-level labor policies. His book *The Broken Table: The Detroit Newspaper Strike and the State of American Labor* (Russell Sage Foundation, 2012) received the 2013 award for best book on labor and labor movements from the American Sociological Association.

Baker A. Rogers is a Professor of Sociology at Georgia Southern University. Their research focuses on inequality, specifically examining the intersections of gender and sexuality in the US South. Their books include: *Conditionally Accepted: Christians' Perspectives on Sexuality and Gay and Lesbian Civil Rights*, 2019; *Trans Men in the South: Becoming Men*, 2020; *King of Hearts: Drag Kings in the American South*, 2021; *Gender and Sexuality in the Classroom: An Educator's Guide*, 2022; and *Trans Men's Incarceration Experiences: Storytelling at the Intersections*, 2025. Their work is also published in numerous academic journals, including *Men and Masculinities; Journal of Interpersonal Violence; Gender & Society;* and *Qualitative Sociology*.

Rogelio Sáenz is a Professor in the Department of Sociology and Demography at the University of Texas at San Antonio. He has written extensively in the areas of demography, Latina/os, race, inequality, immigration, COVID-19, health disparities, aging, public policy, and social justice. He is co-author of the just recently published second edition of *Latina/os in the United States: Diversity and Change* and Co-editor of the *International Handbook of the Demography of Race and Ethnicity*. He is the 2023 Ernest W. Burgess Fellow of the American Academy of Political and Social Sciences.

www.ingramcontent.com/pod-product-compliance
Lightning Source LLC
LaVergne TN
LVHW022000280826
846781LV00023B/220

* 9 7 8 1 8 0 5 9 2 8 5 6 0 *